www.wadsworth.com

wadsworth.com is the World Wide Web site for Wadsworth and is your direct source to dozens of online resources.

At *wadsworth.com* you can find out about supplements, demonstration software, and student resources. You can also send e-mail to many of our authors and preview new publications and exciting new technologies.

wadsworth.com
Changing the way the world learns®

From the Wadsworth Series in Mass Communication and Journalism

General Mass Communication

Biagi, *Media/Impact: An Introduction to Mass Media,* 5th Ed.
Craft, Leigh and Godfrey: *Electronic Media*
Day, *Ethics in Media Communications; Cases and Controversies,* 3rd Ed.
Fortner, *International Communications: History, Conflict, and Control of the Global Metropolis*
Gillmor, Barron and Simon, *Mass Communication Law: Cases and Comment,* 6th Ed.
Gillmor, Barron, Simon and Terry, *Fundamentals of Mass Communication Law*
Jamieson and Campbell, *The Interplay of Influence,* 5th Ed.
Lester, *Visual Communication,* 2nd Ed.
Lont, *Women and Media: Content, Careers, and Criticism*
Straubhaar and LaRose, *Media Now: Communications Media in the Information Age,* 2nd Ed.
Surette, *Media, Crime, and Criminal Justice: Images and Realities,* 2nd Ed.
Whetmore, *Mediamerica, Mediaworld: Form, Content, and Consequence of Mass Communication,* Updated 5th Ed.
Zelezny, *Communications Law: Liberties, Restraints, and the Modern Media,* 3rd Ed.
Zelezny, *Cases in Communications Law,* 3rd Ed.

Journalism

Adams, *Writing Right for Today's Mass Media: A Textbook and Workbook with Language Exercises*
Anderson, *Contemporary Sports Reporting*
Bowles and Borden, *Creative Editing,* 3rd Ed.
Catsis, *Sports Broadcasting*
Chance and McKeen, *Literary Journalism: A Reader*
Dorn, *How to Design and Improve Magazine Layouts,* 2nd Ed.
Fischer, *Sports Journalism at Its Best: Pulitzer Prize-Winning Articles, Cartoons, and Photographs*
Fisher, *The Craft of Corporate Journalism*
Gaines, *Investigative Reporting for Print and Broadcast,* 2nd Ed.
Hausman, *The Decision-Making Process in Journalism*
Hilliard, *Writing for Television, Radio & New Media,* 7th Ed.
Kessler and McDonald, *When Words Collide,* 5th Ed.
Klement and Matalene, *Telling Stories/Taking Risks: Journalism Writing at the Century's Edge*
Laakaniemi, *Newswriting in Transition*
Parrish, *Photojournalism: An Introduction*
Rich, *Writing and Reporting News: A Coaching Method,* 3rd Ed.
Rich, *Workbook for Writing and Reporting News,* 3rd Ed.

Photojournalism and Photography

Parrish, *Photojournalism: An Introduction*
Rosen and DeVries, *Introduction to Photography,* 4th Ed.

Public Relations and Advertising

Hendrix, *Public Relations Cases,* 5th Ed.
Jewler and Drewniany, *Creative Strategy in Advertising,* 7th Ed.
Marlow, *Electronic Public Relations*
Newsom and Carrell, *Public Relations Writing: Form and Style,* 6th Ed.
Newsom, Turk, and Kruckeberg, *This Is PR: The Realities of Public Relations,* 7th Ed.
Sivulka, *Soap, Sex, and Cigarettes: A Cultural History of American Advertising*
Woods, *Advertising and Marketing to the New Majority: A Case Study Approach*

Research and Theory

Babbie, *The Practice of Social Research,* 8th Ed.
Baran and Davis, *Mass Communication Theory: Foundations, Ferment, and Future,* 2nd Ed.
Rubenstein, *Surveying Public Opinion*
Rubin, Rubin, and Piele, *Communication Research: Strategies and Sources,* 5th Ed.
Wimmer and Dominick, *Mass Media Research: An Introduction,* 6th Ed.

Creative Strategy in Advertising

SEVENTH EDITION

A. Jerome Jewler
Bonnie L. Drewniany

College of Journalism and Mass Communications
University of South Carolina, Columbia

 **Wadsworth**
Thomson Learning™

Australia • Canada • Mexico • Singapore • Spain • United Kingdom • United States

Mass Communication Editor: Karen Austin
Executive Editor: Deirdre Cavanaugh
Publisher: Clark Baxter
Executive Marketing Manager: Stacey Purviance
Project Editor: Susan Walters
Print Buyer: Barbara Britton
Permissions Editor: Bob Kauser

Production Service: Melanie Field, Strawberry Field
    Publishing
Copy Editor: Tom Briggs
Cover Designer: Cuttriss and Hambleton
Compositor: TBH Typecast, Inc.
Text and Cover Printer: R. R. Donnelley/Crawfordsville

Wadsworth/Thomson Learning
10 Davis Drive
Belmont, CA 94002-3098
USA

For more information about our products, contact us:
Thomson Learning Academic Resource Center
1-800-423-0563
http://www.wadsworth.com

International Headquarters
Thomson Learning
International Division
290 Harbor Drive, 2nd Floor
Stamford, CT 06902-7477
USA

UK/Europe/Middle East/South Africa
Thomson Learning
Berkshire House
168-173 High Holborn
London WC1V 7AA
United Kingdom

Asia
Thomson Learning
60 Albert Street, #15-01
Albert Complex
Singapore 189969

Canada
Nelson Thomson Learning
1120 Birchmount Road
Toronto, Ontario M1K 5G4
Canada

Library of Congress Cataloging-in-Publication Data
Jewler, A. Jerome.
    Creative strategy in advertising / A. Jerome Jewler, Bonnie L. Drewniany.—7th ed.
        p.   cm.
    Includes bibliographical references and index.
    ISBN 0-534-55783-X
    1. Advertising copy.   2. Advertising layout and typography.   I. Drewniany, Bonnie L.
    II. Title.
    HF5825.J46 2000
    659.13′2—dc21   00-038220

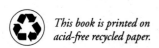

To my family, students, colleagues, and my incredible coauthor who have helped me reach this pinnacle in my life.

JERRY JEWLER

To my father, John Drewniany, who gave me my business sense. And to my mother, Louise Howland Drewniany, who gave me my sense of humor.

BONNIE DREWNIANY

Contents

Preface

Back in 1981, when this book first saw the light of day, we had no idea we'd still be writing it some twenty years later. It remains one of the top sellers in its special field. We guess we must be doing something.

Some things never need to change. And so you'll find the same basic advice in this seventh edition that others found in earlier editions. But other things must change. That's why it was time to regroup and restage *Creative Strategy in Advertising* for a new millennium of learners.

What's special about this book? Admittedly, we're somewhat biased. But because we stubbornly cling to the idea that creativity in advertising demands a structured, step-by-step process, we have structured the book accordingly.

Chapter 1 plunges into a discussion of creativity. What's creative? What's not? How can you become more creative? What pitfalls should you avoid? What about creativity and ethics?

Chapter 2 introduces you to the diverse markets you will be appealing to in your advertisements: women, men, people of color, older people, and more. What are some differences you need to acknowledge as you attempt to reach them through clever phrasing and unusual visuals?

In Chapter 3, as a prelude to strategy, you'll learn where to go digging for the information that's so critical to the creative process. It isn't creative yet, but you have to start somewhere. And that somewhere is at Web sites, in books and magazines, in conversations with clients and consumers, and so forth.

Then Chapter 4 guides you through the strategic process of taking information, adding your own insight, and coming up with a plan for creativity.

Which brings us almost full circle to the opening of the book, but in a different manner. Now, in Chapter 5, you'll explore idea generation. How do you come up with ideas based on a sound strategy? How do you test them? How do you know if they're good or not? And have you struck an appropriate balance between "relevance to the task" and an unexpected creative spark?

Now it's time to explore the major media. Chapter 6 discusses print, while Chapter 7 takes a brief look at design. Chapter 8 talks about radio, while Chapter 9 explores TV. Chapter 10 delves into the magic of direct marketing, while Chapter 11 provides insight into Internet advertising.

Chapter 12 looks at another world of advertising: retail. And Chapters 13 and 14 provide advice on how to present your work successfully and how to land that first job as a writer, designer, computer graphics specialist, Web site specialist, and so forth.

We hope that, as a result of reading this book, you'll come to realize that much of the advertising out there these days isn't very effective, isn't in good taste, or isn't even what advertising should be.

Then we hope you'll take the bull by the horns and show 'em just how *really* creative you can be.

We would like to thank the following people who did take the bull by the horns and helped us make this edition possible: Karen Austin, mass communication editor; Stacey Purviance, executive marketing manager; Melanie Field/Strawberry Field Publishing, production; Susan Walters, project editor; and Tom Briggs, copy editor.

We would also like to thank the following reviewers of this edition: Ed Ackerley, University of Arizona; Linda Cowles, Michigan State University; and Kim Martin, University of Arkansas. Thanks also to the reviewers of previous editions: Katherine Frith, Penn State University; Henry B. Hager, Missouri School of Journalism; Suzette Heiman, University of Missouri; Kevin Keenan, University of Maryland; Peggy Kreshel, University of Georgia; Elizabeth Lester, University of Georgia-Athens; Nancy Mitchell, University of Nebraska, Lincoln; Barbara Mueller, San Diego State University; Philip Patterson, Oklahoma Christian University; Jon Shidler, Southern Illinois University at Carbondale; David Slayden, Southern Methodist University; Ronald E. Spielberger, The University of Memphis; and James Tsao, University of Wisconsin-Oshkosh.

A. Jerome Jewler
Bonnie L. Drewniany

About the Authors

A. JEROME JEWLER is the recipient of the 2000 Distinguished Advertising Educator Award presented by the American Advertising Federation. He is also distinguished professor emeritus in the College of Journalism and Mass Communications, University of South Carolina, Columbia, where he has taught undergraduate and graduate courses in advertising and teaching methods since 1972. He is a graduate of the University of Maryland, with a B.S. in Journalism and an M.A. in American Civilization. He worked as an advertising copywriter before beginning his teaching career in 1972.

He taught briefly at the University of Tennessee; spent a summer with McCann-Erickson, Ltd., London, as a visiting professor; spent another summer in research at the Center for Advertising History of the Smithsonian Institution; and another summer teaching creative strategy to nineteen American students in England.

He has served as co-director for instruction and faculty development for the USC freshman seminar and has led workshops on teaching at more than twenty-five colleges and universities, including the University of Hawaii, the University of Prince Edward Island (Canada), the Art Institute of Houston, and The George Washington University. He and John Gardner are the co-editors of *Your College Experience,* a nationally known college success text. He has had a lifelong interest in film and theatre and recently has performed in several community theatre productions.

BONNIE L. DREWNIANY is sequence chair for advertising and public relations as well as an associate professor in the College of Journalism and Mass Communications, University of South Carolina, Columbia. She has an M.B.A. from Rutgers University with a concentration in Marketing, and a B.S. from Syracuse University, with a concentration in Mass Communications.

Prior to joining the University of South Carolina, she was a visiting professor at Syracuse University's S.I. Newhouse School of Public Communications. She also taught as an adjunct at Parsons School of Design, Rutgers University, and Seton Hall University.

Her professional experience includes ten years with the R.H. Macy Corporation, where she was advertising copy director for the New Jersey division. She has also freelanced for F.A.O. Schwartz, Fortunoff's, and American Express.

Her research interests include advertising's portrayal of minorities, women, and older people. Her findings have been published in *The Wall Street Journal* and various academic publications. She serves on the Academic Committee of the American Advertising Federation and on the ADDY Committee of the Columbia Advertising and Marketing Federation. She spends her summers in Massachusetts.

Creative Strategy in Advertising

SEVENTH EDITION

CHAPTER 1

Creating Unexpected but Relevant Selling Messages

You're exposed to hundreds—perhaps even thousands—of commercial messages each day. But thanks to selective perception, you're able to screen out messages you don't want to see or hear. In fact, one study estimates that the average consumer is exposed to nearly 1500 ads per day yet perceives only 76 of these messages. Richard Kirshenbaum and Jonathan Bond describe this phenomenon as a "radar shield" and urge advertisers to develop under-the-radar communications that are "so ingenious, so interesting, and so creative that consumers barely know they're being sold."[1]

● What Does It Mean to Be Creative?

"If anything is in existence today that only came into existence because of you—that's a creative act." That's what Pat James, who teaches classes in creativity at the Jung Center in Altamonte Springs, Florida, told Linda Shrieves, a reporter for the *Orlando Sentinel,* who interviewed a number of individuals involved in bringing people's suppressed creativity to the surface.[2]

"Most people think creativity is inborn and you either get a dose of it or you don't," says J. Daniel Couger, a business professor at the University of Colorado. Over the years, most of us have had our creativity squashed out of us—by our teachers, our parents, and our employers. "We're taught in the first grade that conformity is good," Couger says. By the time we graduate from high school, most of us are programmed

[1] Jonathan Bond and Richard Kirshenbaum, *Under the Radar: Talking to Today's Cynical Consumer* (New York: Wiley, 1998), p. 34.

[2] Linda Shrieves, *Orlando Sentinel,* 28 Jan. 1996.

to follow the rules and not ask too many questions because we'll be considered a pest. And in the work world, you get even more programming—to conform. If you don't, you may receive a verbal lashing or other, less blunt reminders; you may even get passed over for a promotion.

Patricia Hutchings of Alverno College offers three characteristics of creative people:

- *Risk-taking, or the "right to fail."* All your life, you've been warned against taking risks, especially in school. A creative person takes them anyhow, knowing that little of interest will result otherwise. Try it. If you go too far, it's much easier to pull back than it is to take an ordinary idea and try to push it forward. As Oscar Wilde said, "An idea that is not dangerous is hardly worth calling an idea at all."

- *Divergent thinking.* Albert Einstein failed math as a schoolboy perhaps because he preferred to ask questions rather than merely fill in the blanks. He was a divergent rather than a convergent thinker. Divergent thinkers use more ambiguous, open-ended modes to think through a problem. They don't seek one solution; they want to find as many possibilities as they can. Then they sort them into those-that-work and those-that-don't "stacks." They may even have a third stack of "maybes."

  Divergent thinkers also employ metaphors—using one unrelated idea to describe another—to see things in new ways and to make observations that raise questions rather than provide answers. Looking for a new way to open a can, you might ask, "How does nature deal with openings?" Maybe you consider the openings of a flower, a mouth, or the earth during an earthquake; perhaps you think about the peapod, which opens easily because of its weak seam. In fact, it was from the peapod, the story goes, that the idea of the pop-top can was born.

- *A sense of humor.* Creative people tend to have highly developed senses of humor. Indeed, humor can create an atmosphere conducive to the kind of risk-taking necessary for creativity, for it requires that shift in perspective, that new slant, that unexpected change in direction that is so crucial to problem solving.[3]

Reviving Your Creativity

Shrieves offers these "suggestions from the experts" on reclaiming your natural creativity:

1. *Remind yourself of your goal or dream every day.* Constantly look for ways to bring your dream into your life. If you can't go to New York City, visit the library and check out a book containing photographs and paintings of New York City.

[3]Patricia Hutchings, "Break Out, Be There! Thoughts on Teaching Creativity," *College Teaching,* Spring 1987, pp. 43–48. Copyright 1987. Published by Heldref Publications. Used with permission of the Helen Dwight Reid Educational Foundation.

2. *Write in a journal every day.* Writing keeps your ideas flowing. Don't think of it as creative writing; think of it as "brain dumping." The idea is to get two to three pages of your thoughts on paper daily.

3. *Set aside time to be alone.* For two hours each week, do something by yourself, for that's when most creative ideas come to you. But do something you normally wouldn't do. Visit a museum, wander through the zoo, or go for a walk to revitalize your senses.

4. *Hang out with creative people,* whether in your field or a totally different one.

5. For a week, turn off the TV, stop reading the mail, and don't listen to the radio. A week without all the extra "noise" is the equivalent of meditation.[4]

● Creativity in Advertising

It's been said that an ad is not creative unless it sells. Do we agree with this idea? Yes and no. We agree that an ad needs to contain a persuasive message that convinces people to take action—whether it's to buy a product, send for more information, or view something in a new way. However, that's just the start. A boring ad could persuade you to do these things, but it wouldn't be creative. To be creative, an ad must make a relevant connection with its audience and present a selling idea in an unexpected way.

Look at this headline from Federal Express, for example:

We don't hire Blacks.

We don't hire women.

We don't hire Hispanics.

We don't hire Asians.

We don't hire Jews.

We don't hire Disabled.

We don't hire Whites.

What in the world . . . ? Who *do* they hire, anyway? As the ad text then says, "We hire people." Now that's relevant, and unexpected—and so it's creative. Imagine the impact of this ad compared to one that says, "We don't discriminate in our hiring practices." As in the Federal Express example, creative advertising connects with the targeted consumers and uses an unexpected, yet relevant approach to selling. Advertising legend Bill Bernbach often gave the example of attracting attention to an ad by standing a man on his head. But, he explained, "that is not a good ad unless you're

[4]Linda Shrieves, *Orlando Sentinel,* 28 Jan. 1996.

selling a product that keeps things from falling out of that man's pockets. Then your inventiveness, and your attractiveness, and your cleverness is furthering, and making memorable, the advantage of your product."[5]

Look at some of the ads in this book. See if you can identify the unexpected element in each ad, and see if it passes the test for relevance. Note whether the idea of entertainment has fused with the factual message so that you now want to read the ad. Did the people who created the ad do everything possible to attract the audience they were seeking? Or did they sacrifice a good idea to a funny punch line or an outrageous statement or image? That is, did the entertainment content *intrude* on the message or reinforce it?

● That's Entertainment, but Is It Advertising?

Rance Crain, president and editorial director of Crain Communications, Inc., quoted a letter to the editor from a father: "My 6½-year-old son cut through the mayhem of murderous lizards, a digitally reincarnated Elvis and dancing tomatoes to offer an unwitting, but telling, indictment of Super Bowl ads: 'These commercials are cool. Not like the regular ones where they're trying to sell you something.'"[6] Like that little boy, most viewers love Super Bowl commercials because of their use of humor and celebrities. Unfortunately, the viewers don't always express their enthusiasm for the commercials at the cash register. And Super Bowl commercials are hardly unique in this regard—some of the most popular commercials of all time have been tremendous flops in terms of sales. So does this mean you should avoid humor and celebrities in your ads? No. But it does mean you should use them strategically.

Humor

Consider this TV commercial: An amateur stage production shows two children lost in the forest. The good fairy appears from overhead and starts floating toward them. "Not to fear, little children. I will helpppp—" THUD! She plummets to the stage. Tag line: "Should have used Stren. Stren. The most dependable fishing line in the world." The humor takes us by surprise and shows a situation with which we can empathize. It communicates a relevant, unexpected, and memorable message about the product. It gives us a reason to buy.

Here are some tips on how to use humor in advertising:

1. *Know the difference between humor and jokes.* Once you hear a joke's punch line, it's not as funny the second time. And when you hear the same joke a bunch of times, it can become downright tedious. Humor, by contrast, is more subtle and often contains nuances that make you want to see and hear it again and again. A comedy club understood the difference between jokes and humor when it created a delightful radio spot that promoted what they were selling: laughter. The spot

---

[5] Denis Higgins, *Conversations with William Bernbach, Leo Burnett, George Gribbin, David Ogilvy, Rosser Reeves* (Lincolnwood, IL: NTC Business Books, 1989), pp. 17–18.

[6] Remarks by Rance Crain to the Columbia Advertising and Marketing Federation, Columbia, SC, 17 March 1998.

● FIGURE 1-1

Selling through direct-response catalogs, Lands' End publicizes its goods through print ads such as this. Even the typeface used in the ads mirrors that used in the catalogs, but the similarities hardly end there. Consider the personal tone of the copy in this ad, as well as in the catalogs themselves, a style responsible in part for the overwhelming success of this company. The Lands' End charm is nowhere more self-disparaging than in this headline. Here, the writer compares the misplaced apostrophe in the company name ("a boo-boo from the early days") to the quality control that "was (obviously) a little skimpy" in the early days of the company but that resulted in the company's unconditional guarantee of quality.

To err is human.
To guarantee, divine.

That misplaced apostrophe in our name is a boo-boo from the early days, when our quality control was (obviously) a little skimpy.

Lots of people, especially English teachers, have taken us to task for it. It makes us cringe today. But in a funny way, that out-of-place apostrophe has served our customers very well.

You see, every time we think about it, it reminds us that we're only human. And that we can't ever be *too* careful about what we sell or how we deal with the good folks who favor us with their business.

Truth is, we depend on their trust. As direct merchants, we sell by catalog—classic clothing, soft luggage, home furnishings. Folks have to feel that anything they see in our catalog will deliver as promised.

Still, we know that occasionally we *will* goof. So, we add one more feature to our product line, the Lands' End guarantee:

We accept any return, for any reason, at any time. Without any conditions.

We want no mistakes about *that*.

Guaranteed. Period.® ©1993, Lands' End, Inc.

If you'd like a free catalog, call us any time, 24 hours a day, at **1-800-356-4444**
Or mail this coupon to: 1 Lands' End Lane, Dept. JV, Dodgeville, WI 53595

Name _____

Address _____ Apt. _____

City _____ State _____ Zip _____

Phone (___) _____ Day/Night (*circle one*)

recorded various types of laughter—the chuckle, the giggle, the cackle, the sputtering burst, the snort, and so on. You could hear the spot over and over and laugh each time.

2. *Relate to the human experience.* One of the things that made the comedy club spot so amusing was that listeners could identify people they knew who laughed like that. The spot made a relevant human connection. Allen Kay, whose advertising agency, Korey, Kay & Partners, has won numerous awards for its humorous ads, believes in having a "sense of human." As Kay told *Agency* magazine, "We spell humor h-u-m-a-n. It includes a lot of ironies in life that people recognize and realize and makes them say, 'Yeah, I've been there.'"[7]

3. *Make sure the humor is central to your product message.* Have you ever been so captivated by a commercial that you could repeat almost every detail of it—except for the name of the product it was trying to sell? If the product is obscured by the humor, the ad has flopped. To work, humor must be central to the message you're trying to communicate. Case in point: the quirky beer spots that featured "Dick." In one spot, a giant beaver chewed off a man's wooden leg; in another, in a magic trick, mice appeared under a woman's armpits. Many people found the commercials to be hilarious, and they got a lot of media coverage. Unfortunately, they failed to make any relevant connection to beer, and they didn't sell much beer. Less than two years after its launch, the client dumped the campaign and the agency that created it.

4. *Understand your audience's sense of humor.* The ad should reflect the tastes, aspirations, and sensibilities of its intended audience. Just because you and your friends

● FIGURE 1-2

Most guitar ads feature musicians in contorted positions or are filled with technical jargon. Taylor Guitar ads follow a different strategy. They state, "Taylor Guitars— handcrafted from the finest materials to give the sweetest sound." The copywriter could have run the strategy statement as a headline. But, like all talented artists, he brought it to a new level.

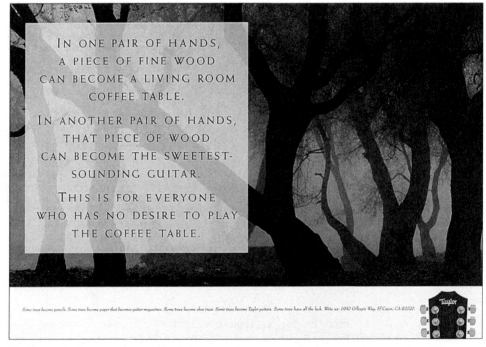

Caption reads: *Some trees become pencils. Some trees become paper that becomes guitar magazines. Some trees become shoe trees. Some trees become Taylor guitars. Some trees have all the luck. Write us: 1940 Gillespie Way, El Cajon, CA 92020.*

[7]Robyn Griggs, "Grinning in the Dark," *Agency,* Fall 1998, pp 16–17.

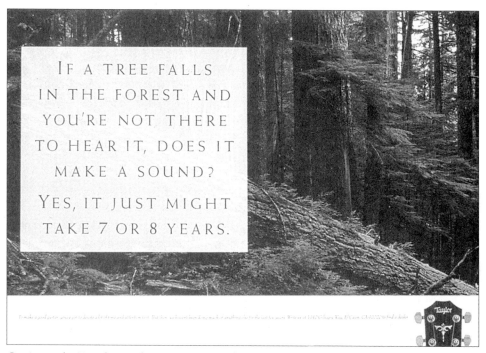

Caption reads: *To make a good guitar, you've got to devote a lot of time and attention to it. But then, we haven't been doing much of anything else for the last few years. Write us at 1940 Gillespie Way, El Cajon, CA 92020 to find a dealer near you.*

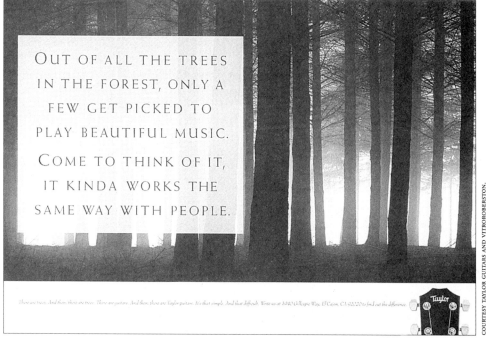

Caption reads: *There are trees. And then, there are trees. There are guitars. And then, there are Taylor guitars. It's that simple. And that difficult. Write us at 1940 Gillespie Way, El Cajon, CA 92020 to find out the difference.*

find something hysterical doesn't mean the rest of the world will. In fact, people may even be insulted by it. So be sure to test your humor on members of your target audience.

5. *Avoid humor that's at the expense of others.* Making fun of, say, ethnic groups, the disabled, and the elderly will very likely backfire on you. A car company offended African-Americans by running an ad in *Jet* magazine that stated, "Unlike your last boyfriend, it goes to work in the morning." And a discount clothing store offended Jewish people by saying, "Dress British. Think Yiddish."

6. *Have fun* with *your product,* but *don't make fun of it.* Self-deprecating humor can work if you turn your supposed shortcomings into an advantage. Motel 6 does this brilliantly. They don't try to hide their lack of amenities but rather flaunt it. At Motel 6, you're not going to get fancy soaps, European chocolates, or fluffy bathrobes. Instead, spokesman Tom Bodett promises, you'll get a comfortable room at a comfortable price.

7. *Don't assume your audience is stupid.* Think of it this way: Would you rather buy something from someone who apparently views you as an idiot or from someone who seems to appreciate your intelligence? Absolut vodka saw a phenomenal growth in its sales following the use of smart, subtle humor in its print ads.

Celebrity Endorsements

Sales of Nike sports bras increased the day after the U.S. women's soccer team won the World Cup and an exuberant Brandi Chastain pulled off her jersey to reveal that she was wearing a Nike sports bra. Although it wasn't a paid commercial message, it did demonstrate the power of a celebrity endorsement. Advantages to using celebrities include the following:

- *They have stopping power.* Celebrities attract attention and help break through the clutter of other ads.

- *They're likable.* Companies hope that the admiration the celebrity enjoys will be transferred to them.

- *They're perceived as experts in their fields.* The trick is to make a relevant connection between a celebrity's expertise and the company or product.

Before you think a celebrity is the answer, however, consider some potential drawbacks:

- *They're expensive.* Many top athletes, actors, and musicians command contracts in the millions of dollars. Smaller companies shouldn't even dream of spending this type of money, nor should companies that are trying to promote their low prices.

- *They're often a quick fix, not a long-term strategy.* Celebrities go in and out of fashion, and as their popularity level shifts, so does their persuasiveness.

- *They may lack credibility.* Sixty-three percent of respondents in a study published in *Advertising Age* said that celebrities are "just doing it for the money," and 43 percent believed celebrities "don't even use the product."[8] The Beef Industry Council learned this lesson the hard way when Cybil Shepherd, who was appearing in their ads, was quoted as saying she did not eat red meat.

- *They may endorse so many products that it confuses people* (and sometimes even themselves). Tiger Woods got into hot water for bouncing a Titleist golf ball on the wedge of a Titleist golf club while shooting a Nike commercial wearing Nike clothing.

- *They can overshadow the message.* Although a celebrity may draw attention to an ad, some consumers focus their attention on the celebrity and fail to note what's being promoted.

- *Bad press about the celebrity can hurt the sponsor.* Kmart canceled its contract with golfing veteran Fuzzy Zoeller after he joked about Tiger Woods eating fried chicken and collard greens. Kodak and Pepsi were mortified when Mike Tyson was first accused of beating his wife and then convicted of raping a woman. And O. J. Simpson, once one of the most popular endorsers, probably won't be asked to appear in many commercials in the near future.

At least initially, you should avoid using celebrities in your ads for two additional reasons:

- *It's very unlikely you'll have that type of budget on your first account.*

- *It doesn't show original thinking.* Your portfolio should show how you can solve problems creatively, not how a famous personality can do it.

● Guidelines for Creating Effective Ads

Creativity doesn't just "happen," and captivating ads don't "write themselves." But there are a number of things you can do to fuel the creative process, including the following:

1. *Forget about hard and fast rules, but* know *the rules.* Before you can break the rules effectively, you have to know them.

2. *Begin with a sound strategy or plan.* In Chapter 4, you will learn how to develop a creative strategy that serves as the basis and justification for your entire campaign.

3. *Remember that most products are not unique.* Clients will tell you differently, but a refrigerator is a refrigerator, a car is a car, and so on. It's how you present them in the ad that makes the real difference.

[8]Dave Vadehra, "Celebs Remain Entertaining, If Not Believable," *Advertising Age,* 2 Sept. 1996, p. 18.

4. *Show an understanding of the people you are trying to reach.* Make your target think, "Hey, this really is me they're talking about."

5. *Remember that your audience isn't very interested in what you have to say.* Therefore, your message must be crafted so that your target (think one consumer) will take notice. *How* you communicate is just as important as *what* you communicate.

6. *Do your own research.* The client can be helpful in narrowing the target market and filling you in on the product and the competition, but you need to do some digging on your own (see Chapter 3). Ultimately, you need to find a way to build that all-important relationship between the brand and potential consumers of that brand.

7. *Ask a lot of questions when you're interviewing consumers.* Always remember that they may not want to reveal the real reasons they do or don't like a product. A mom in England told a market researcher that milk was best for her kids while soda pop was terrible. Then he asked what she bought for them and she replied, "Soda pop. They hate milk." What could you do with this information if you had to sell milk?

8. *Be aware that people are often irrational in their buying habits.* So most advertising relies to some extent on emotional appeal, and some advertising relies on it completely. How consumers feel about a competitor's product or activity may also affect how you choose to develop your advertising strategy.

9. *Never overpromise.* Make meaningful promises to your targeted audience, promises that you can keep.

10. *Stress benefits over selling points.* "Women don't buy lipstick, they buy hope," Revlon founder Charles Revson once told his staff. A tire ad should emphasize safety and smooth riding, not unique tread design. A computer ad should stress user-friendliness, not the sophisticated circuitry that makes it possible. Remember, emotional benefits are often more convincing than logical ones.

11. *Keep it simple.* If a campaign or slogan is simple and effective, chances are it wasn't easy to invent. The phrase "Courage for your head" sounds simple and makes its point, but it didn't just pop into the minds of the Bell Helmets creative group by itself (see the BriefCase at the end of the chapter). As Nathaniel Hawthorne said, "Easy reading is damned hard writing."

12. *Build a relationship.* Ads don't produce instantaneous results. Even retail, point-of-purchase, and direct advertising—which use urgency to get you to buy as soon as possible—are limited in their ability to make you part with your money. What advertising does best is establish that special relationship between product and consumer. If you feel good about the ad, you may eventually try the product.

COURTESY GYNECOLOGICAL CANCER FOUNDATION. PRO BONO WORK DONATED BY SUSAN FOWLER CREDLE (COPY) AND STEVE RUTTER (ART DIRECTION).

● FIGURE 1-3

Before this pro bono (for the public good) ad for the Gynecological Cancer Foundation ran in space donated by *People Weekly*, the foundation was receiving an average of 500 calls monthly to its 800 number. The month the ad ran, 1278 women called for information and an additional 425 responded by mail. Even two months later, the number of calls (974) was still well above the monthly average prior to the ad. Despite budget restraints on production and the absence of visuals, the ad worked. What made so many women respond to this ad?

Odds are a woman is more likely

to cut out a coupon to save 25 cents

than one to save her life.

Of course, we've never chosen to do what we do

based on odds. After all, 20 years ago,

the chances were a woman diagnosed with cancer

would die.

That didn't stop doctors from trying.

And the result has been that the statistics

have changed dramatically.

Cancer is no longer a death sentence. Today, women

can continue to increase the odds of beating cancer,

simply by taking the time

to find out

how to get

the best care.

For a free brochure on gynecologic cancers and a directory of specialists, call 1-800-444-4441, or write: Gynecological Cancer Foundation, 401 N. Michigan Avenue, Chicago, IL 60611-4267

Name_____

Address_____

City_____ State _____ Zip _____

13. *Avoid clichés.* Clichés in advertising are just as off-putting as they are anywhere else—and people simply tune them out. Puns become clichés if you try to use one in every headline. Rhymes have limited shelf life, too.

14. *Revise.* Even the pros don't write the magic punch line the first time. Before Goodby, Silverstein & Partners arrived at "Courage for your head" for client Bell Helmets (see the BriefCase), they visited the client, viewed the manufacturing process, and absorbed hours of information, which led to a group-think session in which the tag line finally emerged.

Anyone can dash off an ad in minutes; you see or hear those every day in print, on radio or TV, in your mailbox, on billboards, and on the Internet. Most of the "instant ads" are merely background clutter for the few great ads that burn their messages into our memory and make us feel something.

● A Mandate for Social Responsibility

Myths, stereotypes, and cultural signs abound in advertising messages. Try as they may to avoid perpetuating negative values in the context of a message, a number of advertisers, intentionally or not, cause certain consumers to feel they're not "good enough" or "pretty enough" or "successful enough." As you read the following messages, decide which parts are myths and which parts contain some truth. Do you see any consequences—positive and negative—from using them to sell a product or service?

- *The children:* Let's be sure our children get all the things we didn't (more games and toys, fancier clothes, more exotic vacations, and so on).

- *Men and women:* For men, it's smart to be strong and sensible, to work hard for success, to rein in emotions. Of course, women can cry.

- *The materialistic ideal:* What you are depends to a large extent on the products and services you own and use, as opposed to your values, personality, ethics, and interests.

- *Technology:* The more technology, the better the life, so be sure your TV is theater quality in terms of both screen size and sound.

- *The egalitarian ideal:* We're all in this together. And on and on. . .

- *The elitist dream:* We're *not* all in this together! Other people need to be smart to keep up with me.

- *What's good for America:* You're unpatriotic if you drive a Honda, shave with a Braun, or drink French wine. (Used only to sell American brands, of course.)

- *The perfect host:* If you're not the perfect cook, decorator, party host, and so on, what's wrong with you?

- *Sex:* No matter what the question is sex is the answer. All it takes is x product to make you irresistible. Use it and you will be loved. And when it doesn't work, it's your fault.

- *Fear and guilt:* You'll be offensive if you don't use this deodorant. You'll lose your home if you don't have the proper protection. You're a goof if you dress like one.

- *Being "real"—the denial of fantasy:* This one is tricky because the advertiser seems to be leveling with you. "We know advertising is full of tricks," they seem to be saying, "so we're going to level with you." (But are they really?)

- *Body language:* The lowered eye, the sidelong glance, the disapproving frown, the gawky stance—these nonverbal messages often communicate more strongly than words.

What Kind of Advertising Are You Going to Create?

In *The Book of Daniel,* novelist E. L. Doctorow condemns the impact of television commercials:

> Everyone is digging the commercials. That's today's school, man. In less than a minute a TV commercial can carry you through a lifetime. It shows you the baby, the home, the car, the graduation. . . . It makes you laugh and makes your eyes water with nostalgia . . . telling you how cool you are and how cool you can be. Commercials are learning units.

Indeed they are. Advertisers have installed video units above public phones in schools and have offered to provide free TV sets, satellite dishes, and wiring to classrooms, as well as twelve minutes of news, in exchange for being allowed to run two minutes of commercials. Jeffrey Goldfarb reports a variety of other ways that commercialism has entered the classroom.[9] A popular middle-school math book asks students to determine the fat grams in a Whopper, figure the length of the Oscar Mayer Weinermobile, and calculate the surface area of a box of Cocoa Frosted Flakes. Some grade-school children learn how to add and subtract by using the M&M's counting book. And in Georgia, a student was suspended for wearing a Pepsi T-shirt during the school's "Coke in Education Day." (The school was competing for a cash prize by having students spell out "COKE" in the parking lot.) Goldfarb reminds us that ads in schools can be traced back to logo-imprinted rulers given to students in the nineteenth century. Even so, Goldfarb and other critics question whether commercialism has gone too far.

Advertisers also retouch images to perfect what is imperfect, to appeal to feelings while discouraging thinking, and to urge consumers to measure up to some vague "status quo." As far back as the seventeenth century, brochures published in England

[9]Jeffrey Goldfarb, "Today's Lesson: How to Ad," *American Advertising,* Fall 1999, pp. 19–21.

lured settlers to the New World with hopeful overstatements, half-truths, and down-right lies. And as early as 1930, one trade magazine claimed that advertising "helps to keep the masses dissatisfied with their mode of life, discontented with the ugly things around them. Satisfied customers are not as profitable as discontented ones."

Now ask yourself these questions about advertising: Should profit or prudence prevail when surveys indicate that women, Hispanic-Americans, and African-Americans are prime targets for cigarettes and alcohol at a time when most consumers are consuming less of both? Should a commercial for a popular pain reliever reveal that the reason "more hospitals choose our brand" is that it is supplied at a reduced price? Should an automobile maker show a sports car outracing a jet plane in an age when speeding motorists are killed daily?

Should advertisers cast television commercials using such imperatives as "she should be blond—or if brunette, not too brunette, and pretty but not too pretty," or "midwestern in speech, middle-class looking, gentile," or "if we're using blacks, make them upscale"?

Should advertisers be sensitive to ethnic issues? In Australia, TV spots for Colgate-Palmolive's UV sunscreen showed a group of black men joking about whites' needs for suntan lotion. The conclusion is that, since blacks have natural protection, "Mother Nature must be black." All laugh heartily as the spot closes. Some viewers thought the ads were funny, but the New York–based agency pulled them after receiving five complaints, some reportedly from African-Americans living in Australia.

Is even a mock representation of violence and domination appropriate in commercial speech? One ad for a woman's fragrance showed a woman's fingernails making scratches down the skin of a man's back as the headline proclaims, "Leave your mark on a man." A TV ad for a mall that has "21 places to buy underwear" showed a man stepping in front of a speeding truck and being so terrified that . . . well, you know . . . Fashion leader Kenneth Lane headlined a three-page spread with, "If there were a public execution, would you go watch it?" Turn the page and, above a display of shoes, bags, and sunglasses is the phrase, "What would you wear?"

What about sexual inuendo? Rally's introduced its new big hamburger with a commercial in which women oohed and ahhhed over a guy's "Big Buford," the name of the new product. And a brand of tequila used the front and back of a magazine page to shock readers. Over a picture of a beautiful woman in a scanty costume, the headline read, "She's blonde. She's beautiful. She's headed your way." The reverse side showed the same photo, except the headline now read, "She's a he. Life is harsh. Your tequila shouldn't be."

What do such ads communicate to consumers about values? What do they suggest about the men and women who create the messages? Is it essential to grasp the reader's attention at any cost? That's something only you can decide. As you think about your answer, read on.

● FIGURE 1-4

How do you convince customers that your fishing line is really, really strong? The obvious way would be to show a giant fish that's just been hooked. But that's been done before. Ad from Carmichael Lynch for Stren is unexpected, but relevant.

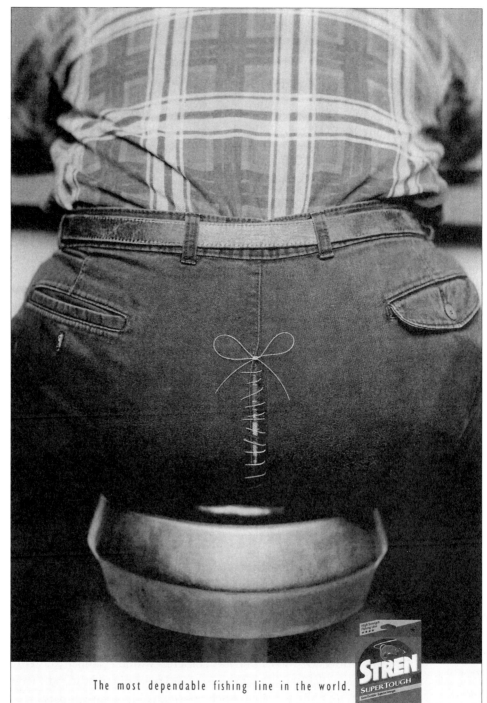

The most dependable fishing line in the world.

● Creativity Run Amuck

As the preceding examples suggest, advertisers sometimes go too far in their attempts to lure consumers. Here are some cautions to be aware of:

1. *Don't let your creativity or your ego get in the way of good judgment.* A woman, annoyed when she saw an ad promoting a nighttime TV soap opera that showed three female characters under the headline "BITCH, BITCH, BITCH," wrote a letter of complaint to the agency that created the ad. Rather than apologize, an employee at the agency sent her a photo of an African child kissing the rear end of a cow and suggested that she should visit the Dinka tribe in East Africa and put a stop to their horrible social practices. When she contacted the agency heads, their response was even more juvenile. They offered to buy the woman a one-way ticket to Africa and sent her a map of Africa, a pith helmet, and mosquito net. Upon receiving their response, the woman copied the entire set of correspondence and sent it to the agency's clients. That got results. One of the major clients withdrew its $10 million account from the agency, and for months the agency was in a damage-control mode due to negative publicity prompted by the incident.

2. *Avoid doing something in questionable taste.* As the previous example illustrates, bad taste is also bad business. The media may reject your ad if it violates the things they believe in. For example, *Elle* magazine left a page blank rather than run a Benetton ad that portrayed a man dying of AIDS. Consumer groups can bring pressure on you as well. Mothers Against Drunk Driving (MADD) will protest any message that glamorizes irresponsible drinking, such as Abercrombie & Fitch's 1998 back-to-school catalog, which included a section called "Drinking 101" and recipes for drinks named the "Brain Hemorrhage," the "Orgasm," and the "Dirty Girl Scout Cookie."

3. *If you make a claim, be prepared to substantiate it.* You may be tempted to promote a health benefit or state that your product is better than another company's. Before you do this, be aware that the Federal Trade Commission (FTC), the Food and Drug Administration (FDA), or the National Association of Attorney Generals may require you to substantiate your claims. If you can't, they can order you to do a variety of things.

For years, ads for Listerine mouthwash claimed that it could prevent colds and sore throats. In 1975, the FTC ordered Warner-Lambert, Listerine's parent company, to spend $10 million on corrective advertising that stated, "Contrary to prior advertising, Listerine will not help prevent colds or sore throats or lessen their severity."

The FTC also challenged ads for Campbell's Soup that used the implied claim that "most of its soups make a positive contribution to a diet that reduces the risk of heart disease." The claim was unsubstantiated and misleading because the soup's high sodium content could contribute to heart problems.

Competitors can sue if your ad "misrepresents the nature, characteristics, qualities, or geographic origin of his or her or another person's goods, services, or commercial activities." John Deere & Co. stopped MDT Products from using the John Deere logo in a disparaging manner. And Wilkinson Sword was ordered to pay Gillette $953,000 in damages after making deceptive superiority claims.

4. *Don't copy creative ideas from other campaigns.* Regardless of what you may have heard, imitation is not always the most sincere form of flattery. Nike forced Volkswagen to pull a print ad that used an "Air Jorgen" headline because it was too close to Nike's "Air Jordan" trademark.

5. *Don't copy other people's likeness.* Tom Waits won a $2.4-million lawsuit against Frito-Lay and ad agency Tracy Locke after they used a soundalike of Waits in a radio campaign for Doritos. Vanna White won $400,000 from Samsung after it used a female robot dressed in an evening gown and blond wig, standing in front of a letter board.

6. *Respect other companies' trademarks.* Tony the Tiger and the Exxon tiger co-existed peacefully for more than 30 years. But when Exxon started using its tiger to sell food, Kellogg's sued for infringement of its tiger trademark.

7. *Watch what you say in front of children.* Advertising claims that may be perfectly suitable for adults may be unacceptable for children, who are more vulnerable to advertising claims. A Post Grape Nuts commercial was deemed unfair because a spokesman compared the "natural goodness" of Grape Nuts to the wild nuts and berries he picked in the woods, since some nuts and berries found in the wild are poisonous.

To see how creativity can run amuck in another manner, see the box on pages 18 and 19.

● The Creative Challenge

The bottom line is, we want you to come up with unexpected solutions to advertising problems. But we want these solutions to make a relevant connection to your target audience. We want you to capture people's attention without insulting them in the process. We want you to convince potential consumers of the merits of your product without tricking them through the use of unsubstantiated claims. We want you to be clever without borrowing other people's cleverness. In other words, we want you to be creative.

Creative advertising makes relevant and unexpected connections in order to build a positive relationship between product and consumer. The relevance comes from the facts, while the unexpected connection is the inspiration of the writer and art director—the added ingredient that gets the message noticed. That's what this book is all

How to Make a Mess Out of a Miracle

Ohrbach's, a bargain clothing store in New York, was famous for its witty ads, which were created by the legendary Bill Bernbach. One of its most famous ads showed a cat, wearing a woman's hat and clenching a long cigarette holder, above the headline "I found out about Joan." The copy continued, "The way she talks, you'd think she was in Who's Who. Well! I found out what's what with her. Her husband owns a bank? Sweetie, not even a bank account. Why that palace of theirs has wall-to-wall mortgages! And that car? Darling, that's horsepower, not earning power. They won it in a fifty-cent raffle! Can you imagine? And those clothes! Of course she does dress divinely. But really . . . a mink stole, and Paris suits, and all those dresses . . . on his income? Well darling. I found out about that too. I just happened to be going her way and I saw Joan come out of Ohrbach's!"

What an original, clever way to advertise bargain clothes in a sophisticated way! But think what might happen if someone "followed the rules."

1. "A good ad always has the name of the advertiser in the headline. Let's include Ohrbach's in the headline, just in case customers miss it at the bottom of the ad."

2. "Let's tell customers they'll save at Ohrbach's. Make the headline bigger. And the cat smaller. And be sure to include the price of the hat."

3. Let's tell customers how much they'll save in 72-point type. And let's have the word "SAVE" in a starburst. Make sure we have a giant 'X' through the suggested retail price of the hat and blow up the Ohrbach's price."

4. "You know, customers might think all we sell is hats. Let's list all the other things we sell."

5. "Let's drop the cat and run a huge savings headline. After all, customers care about themselves. Not about some dumb cat. Let's add a sense of urgency. Say something like, 'Today only!' And in the body copy, let's run some examples of the savings customers will find."

Bernbach's ad positioned the store as a fantastic place to save money on good fashions. What did the resultant "revisions" we've created (and we use that term loosely!) do to that message?

● FIGURE 1-5

Why waste unnecessary words describing a product's attributes? Sometimes a picture *is* worth a thousand words.

about: identifying the advertising problem, gathering the facts, and—through a process of critical and creative thinking—adding your own insight to create a memorable ad that not only commands attention but also delivers the right message to the right audience in a language they understand and accept.

● Suggested Activities

1. Take inventory of the number of advertising messages you see or hear in a single day. How many did you count, how many do you remember vividly, and what were some of the more unusual places in which you found advertising?

2. Find examples of advertisements that you believe (a) promise "miracles" through products, (b) offer stereotypes of people to sell products, (c) play on fears to convince us to buy, (d) state questionable "truths," and (e) are in bad taste. What could the advertisers have done to eliminate such qualities without diminishing the impact of the selling message?

3. Make an inventory of your "creative resources," and seek new worlds to conquer. First, make a list of your favorite films, entertainers, music, fiction and nonfiction books, magazines, live plays and musicals, live concert performances, television programs, and leisure activities. Share these with classmates and your teacher. Now make a concerted effort to add something different to that list. If you watch TV sitcoms, spend an hour or more watching a nature program, a ballet performance, or a historical documentary. If you like country music, try a symphony. What did you learn about yourself as a result of this exercise?

4. After reading what this chapter has said about being creative, what do you regard as your strengths in this area? Your weaknesses? How can you capitalize on the former and improve on the latter?

5. Although some might argue that it's impossible to be creative about ordinary products, advertising professionals will retort, "Boring is no excuse!" Writer James Gorman takes nearly three magazine pages exploring the charm of the lowly pencil. In part, he writes:

> Remember pencils? Remember the smell of cedar shavings, the pleasure of writing on clean paper with that first, sharp point, the sense of guilt and personal inadequacy that comes from seeing the gnawed and stubby evidence of your own anxiety neurosis next to some obsessive's long, sharp points and untoothed hexagonal pencil bodies? I had forgotten about pencils until recently, when I overdosed on computers and decided I needed a rest cure. Pencils. Do people still use them? Are there living pencil devotees? Or have the laser printer and the felt tip pen conquered all?[10]

[10] "Pencil Facts, from James Gorman," adapted from *Wigwag*, Feb. 1990. Used by permission.

Gorman adds that he called the Pencil Makers Association in Moorestown, New Jersey, and discovered that "pencils are doing fine." About 2 billion pencils are made each year by U.S. companies, he learned. He also discovered that pencils got their start in 1564, when a large graphite deposit was uncovered in England. Gradually, folks figured out what to put around the graphite, what to mix it with, and how to cook it to make it stronger and better for writing. Ernest Hemingway and Walt Whitman used pencils, not pens or typewriters. So did Vladimir Nabokov and Herbert Hoover. Henry Thoreau ran a family pencil-making business. Finally, Gorman learned that "you could eat one every day without harming yourself," mainly because the "lead" in a pencil is not lead at all, but graphite.

If Gorman can take three full pages to entertain you about pencils, can you create a single advertisement to provide the pencil with a personality so appealing that readers will clamor for more pencils? Try it.

6. Find an ad in a national magazine, or describe a commercial from radio or TV. Critique it using the following guidelines:

   a. Does the ad gain your attention without confusing you? Would it stand out in a magazine or newspaper full of ads (or on television or radio, as the case may be)?

   b. Does the ad show empathy with the target audience? Is the target clearly defined? Is there a sense of involvement—that is, does the ad make you exclaim, "That's me they're talking about"?

   c. Does the ad clearly communicate the key benefits? Is there a reason to consider purchase, whether rational or emotional, overt or implied? If implied, is it clear enough?

   d. Does the ad use a memorable device to make you remember something important? Is there a line or phrase in the copy that is especially outstanding?

   e. Does the ad make you feel positive about the product, the ad, the manufacturer, and yourself?

   f. Is there anything about the ad, however small, that might be improved? How could it be improved?

7. Take inventory of your creative attributes. In a short paper, write about an event in your life in which you demonstrated your ability to be creative. It doesn't have to deal with advertising or school.

8. Take a "learning style inventory" at your campus career or counseling center. Such inventories can help you discover how you use knowledge and how you make decisions. Understanding how you learn helps you build on your strengths and correct your weaknesses.

Search Online! Discovering More About Creativity

Using InfoTrac® College Edition, try these phrases and others for Key Words and Subject Guide searches: *creativity, creative thinking, creative and relevant, divergent thinking, William Bernbach, David Ogilvy, humanize, humor, celebrity endorsement, irrational decision, advertising myths, advertising stereotypes, advertising and society.*

BriefCase

Bell Helmets: Courage for Your Head

How did Goodby, Silverstein & Partners create the remarkable campaign you see on these pages for its client, Bell Helmets? First, by finding out as much as they could about the company and the market. From the start, it was evident that the target consumers were divided into two groups: the "adult biker enthusiast" and the "young biker," whose mother usually participated in the choice of helmet once she managed to convince her youngster to wear one.

Through firsthand research, the agency team found that mass merchants (instead of independent bike shops) were selling the majority of bike helmets, that the market was growing steadily due to new helmet laws, and that people perceived all helmets to be alike, with the result that prices and profit margins were being pushed downward.

From their San Francisco offices, the agency team drove into the hills north of the city to ask mountain bikers how they chose a helmet. Back in the city, they interviewed youngsters in one focus group who biked regularly and then interviewed their mothers in a separate focus group.

"We were amazed that, young or adult, most bikers had no idea what brand of helmet they were wearing," admits Mary Sturvinou, Goodby's strategic planner on the Bell Helmets account. One person, when asked to name the brand, actually said, "What does it say on my helmet?"

In the focus groups with children and their moms, the agency team learned that the majority of youth helmets were purchased at toy and discount stores. "If a store sells it as a bicycle helmet, it must be okay," was the general attitude among these groups. When youngsters were given a variety of brands to examine and asked to pick the helmet they liked best, brand names were of little consequence. Many referred to their choice as the "youth" brand because the word appeared on the package to indicate the helmet size!

But when the agency team visited the Bell Helmets factory, they were impressed with the lengths to which Bell went to test the safety of each model. They learned that a number of Indy racers who had crashed credited Bell Helmets with saving their lives.

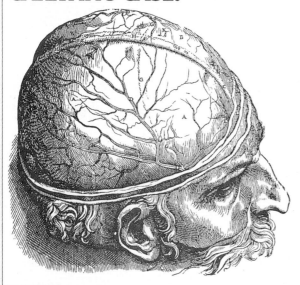

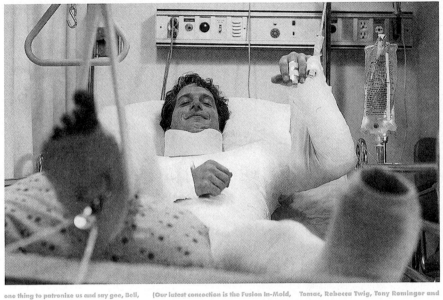

What next? Goodby's brief on the case sets several important goals, including the following: (1) Correct the perception that all helmets are created equal. By making Bell top-of-mind in a category with no real brand registration, and (2) begin reversing youngster's perceptions that "helmets equal corrective shoes." Another insight from the team was that the link between the most serious road-racer and the eight-year-old kid just learning to skate or bike is the spirit (or coolness) of their sport. Everyone wants the freedom and courage to pursue their sport to its fullest, even if they never actually exercise this opportunity.

The strategy was a natural outgrowth of this line of thinking: Bell Helmets are the safest you can buy. Bell allows you to pursue your sport to its fullest. To the trade, the message was, "Only Bell has been here for 40 years and, thanks to their tradition of testing, will be here 40 years from now."

In brainstorming sessions, the team agreed that Bell should be a star in a field that had little brand awareness. "Bell should *own* helmets," said one of the Goodby folks. And someone else added, "When you wear a helmet you can trust, it gives you the courage you need to tackle a sport all the way." Writer Paul Venables jumped from that thought to the idea that Bell Helmets were "courage for your head," which became the tag line for the campaign. With Jeremy Postaer's unusual use of heavy

BriefCase

borders, bold headlines, and screened body copy, the two-page magazine ads stood out instantly. Television spots echoed the same theme, using grainy footage of bikers, racers, and other daredevils crashing their vehicles as a gentle whistler fills the soundtrack to suggest that "these guys are cool because they've protected their heads." In between the action shots, full-screen titles completed the story, and the signoff used a full-screen Bell Helmets logo followed by a helmet wrapping itself around a model of the human brain with the chin strap locking into place as the announcer stated, "Bell Helmets: Courage for your head." (See Figure 9-1 for a copy of one of these scripts.)

The result? Bell's total market share increased eight points in eight months in a shrinking market (from 40 percent to 48 percent). Distribution in independent bike stores increased where Bell had anticipated a decline. In qualitative research, the team discovered that after exposure to the advertising youngsters did not feel as negative about wearing helmets while parents felt very strongly that "there must be a difference in helmet quality" and "I should buy the best."

Amazing what first-rate strategic planning, exhaustive research, and creative thinking can do, isn't it?

CHAPTER 2

Targeting a Diverse Marketplace

Effective advertising makes relevant connections with its target audience. To be successful, advertisers must understand, respect, and embrace the diversity of American consumers.

Currently, one in four Americans is a person of color. By the year 2005, that ratio will be one in three, and by 2050, people of color will represent 55 percent of the U.S. population, according to U.S. Census Bureau projections. The buying power of ethnic Americans is also changing. Hispanic-Americans, African-Americans, and Asian-Americans are expected to triple their buying power in the next twelve years while the general market's buying power will only double. Furthermore, the Multicultural "American Dream" Index study reports that Asian-Americans, Hispanic-Americans, and African-Americans are increasing household income, obtaining mortgages, owning small businesses, and earning college degrees more than three times as quickly as other Americans.

Interesting things are happening to the age of Americans, too. Today, one in three Americans is a grandparent, according to Roper Starch Worldwide. By the year 2010, grandparents are expected to number 80 million, up dramatically from today's already impressive number of 60 million. Women age 40–64 will soon be America's largest age segment, accounting for 24 percent of the U.S. population by 2002 and 32 percent by 2015, according to U.S. Census Bureau projections.

● African-Americans

African-Americans, at 33 million strong, are the nation's largest minority group. Their annual purchasing power of $447 billion makes them very attractive to advertisers. Furthermore, they're very brand loyal—with an 86.7 percent brand loyalty for food products, 81.1 percent for cars, and 79.5 percent for electronic equipment, according to the Urban Consumer Market Report.

Unlike many of their Anglo counterparts, African-Americans love to shop. *American Demographics* reports that 60 percent of African-Americans find it "fun and exciting" to shop for clothes while only 35 percent of Anglo-Americans feel the same way. African-American households spend more than the average American on hosiery, shoes, women's accessories, jewelry, and personal-care services.

But it's not just fashion and beauty products that distinguish African-Americans from other groups. According to the Consumer Expenditure Survey, a typical African-American household spends more on sugar than the average white household. When they buy soft drinks, African-Americans prefer to buy larger-size bottles, and when they drink coffee, they use larger portions of sugar, cream, and nondairy creamer than other groups.

Before you try to reach this market, it's important to understand what distinguishes African-Americans from other market segments. Unlike other immigrants who came to the United States to better themselves, most African-Americans originally were brought to this country against their will. Because they were victims of slavery and generations of discrimination, African-Americans seek products that give them a sense of empowerment and that show they are important members of society, according to Ken Smikle, publisher of *Target Market News.*

The quest for empowerment may explain certain buying patterns. Eugene Morris, president of E. Morris, LTD, points to the fact that many lower-income African-Americans buy expensive liquor to make a statement about themselves because it is an affordable status symbol. Likewise, Byron Lewis, chairman of UniWorld Group, states that many African-Americans focus their spending on status symbols such as cars, electronics, and jewelry because they can't acquire the home they want. Marlene R. Rossman, author of *Multicultural Marketing,* also suggests that the need for status may explain why less affluent African-Americans prefer to buy branded goods while more upscale African-Americans are willing to buy less expensive private-label and generic goods.

● Hispanic-Americans

The nation's 32 million Hispanic-Americans make up the second largest minority group and are expected to outnumber African-Americans by the year 2005. They originate from many different places, including Mexico, Cuba, Puerto Rico, Central and South America, and Europe. The majority choose to live in major cities, with 37 percent of Hispanic-Americans living in Los Angeles, New York City, and Miami.

As a result of the diversity of their roots, Hispanic-Americans have varied tastes in food, clothing, and music. Advertisers should pay attention to these cultural subtle-

● FIGURE 2-1

People from all over the country have stories about loved ones who were killed by a drunk driver. This urgent plea to stop friends from driving drunk has been translated into Spanish to reach Hispanic-Americans.

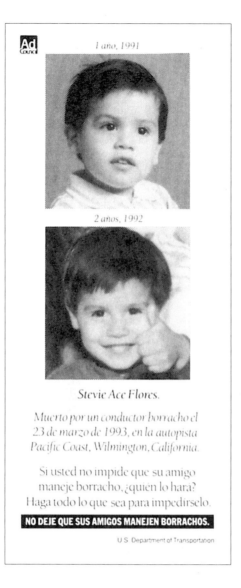

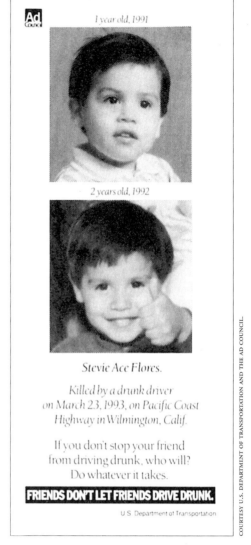

ties, as Coca-Cola did when it ran three versions of an ad for Hispanics. Each ad featured the Coca-Cola logo and a can of Coke, along with the words "*y su comida favorita*" (and your favorite meal). But the food next to the Coke was changed to reflect different cultural preferences. Tacos were featured for the western Mexican-American segment, pork loin for the southeastern Cuban-American segment, and arroz con pollo (chicken and rice) for the northeastern Puerto Rican segment.

Spanish words can have different meanings, depending on national heritage. The word *bichos,* for example, means bugs to Mexicans and a man's private parts to Puerto Ricans. Imagine you were writing an ad for an insecticide and weren't aware of this little subtlety!

Although it's complex, the Hispanic-American market is attractive to advertisers. According to Market Segment Research, Hispanic families buy more groceries than any other ethnic group, spending an average of $91 on groceries each week, compared to $65 by the general market. They purchase more regular soft drinks, dry seasoning, breath mints, canned vegetables, cooking oil, analgesics, deodorant, and bathroom tissue than any other ethnic group. They also spend twice as much as general-market consumers on long-distance calls.

Part of the reason for these expenditures is that Hispanic-Americans tend to have larger families, with almost 3.5 people per household compared to the national average of just over 2.5. To reach Hispanics successfully, advertisers should recognize the importance placed on the family and tradition. A radio station learned this lesson after it promoted a sweepstakes that offered a prize of two tickets to Disneyland and received a limited response from Hispanics. The reason? Hispanics didn't want to choose which family member should go.

Marketers must also pay close attention to the ages of their target groups. The median age of Hispanic-Americans is 26, which is eight years younger than the overall population. Nearly 35 percent of Hispanics are under the age of 18, and they're big spenders. Overall, Hispanic teens spend 7.8 percent more than the average teen does, according to Teenage Research Unlimited. And Hispanic girls spend more than twice as much on hair products and makeup as other female teens. As you might expect, age plays a major role in shaping attitudes, styles of dress, and choice of music. But there's an interesting twist: The younger generation of Hispanics are often more in tune with their ancestry than their parents are.

According to a special *Newsweek* poll, those over 35 are more likely to identify themselves as American, while those under 35 are more likely to identify themselves as Hispanic or Latino. To reach Hispanic-American youths, advertisers should stop thinking in terms of Generation X or Y, and instead think Generation Ñ. Bill Teck, who coined the term *Generation Ñ,* explains: "If you know all the words to [the merengue hit] 'Abusadora' and 'Stairway to Heaven,' if you grew up on cafe, black beans and 'Three's Company,'. . . if you're thinking of borrowing one of your father's guayaberas, . . . you're Generation Ñ."[1]

● Asian-Americans

Although Asian-Americans represent only 3 percent of the U.S. population, they are the nation's fastest-growing and most affluent minority group. The median income for Asian-American households is $45,248, which is significantly higher than the $37,004 median income of all U.S. households. Furthermore, 42 percent of Asian-Americans and Pacific Islanders have at least a bachelor's degree, compared to

---

[1]John Leland and Veronica Chambers, "Generation Ñ," *Newsweek,* 12 July 1999, p. 53

24 percent of the general U.S. population. And when it comes to the Web, Asian-Americans are in the fast lane. *Newsweek* reports that 64 percent of Asian-Americans are online, compared to 33 percent of total households, 36 percent of Hispanic-American households, and 23 percent of African-American households.

Advertisers have been slow to target Asian-Americans because of the complexity of their varied languages and cultures. Many nationalities are included in this minority group, among them Chinese, Japanese, Korean, Filipino, Vietnamese, and Asian-Indian. And there's not a common language among them. People of Chinese origin, the largest subgroup, speak dozens of different dialects, with Mandarin, Cantonese, and Taiwanese being the most common.

As you can imagine, horror stories about advertisers who have inadvertently alienated this market abound. Marlene L. Rossman points to a number of such stories. One advertiser wished Chinese-Americans a "Year New Happy" rather than a "Happy New Year." Another used Korean models to target the Vietnamese community, oblivious to the fact that the two groups rarely look anything alike. And a footwear manufacturer depicted Japanese women performing footbinding; as Rossman observed, this not only stereotyped Japanese people as "Shogun" characters but also displayed the company's ignorance about Asian cultures, given that footbinding was practiced exclusively in China.[2]

Although each nationality has distinct cultures and traditions, there are two important commonalities: the importance of family and of tradition. In Asian cultures, it is inappropriate to call attention to oneself; therefore, tactful ads targeted at Asian-Americans don't show an individual standing out from the crowd or achieving personal gain by using the product. Instead, culturally conscious ads focus on how the family or group benefits. And with the great importance placed on tradition, "new and improved" claims are far less effective than those that stress a company's or product's many years of excellence.

Whether it's a result of their wealth and education, their respect for tradition, or a combination of the two, Asian-Americans don't look for off-brand bargains when shopping. They tend to buy top-of-the-line, high-ticket items, and they prefer name department stores to discount stores. When they go grocery shopping, Asian-Americans avoid canned vegetables, preferring fresh fruits and vegetables purchased on a daily basis as needed.

● Native Americans

The estimated 1.8 million Native Americans make up less than 0.8 percent of the nation's population, and approximately one-third live at or below the poverty line. As a result, few marketing efforts are aimed at this group. Although companies

[2] Marlene L. Rossman, *Multicultural Marketing: Selling to a Diverse America* (New York: American Management Association, 1994).

And you thought the pink Energizer bunny kept going and going and going! This true story demonstrates that Coleman stoves and their owners are unbelievably tough, regardless of age.

L.C. Shaffer's 1924 Two-Owner Classic
(An Unbelievable True Story)

In 1951, L.C. was given a Coleman® stove that its original owner had used since 1924. L.C. thought it might still have some life in it. So for the next 40-odd years, he fired it up on every hunting trip and at every fishing hole. And used it every day at every construction site he worked. Including a big job in Nevada when he cooked three meals a day on it for nine months. L.C. is now 81, and his Coleman stove is 69. L.C. says they're both a long way from retirement.

UNBELIEVABLY TOUGH

COURTESY THE COLEMAN COMPANY, INC., AND LEE CRUM, PHOTOGRAPHER.

don't often target this group in advertising campaigns, they make frequent use of Native American names and symbolism. For example, Chrysler uses the name "Cherokee" for one of its jeeps, and Land O' Lakes butter features an Indian on its package. Ironically, "Crazy Horse" malt liquor was named after the Sioux leader who was opposed to alcohol consumption among his people. Needless to say, these images are insulting to Native Americans.

Gail Baker Woods, author of *Advertising and Marketing to the New Majority,* points to the fact that Native Americans are becoming better educated and that tribes have begun to develop their own businesses and to use their land as an economic resource. If, as Woods says, these economic and educational trends continue for Native Americans, "marketers will surely find them in their search for new consumers."[3]

● How to Reach Ethnic Minorities

Savvy advertisers know several methods for reaching ethnic minorities:

1. *Feature minorities in starring roles, and not just in the background.* Pepsi connected to young Hispanic-Americans with commercials featuring pop singer Gloria Estefan and the Miami Sound Machine. After Reebok ran an ad featuring the Chinese-American tennis star Michael Chang, Reebok's sales to Asian-Americans skyrocketed. Similarly, sales to African-Americans in an Atlanta mall soared when the mall hired a black Santa. In addition to making a positive connection to the ethnic group portrayed, research shows that advertisements featuring minorities are favorably received by general audiences.

2. *Seek the opinions of people who hail from the culture you are targeting.* However, be aware that traditional research methods may not work. For example, a survey written in English won't get results that are representative of all American households because 15 percent of the U.S. population doesn't speak English at home. In addition, many Hispanic and Asian immigrants are uncomfortable giving out information to strangers over the telephone or through the mail.

3. *Be sensitive to nuances in language.* It's not enough merely to translate the English copy of a campaign into another language. Frank Perdue found this out the hard way when the line "It takes a tough man to make a tender chicken" was translated into Spanish by someone unfamiliar with regional slang. The translation came out something like, "It takes a sexually stimulated man to make a chicken affectionate." For some other examples of mistranslations, see the box on page 36.

Also, be aware of different uses of English words, because they can mean different things to different groups. For example, sales of Stove Top stuffing improved among African-Americans after the company realized this group uses the word "dressing," rather than "stuffing."

You must also be sensitive to how you refer to different groups. Ethnic groups use a variety of names to describe themselves. For example, this book uses "Hispanic-American" rather than "Latino" because it is the designation used by the U.S. Census Bureau. We use "African-American" because this book is targeted to college students

---

[3]Gail Baker Woods, *Advertising and Marketing to the New Majority* (Belmont, CA: Wadsworth, 1995), p. 50.

Diverse Goofs: Translating American Advertising into Other Languages

- When Braniff Airlines touted its upholstery by saying "Fly in leather," it came out in Spanish as "Fly naked."

- Coors' slogan "Turn it loose" means "Suffer from diarrhea" in Spanish.

- The Spanish translation for chicken magnate Frank Perdue's line "It takes a tough man to make a tender chicken" is "It takes a sexually stimulated man to make a chicken affectionate."

- When Vicks first introduced its cough drops in Germany, they discovered that Germans pronounce "v" as "f," which made their trade name reminiscent of the German word for sexual penetration.

- Puffs tissues learned its lesson in Germany, too. "Puff" in German is a colloquial term for a whorehouse.

- The Chevy Nova never sold well in Spanish-speaking countries, perhaps because "*No va*" means "It does not go."

- Nor did the Ford Pinto, since its name was used to describe men with smaller-than-average private parts.

- When Pepsi's old campaign, "Come Alive. You're in the Pepsi Generation," was translated into Chinese, it announced that "Pepsi will bring your ancestors back from the grave."

- GM's "body by Fisher" translated, in some languages, into "corpse by Fisher," something you would not want associated with automotive design.

- Coke discovered problems in China when they used Chinese characters that, when pronounced, sounded like "Coca-Cola" but meant "Bite the wax tadpole."

and young copywriters, who prefer that term. However, older persons often prefer "black" or "person of color."

4. *Show the diversity of each group.* African-Americans come in 35 different shades and color hues, and just as many hair textures and eye shadings, according to Georgia Lee Clark of the Communications Publishing Group. Likewise, Asian-Americans and Hispanic-Americans hail from many different countries and, contrary to what poorly informed people think, don't all look alike.

5. *Learn about their heritage.* It's important to show respect for ethnic holidays, whether it's the Chinese New Year, the African-American holiday Kwaanza, or Cinco

de Mayo, a holiday commemorating Mexico's triumph over France. It's also important to pay close attention to details and learn about preferences in food, icons, customs, and clothing. For example, McDonald's was praised for a commercial that featured a celebration that looked like a simple birthday party to most viewers but was recognized by Hispanics as the *quinceañera*, the celebration of a girl's coming of age at 15.

● The 50-Plus Market

The 50-plus American population is 65 million strong and is growing larger every day. Every 8 seconds, a Baby Boomer turns 50. Furthermore, those in the 50-plus population control 55 percent of the discretionary income in the United States and account for the majority of personal assets—upwards of 80 percent of the money in savings and loans and 70 percent of the net worth of U.S. households.

But older people aren't just saving money; they're also spending it. According to recent statistics, the 50-plus population purchases 48 percent of all luxury cars, 37 percent of all spa memberships, and 80 percent of all luxury trips.

Despite these impressive figures, advertisers haven't done a good job reaching older people and have been accused of ignoring and insulting this market through negative stereotypes that portray them as doddering and senile. So how do you reach this important market? Here are some tips:

1. *Don't think of older people as just one market.* Think about some of the older people you know: grandparents, neighbors, professors, community leaders. Chances are, these people are quite different from one another. They have different political views, different senses of humor, different lifestyles, and so on. Like any group, the older population is comprised of people with varied incomes, education levels, ethnic backgrounds, and life experiences. Using one message to reach all these people is about as absurd as saying one message will work for all people aged 18 to 49.

2. *Don't specify age.* Research has shown most older people feel younger than their birth certificate indicates. As Bernard Baruch said, "To me, old age is fifteen years older than I am." Several years ago, an advertising campaign featured the claim "the first shampoo created for hair over 40." It bombed. The problem? Younger people refused to buy a product aimed at older people, and older people didn't want to be reminded they had older hair.

3. *Cast models who reflect the way your audience feels.* Use models who portray an upbeat, positive image, not those who reinforce the negative stereotypes of frailty and senility. But don't go to the opposite extreme. Although you may be tempted to show a person in his 80s who bungee-jumps, most older people won't identify with this portrayal.

The Classic Account. Another honor for those who served with Elvis.

If you're turning 50, you may have buttoned on a uniform about the time Elvis helped to defend us.

Whether you did—or whether it still fits—isn't the point, of course. It's that now South Carolina National has a banking package that fits you very well.

And the only requirement is that you're 50 or older.

If you are, you're eligible for free checking, free checks, free travelers checks and money orders.

Interest on every dollar in your account. Discounts on a safe deposit box. A special Health Care CD. And more.

You can even apply for a special SCN Palmetto VISA® card.

Our Classic Account is the kind of honor most banks won't offer till you turn 55. But we figure it's time someone gave special consideration to the generation that grew up with rock 'n roll.

See your SCN banker. Or call Ann Singer at 1-800-922-5560. (771-3939 in Columbia.)

FLEXBANKING℠
South Carolina National
Equal Opportunity Lender. Member FDIC.

COURTESY FLEX BANKING.

● FIGURE 2-3
....

The king of rock 'n' roll lives in the hearts of many people, particularly those in the 50-plus set. This humorous visual laughs with the audience, not at them. After all, the last time someone saw Elvis, he couldn't fit into his uniform, either.

Cast models who represent the age your audience feels. Remember how you identified with the "big" kids when you were younger? Well, the opposite is true as you get older. Most older people see themselves as ten to fifteen years younger than their birth certificates indicate. Therefore, use models who are younger than your target audience.

4. *Tell the whole story.* While commercials with fast editing cuts and very little copy may appeal to younger audiences, older audiences prefer a narrative style, with a beginning, a middle, and an end. As Grey Advertising summed it up, this generation is MGM, not MTV.

When writing copy, give facts, not fluff. After years of shopping, older people are not going to be fooled into buying your product simply because you tell them that it's "new" or "the best." After all, these folks remember product flops like the Edsel, and they want facts to back up your claims. Give them a compelling reason to try your product, and they'll be willing to read lengthy copy or listen to a detailed pitch.

5. *Don't remind older people of their vulnerability.* It's a fact of life: Arthritis, high blood pressure, heart problems, and other ailments bother more older people than younger people. However, older people know they have aches and pains without being reminded by you. Rather than dwell on the problems, your advertising should show how your product offers solutions.

6. *Show older people as they are, happy with themselves.* Show them enjoying life, playing with their grandchildren, volunteering their time, starting new hobbies, and learning new things. Advertisements for Fox Hill Village, a retirement community in Massachusetts, used to show smiling retirees on balconies admiring the beautiful landscape. But when the community ran a series of ads featuring Ben Franklin, Clara Barton, Noah Webster, and other individuals who became famous during their later years, inquiries went up 25 percent.

● Women

Women comprise 51 percent of the U.S. population, so it may seem odd to include them in a chapter about minority groups. However, because women are still fighting issues of empowerment, they are included here.

Vamps. Tramps. Trophy wives. Old maids. Sexy babes. Dumb blondes. Bimbos. Bulimic models. Bitchy bosses. Chronic PMS. You name the insult, and advertising has used it. Even the tag line that was supposed to show how liberated women had become, "You've come a long way, baby," was insulting.

Although advertising can always be improved, we are light years from the era when blonde bombshells were used to sell cars to men (just look at any ad from Saturn to see how far advertising has progressed). Smart advertisers pay attention to the stats, which show they can't afford to ignore or insult women. According to J. D. Power &

Figure 2-4

Jamaicans living in the United States should certainly be attracted to a long-distance offer that provides discounts on all calls to Jamaica, but the ad on the left failed to produce responses. While the primitive artwork might appeal to tourists, it left native Jamaicans cold. The revised campaign (right) reflected the strong emotional ties Jamaicans maintain with their extended families (not palm trees or beaches). The agency also understood that Jamaicans take great pride in their independence, whether they live in New York or Jamaica. Pictures of Jamaican children on an interactive puzzle postcard, along with copy on the back celebrating the nation's independence, connected to the heritage that Jamaicans hold dear.

We can offer you the world. Unless, of course, you'd rather have your own country.

Now you can get discounts on every call you make to Jamaica with the new AT&T Special Country℠ Plan. Or you can go further than that, with the AT&T Reach Out® World Plan, and save on AT&T calls to Jamaica plus more than

INTRODUCING THE PERFECT PLAN TO CALL JAMAICA.

50 other countries and locations during plan hours. Either way, we've got an international calling plan that's just what you're looking for. To find out which one is right for you, call us at 1 800 523-WORLD, Ext. 4375.

AT&T

These plans may not be combined with each other or with certain other AT&T optional calling plans. Discounts apply to basic AT&T International Long Distance prices on direct-dialed calls. Other conditions and exclusions also apply. Subject to billing availability. © 1993 AT&T

A POSTAL PUZZLE
FOR YOU!
YOUR SPECIAL POST CARD IS A POSTAL PUZZLE.
Your puzzle comes apart easily so you can put it together again.

Dear Valued Customer,

The spirit of independence. It's what being an individual is all about. No one understands that better than the folks back home. Give them a call this Independence Day.

Satisfying your individual communications needs is what **The _i_ Plan** from AT&T is all about. **The _i_ Plan** offers a menu of savings and service options to pick and choose from depending on when, where and how often you call. Because everybody's different, every **_i_ Plan** is different. Call us to help design yours.

1 800 523-9675, Ext. 6025

_i_ is for individual.

© AT&T 1993
Printed in U.S.A.

```
FIRST-CLASS MAIL
U.S. POSTAGE
PAID
SCHENEVUS, NY
Permit No. 1
```

TO OPEN:
Score on perforation lines! Pull off on perforated lines! Puzzle removes easily for your entertainment!

BEND TO BREAK PLASTIC
ON DOTTED LINE

PULL OFF ON
DOTTED LINE

PATENT PENDING

Associates, women influence 80 percent of car purchases. The Roper Organization says that women have greater influence than men over purchasing decisions about most household products, grocery items, children's toys, and clothing. The National Retail Hardware Association/Home Center Institute reports that the majority of today's women own a monkey wrench, a ladder, a pipe declogger, and a plunger. And MediaMark Research reports that women own slightly more than 50 percent of all life insurance policies.

● People with Disabilities

An estimated 43 million Americans, or 14.5 percent of the working population, have disabilities. Once nearly invisible in ads, people with disabilities now have starring roles. McDonald's showed that people with disabilities can work and be productive citizens through a heartwarming commercial narrated by an employee named Mike, who has Down syndrome. Wal-Mart's advertising regularly features employees and customers in wheelchairs, and one of their TV commercials stars a hearing-impaired employee signing to a deaf customer.

Although many people praise these ads, some question the motives behind them. Bob Garfield, a critic for *Advertising Age,* states that jumping from not showing disabled people at all to portraying them as superhuman or as tokens does not help disabled people or the advertiser in the long run. Screenwriter Mark Moss, who ended up in a wheelchair after a diving accident, told the *Boston Globe,* "Advertisers know that using people with disabilities is politically correct and a viable way to catch people's attention. I look at the phenomenon like I do politicians kissing babies. It's good for the babies . . . it's good for the politicians . . . but we can't be blamed for looking at it with cynicism."[4]

As with any target group, it's important to ask group members what they think. For example, a major fast-food chain ran a newspaper ad with the headline "Introducing our new easy-to-read menu," which was printed over a design that looked like braille. A blind student appropriately asked, "Why didn't they actually print the ad in braille? If they printed it on a heavier stock and inserted it into the paper, then I could keep it for future reference."

● Gays and Lesbians

The policy of "Don't ask, don't tell" reaches far beyond the U.S. military. Even the all-knowing U.S. Census Bureau doesn't ask. As a result, there are varying opinions on this market's size and spending power. Overlooked Opinions, a gay and lesbian market research firm, reports there are nearly 18.5 million gay and lesbian adults in the United States. To arrive at these figures, Overlooked Opinions used findings from the Kinsey Institute, which stated that 10 percent of the U.S. popula-

[4]Maggie Farley, "Ads with a Soul Touch an Untapped Market," *Boston Globe,* 6 July 1992, p. 10.

tion is gay. However, lower figures are reported in other studies that ask people to state whether they identify themselves as gay or lesbian. A study from Yankelovich Partners reports that 6 percent of the U.S. population is gay, and a study from the University of Chicago reports that 2.8 percent of adult men and 1.5 percent of adult women identify themselves as homosexual or bisexual.

As a result of this confusion, some mainstream companies say they don't target gays and lesbians because they don't have enough data. Others fear backlash from conservative Americans. However some companies, such as Absolut Vodka, which has been advertising in gay publications since 1979, have taken the gamble. Does it work? According to *Advertising Age,* people in gay bars don't ask for vodka; they want Absolut. Other companies that have targeted gays include American Express, Anheuser-Busch, AT&T, Continental Airlines, Hiram Walker, Ikea, MCI, Miller, Saab, Saturn, Subaru, and Virgin Atlantic Airways.

Several factors account for the increase in the number of companies targeting gays and lesbians. For starters, gays and lesbians are more affluent than the mainstream population. A 1998 study by Greenfield Online reported average yearly household income among gays and lesbians to be $57,300, with 11 percent surpassing $100,000 annually. Simmons Market Research Bureau reports an even higher percentage of affluent gays, with 21 percent of gay and lesbian households surpassing $100,000 in annual income.

Furthermore, Simmons notes that this market segment is exceptionally loyal, with 89 percent reporting they would buy products or services that advertised in gay publications. A spokesman for Hiram Walker & Sons confirmed this, telling *Advertising Age,* "I have a file of letters an inch or two thick from gay consumers thanking us and vowing their loyalty. A straight consumer wouldn't take the time and say thank you for validating us."[5]

To reach this affluent market segment, some companies run existing ads from their current campaign in gay publications. Others incorporate gay themes in their ads. A brochure for AT&T, for example, features same-sex couples talking about long-distance communications. One panel of the brochure shows a photo of two men with the caption, "When David's away on business, we like to stay close. I love to know what he's doing and what's on his mind." Subaru, which discovered that lesbians are four times likely to own a Subaru as people in the general market, ran an ad featuring two women with the headline, "It loves camping, dogs and long-term commitment. Too bad it's only a car."

A reader poll from *The Advocate* supports the decision to focus on gay themes. In the survey of 5000 readers, 54 percent said they want ads that address gay and lesbian themes. However, another 33 percent said, "It depends on how gay content is handled in the ad," and 13 percent responded, "Concentrate on the product, not the consumer."

[5]Nancy Coltun Webster, "Playing to Gay Segments Opens Doors to Marketers," *Advertising Age,* 30 May 1994, pp. 5–6.

● Lessons That Apply to All Segments

Whatever group you are targeting, certain basic principles apply, including the following:

1. *Look at the whole person, not one demographic characteristic.* To understand your target audience, you must factor in other demographic aspects, as well as psychographic issues such as values, attitudes, personality, and lifestyle. For example, a middle-age Hispanic-American business executive living in the suburbs is likely to have very different attitudes from an inner-city Hispanic-American youth living below the poverty line or a single, working Hispanic-American mother earning minimum wage. Second- or third-generation Americans have different views than recent immigrants. African-Americans who formed their core values before the 1960s will have one outlook, those who were a part of the civil rights movement will have another, and teenagers will have still another.

2. *Avoid stereotypes.* Taco Bell offended Mexican-Americans with its border search commercial because it looked like a search for illegal immigrants. The state of Pennsylvania offended Chinese-Americans with its state lottery promotion, which featured the line "No tickee—no money." Dow Chemical insulted African-Americans with a commercial in which a robust black woman exclaimed, "Ooh-wee!" because it was a reminder of the black mammy stereotype. Native American activists protested when a brewer tried to introduce a malt liquor called "Crazy Horse." Unfortunately, this list of insulting ads could go on and on. Your job is to change that.

Be wary even of "positive" stereotypes. Not all African-Americans are great athletes, musicians, or dancers, yet advertising often portrays them this way. Likewise, not all Asian-Americans are good at math or science. In fact, when figure skater Kristi Yamaguchi won the Olympic gold medal, the *New York Times* printed an anonymous comment: "We are not all math or science wizards or laundry operators or restaurant owners, but skaters, architects, writers. And more. And less." The same holds true for every group you'll ever want to reach in your advertising.

3. *Laugh with them, not at them.* Humor does have a place—if it doesn't rely on insulting stereotypes. To test whether your humor might be insulting to some group, consider replacing one of the characters with a person from a different market segment. For example, if you wanted to make sure customers remembered your client's name, you might be tempted to create a humorous commercial featuring an older person who is hard of hearing and needs to have everything repeated, as Country Time Lemonade did. Or you might feature an older woman who keeps forgetting the name and needs to be constantly reminded, as another company did. However, would it be as funny if a young, physically active college student couldn't hear or remember the name? Probably not. What if you replaced the older woman with a

college student who was high on drugs? Would it be a fair portrayal of college students? Of course not.

4. *Make relevant ties to their special causes.* Consider donating a portion of your sales to causes that are dear to their hearts, such as AIDS research, the Council on Aging, the Special Olympics, the Rape Crisis Center, the Native American Arts Foundation, the Sickle Cell Disease Foundation, the United Negro College Fund, or ASPIRA, a scholarship fund for Hispanics. However, make it a long-term commitment, not a one-shot deal.

5. *Test your ads on a member of the target audience.* You may find an embarrassing mistake in time to correct it before it runs. For example, the Publix grocery chain might have saved itself from the embarrassment of wishing their customers "a quiet, peaceful Yom Kippur" right below an announcement of a sale on center cut pork chops and fresh pork shoulder picnics if they had double-checked with someone who is Jewish.

6. *Show diversity in your ads.* As America becomes more diverse, it's not only the right thing to do but the smart thing to do.

● Suggested Activities

1. Watch 2 hours of prime-time television, and record the way the groups mentioned in this chapter are portrayed. How many are in starring roles? How many reflect stereotypes? What products are they selling?

2. Compare print ads for fashion, liquor, and travel that appear in general-interest magazines (such as *Cosmopolitan, Vogue, Sports Illustrated,* and *Newsweek*) to those that appear in special-interest magazines (such as *Essence* and *Ebony,* which target African-Americans; *Latina* and *People en Español* which target Hispanic-Americans; and *New Choices* and *Modern Maturity,* which target older people). Are the ads similar? If not, comment on the differences in visuals and text that appear to reflect different targeted audiences.

3. Choose an ad (such as for toothpaste, soap, or potato chips), and rewrite the copy to appeal directly to an ethnic minority.

4. Write headlines for the following products: (a) an arthritic pain reliever, (b) a denture adhesive, and (c) an undergarment for adults with bladder control problems.

5. Look at automobile ads from recent decades, and comment on the changes in the way people are portrayed. (Your library should have bound editions of back issues of magazines such as *Time* and *Newsweek.*)

Search Online! Discovering More About Targeting and Diversity

Using InfoTrac® College Edition, try these phrases and others for Key Words and Subject Guide searches: *ethnic consumers, ethnic buying habits, African-American brand loyalty, African-American empowerment, African-American consumer, Hispanic-American consumer, Asian-American consumer, Native American consumer, translating advertising copy, 50-plus consumer, women and advertising stereotypes, Virginia Slims campaign, disabled consumer, gay and lesbian consumer.*

BriefCase

Tide en Español

Some brands linger for decades and slowly fade into obscurity. But if you take a brand and continually extend it with new technologies, forms, and benefits without losing sight of the original, you can run with it for years.

Procter & Gamble has done this with Tide detergent, now celebrating more than 50 years as the leader in its category. Tide has endured because, as a corporate spokesperson puts it, "It is kept up-to-date, meeting consumer needs and doing so in ways that provide steadily improving performance and value."

Of course, advertising must keep pace with such changes. A 1953 advertisement for Tide, showing a woman in an apron high-kicking with joy as she holds a box of Tide, was headlined, "You never had it so clean. Never before Tide was it possible to get your family wash so clean." Great positioning for its time, but we're in a new millennium, remember?

Women work today. They need to manage home and family as well as office tasks. With flextime, some work extra hours each day so they can take a day off during the week to shop, do laundry, and catch the school play. This takes planning. Lots of it. And choosing a detergent brand is a comparatively minor issue in their lives, while time is of the essence.

So the new Tide ads speak to the millennium woman. They speak with humor, because she appreciates it. They acknowledge that life is full of problems, some of which their detergent can solve. They don't promise results; they imply them.

"Recess. Gym class. Food fights. Any questions?" reads one in English.

But idiomatic phrases don't translate well. So for its Hispanic campaign, the words, as well as the language, are different.

"La salsa se baila no se viste" translates as "Salsa is meant to be danced, not worn," which plays on the fact that *salsa* is also a dance.

"¿Para que usar la servilleta cuando existe la camiseta?" translates as "Why do you need a napkin when you have a T-shirt?"—a play on the Spanish words *servilleta* (napkin) and *camiseta* (T-shirt).

A third ad uses the rhyme "De la cuchara a la boca, se cae la sopa" ("From the table to the mouth, the soup spills out"), which is an old saying used to teach table manners to children.

The campaign, without merely translating English copy, has the same smart tone as the general-market campaign, but was obviously created for the Hispanic market.

Using the person's life as the context of the message can be a strong way to maintain top-of-mind awareness, especially for established brands. In any language, Tide has proved that.

CHAPTER 3

Fact-Finding: The Basis for Effective Creative Work

P art of the fun of working in advertising is digging for information. Thorough searches can help you uncover new uses for products, learn about new market areas, spot new trends, and discover what makes people tick. By doing a complete job in the research stage, you'll find that coming up with the big idea is much easier. So where do you start?

● Step 1: State Your Question(s)

B efore you do your research, you need to define the question or problem you're investigating. For example, you may want to know who is the most likely prospect for the product. What real or perceived differences make the product better than a competitor's? How should this be communicated? How is the current campaign perceived by customers? By carefully defining your question(s), you avoid gathering irrelevant information and wasting time.

● Step 2: Dig Through Secondary Sources

O nce you've got a clear statement of the question, look for answers from information that already exists.

Company Records

A good place to start is with your client's own records.

Annual reports   In addition to financial data, an annual report contains information about the corporate philosophy, the competition, and future goals. However, even any bad news in such reports usually has an optimistic slant to it. Therefore, annual reports should be primarily used as a starting point.

Customer profiles   If you've ever filled out a product warranty card, entered a sweepstakes, applied for a credit card, or sent for a rebate, you've supplied important information, such as your age, sex, income, education, family size, and living situation. And you've been contributing to a database. You may also have been asked to state how you learned about the product, where you bought it, and whether you have owned that brand before. Your client may have all this information; it can be compiled to create a profile of current customers.

Public relations files   The public relations department collects press clippings and letters from satisfied customers that are sometimes so glowing they warrant being reprinted as an ad. And, with a bit of inspiration, even negative publicity can be turned to the client's advantage. For example, after the media ran stories claiming that Leona Helmsley was a tyrant to her hotel employees, her advertising agency turned her insistence on perfection into a positive attribute. One ad showed letters from satisfied guests with the headline "She knows people talk about her. She'll even show you what they say."

Technical reports   Granted, much of the information in these reports may sound like gobbledygook to the average reader, but you never know when you'll happen on the perfect line. Like Harley Procter, when one of his chemists reported that Ivory Soap was "99 and $^{44}/_{100}$th's percent pure." Or like David Ogilvy, when he wrote an ad for Rolls-Royce using an engineer's statement: "At 60 miles an hour the loudest noise in this new Rolls-Royce comes from the electric clock." But don't think you'll get instant results. Ogilvy spent three weeks reading about Rolls-Royce before he wrote his classic ad.

Trade Associations   Name a trade or area of interest, and there's bound to be an association for it, staffed with knowledgeable people. Some of the more offbeat associations include the Flying Funeral Directors of America, the Committee to Abolish Legal-Sized Files, and the International Barbed Wire Collectors Association. There's even an association of associations, the American Society of Association Executives. To find an association for your client's product or service, refer to the *Encyclopedia of Associations* published by Gale, available at most libraries.

Libraries   A good place to start is with a guidebook to business information, such as *Business Information Sources,* the *Handbook of Business Information,* and *Marketing Information: A Professional Reference Guide.*

Indexes to articles in periodicals   You probably used the *Readers' Guide to Periodical Literature* in high school. Although it's a good index of articles from general-interest magazines, it's not likely to list much on advertising or in-depth product coverage. Therefore, you'll want to consult the following indexes:

- *Business Periodicals Index* is a subject index of over 300 business journals including *Advertising Age, Adweek, American Demographics, Journal of Advertising Research,*

Marketing Communications, Sales and Marketing Management, and the *Wall Street Journal.*

- *Communication Abstracts* is arranged by subjects such as advertising, mass communications, journalism, and public communication.

- *Guide to Industry Special Issues* is an index to special issues of regularly published business journals including *Advertising Age* and *Adweek.*

- *Topicator* is a classified index to journals in the fields of advertising, communications, and marketing.

Sources of statistical information   The U.S. Government Printing Office publishes thousands of books and pamphlets, many of which are available at your library. A quick way to find these publications is in the *Subject Bibliography Index,* which lists over 15,000 different government publications. Specific sources of statistical information include the following:

- *County and City Data Book* gives information on states, counties, and cities in the United States on a variety of subjects including education, labor, income, housing, and retail and wholesale trade.

- *Statistical Abstract of the United States* is considered the "bible" of social, political, industrial, and economic statistical information of the United States. It contains information on everything from the retail sales of men's fragrances to the number of eye operations performed.

- *U.S. Census* is totally updated every ten years and provides population, ancestry, marital status, education, geographic mobility, occupation, income, and other demographic data. One of the few things it doesn't report, because of the constitutional separation of church and state, is religious data.

- *U.S. Industrial Outlook* gives statistics on the current situations and long-term prospects for approximately 50 major industries.

Market guides   A number of guides offer a detailed look at the lifestyles and shopping habits of various U.S. markets. Here's a sample:

- *Editor and Publisher Market Guide* gives market information on U.S. and Canadian cities in which a daily newspaper is published. It includes data on population, number of households, disposable personal income, and retail sales.

- *Lifestyle Market Analyst* breaks down the American population geographically and demographically and includes information on the interests, hobbies, and activities popular in each geographic and demographic market.

- *MediaMark Research* (often referred to as MRI) provides information on heavy, medium, and light users of various product categories and specific brands and gives the media usage patterns of these groups.

● FIGURE 3-1

A classic warranty card designed for manufacturers by the Polk Company, one of the nation's leading information gatherers, indicates the scope and nature of data that a majority of consumers are willing to share with companies. While the form allows space for "Product & Purchase Related Questions" on the left side, the balance of the questions (usually answered by an overwhelming majority of recipients), cover both demographics, lifestyles, shopping habits, and ownership or preferences for pets, computers, internet services, and large/tall sizes, among other things. Imagine how valuable such information might be, not only to the company whose product the consumer purchased but for thousands of other companies that use Polk's data services.

POlk.
Multi-Dimensional Intelligence™

IMPORTANT!   IMPORTANT!
Please complete and return within the next 10 days!

1. 1. ☐ Mr.   2. ☐ Mrs.   3. ☐ Ms.   4. ☐ Miss
First Name   Initial   Last Name

Street   Apt. No.

City   State   ZIP Code

Product & Purchase Related Questions Appear Here

9. Your date of birth: |__|__| 19 |__|__|
                           Month   Year

10. Marital status: 1. ☐ Married   2. ☐ Single

11. *Not including yourself*, what is the GENDER and AGE (in years) of children and other adults living in your household?
   1. ☐ No one else in household   2. ☐ Child under 1 year

Male	Female	Age		Male	Female	Age
1. ☐	2. ☐	|__|years		1. ☐	2. ☐	|__|years
1. ☐	2. ☐	|__|years		1. ☐	2. ☐	|__|years

12. Occupation: *(check all that apply)*   You   Spouse
   Professional/Technical .... ☐   1. ☐
   Upper Management/Executive .... ☐   2. ☐
   Middle Management .... ☐   3. ☐
   Sales/Marketing .... ☐   4. ☐
   Clerical/Service Worker .... ☐   5. ☐
   Tradesman/Machine Operator/Laborer.... ☐   6. ☐

13. Are you or your spouse: You   Spouse
   A Homemaker? .... ☐   1. ☐
   Retired? .... ☐   2. ☐
   A Student? .... ☐   3. ☐
   Self Employed/Business Owner? .... ☐   4. ☐
   Working from a Home Office? .... ☐   5. ☐
   In the Military? .... ☐   6. ☐
   A Federal Employee? .... ☐   7. ☐

14. Which group describes your annual family income?
   01. ☐ Under $15,000   08. ☐ $45,000-$49,999
   02. ☐ $15,000-$19,999   09. ☐ $50,000-$59,999
   03. ☐ $20,000-$24,999   10. ☐ $60,000-$74,999
   04. ☐ $25,000-$29,999   11. ☐ $75,000-$99,999
   05. ☐ $30,000-$34,999   12. ☐ $100,000-$124,999
   06. ☐ $35,000-$39,999   13. ☐ $125,000-$149,999
   07. ☐ $40,000-$44,999   14. ☐ $150,000 & over

15. Level of education: *(check highest level completed)*
   1. ☐ Completed High School
   2. ☐ Completed College
   3. ☐ Completed Graduate School

16. Which credit cards do you use regularly?
   1. ☐ American Express, Diners Club
   2. ☐ MasterCard, Visa, Discover
   3. ☐ Department Store, Oil Company, etc.
   4. ☐ Do not use credit cards

17. For your primary residence, do you:
   1. ☐ Own?   2. ☐ Rent?

18. Which of the following do you plan to do within the next 6 or 12 months?

	1-6 Months		7-12 Months
Get Married .... ☐	1.	☐
Have a Baby .... ☐	2.	☐
Buy a House .... ☐	3.	☐
Remodel a Home .... ☐	4.	☐
Move to a New Residence .... ☐	5.	☐
Buy a Personal Computer..... ☐	6.	☐
Buy/Lease a New Vehicle..... ☐	7.	☐
Buy/Lease a Used Vehicle .... ☐	8.	☐

PLEASE CONTINUE ON BACK!

Please send products and
other correspondence to:

‖ ‖ ‖

Polk.
Multi-Dimensional Intelligence™

**PO BOX 17XXXX
DENVER CO 80217-XXXX**

•

Standard 7.3

(7/96)

Please fold here.

19. To help us understand our customers' lifestyles, please indicate the interests and activities in which *you* or *your spouse* enjoy participating on a *regular* basis.

01. ☐ Bicycling	21. ☐ Automotive Work	41. ☐ Our Nation's Heritage
02. ☐ Golf	22. ☐ Electronics	42. ☐ Real Estate Investments
03. ☐ Physical Fitness/Exercise	23. ☐ Home Workshop/Do-It-Yourself	43. ☐ Stock/Bond Investments
04. ☐ Running/Jogging	24. ☐ Recreational Vehicles	44. ☐ Mutual Funds
05. ☐ Snow Skiing	25. ☐ Listen to Records/Tapes/CDs	45. ☐ Entering Sweepstakes
06. ☐ Tennis	26. ☐ Avid Book Reading	46. ☐ Casino Gambling
07. ☐ Camping/Hiking	27. ☐ Bible/Devotional Reading	47. ☐ Science Fiction
08. ☐ Fishing	28. ☐ Health/Natural Foods	48. ☐ Wildlife/Environmental Issues
09. ☐ Hunting/Shooting	29. ☐ Photography	49. ☐ Dieting/Weight Control
10. ☐ Power Boating	30. ☐ Home Decorating/Furnishing	50. ☐ Science/New Technology
11. ☐ Horseback Riding	31. ☐ Attending Cultural/Arts Events	51. ☐ Self-Improvement
12. ☐ Sailing	32. ☐ Fashion Clothing	52. ☐ Walking for Health
13. ☐ House Plants	33. ☐ Fine Art/Antiques	53. ☐ Watching Sports on TV
14. ☐ Grandchildren	34. ☐ Foreign Travel	54. ☐ Community/Civic Activities
15. ☐ Needlework/Knitting	35. ☐ Cruise Ship Vacations	55. ☐ Home Video Games
16. ☐ Flower Gardening	36. ☐ Travel in USA	56. ☐ Motorcycles
17. ☐ Vegetable Gardening	37. ☐ Gourmet Cooking/Fine Foods	57. ☐ Watch Cable TV
18. ☐ Sewing	38. ☐ Wines	58. ☐ Home Video Recording
19. ☐ Crafts	39. ☐ Coin/Stamp Collecting	59. ☐ Moneymaking Opportunities
20. ☐ Buy Pre-Recorded Videos	40. ☐ Collectibles/Collections	60. ☐ Current Affairs/Politics

20. Using the numbers in the above list, please indicate your 3 most important activities: |__|__| |__|__| |__|__|

21. Please check all that apply to your household.

01. ☐ Shop by Catalog/Mail	06. ☐ Own a Compact Disc Player	11. ☐ Subscribe to an Online/Internet Service
02. ☐ Member of Frequent Flyer Program	07. ☐ Own a Camcorder	12. ☐ Own an IBM or Compatible Computer
03. ☐ Donate to Charitable Causes	08. ☐ Have a Dog	13. ☐ Own an Apple/Macintosh Computer
04. ☐ Wear Women's Large/Tall Sizes	09. ☐ Have a Cat	14. ☐ Own a CD-ROM
05. ☐ Wear Men's Large/Tall Sizes	10. ☐ Own a Cellular Phone	15. ☐ Speak Spanish at Home

Thanks for taking the time to fill out this questionnaire. Your answers will be used for market research studies and reports. They will also allow you to receive important mailings and special offers from a number of fine companies whose products and services relate directly to the specific interests, hobbies, and other information indicated above. Through this selective program, you will be able to obtain more information about activities in which you are involved and less about those in which you are not. Please check here if, for some reason, you would prefer *not* to participate in this opportunity. ☐

If you have comments or suggestions about our product, please write to:
Customer Service • XXYZZ Inc. • 123 Road Ave. • Anywhere, USA 12345

Copyright © 1996 The Polk Company All Rights Reserved   Please seal with tape. Do not staple.

- *Simmons Study of Media and Markets* (SMRB) is one of the most widely used sources of product usage and media audience data. Similar to MRI, SMRB provides market information on 750 product and service categories.

- *Survey of Buying Power* ranks zip code areas in special characteristics such as Asian-American population, children under 5 years of age, and households in mobile homes. It also gives five-year projections and percentage of change for population, buying income, and retail spending in all U.S. counties.

Computer databases and online services   Your library subscribes to a variety of services that enable you to access information from all over the world. Here are a few that are useful for business searches:

- *InfoTrac® Business Index* contains more than 3 million citations, some with complete articles from more than 1000 business journals and news sources.

- *Business Periodicals on Disc* contains citations with abstracts to articles appearing in more than 900 business periodicals.

- *Compact Disclosure* contains complete Securities and Exchange Commission (SEC) filings for 12,500 publically held companies.

- *Newspaper Abstracts* is an index, with abstracts, to the *Wall Street Journal, New York Times, Los Angeles Times, Boston Globe, Atlanta Constitution/Journal, Chicago Tribune, Christian Science Monitor,* and *USA Today.*

Web Sites

The following list is a sampling of Web sites that contain information useful to advertisers:

- *Business Index* (http://www.dis.strath.ac.uk/business/index.html) is an annotated guide to business information sources across the Web.

- *Business Researcher's Interests* (http://www.brint.com) offers more than 2000 links to online research tools, including newspapers, full-text databases, online libraries, and free reports.

- *BusinessWire* (http://www.businesswire.com) is an electronic distributor of press releases and business news.

- *Census Bureau* (http://www.census.gov) allows you to search the U.S. Census Bureau database, read press releases, check the population clock, and listen to clips from its radio broadcasts.

- *CNNfn* (http://www.cnnfn.com) is the Web site for CNN's business and finance network.

- *County and City Data Books* (http://www.fisher.lib.virginia.edu/ccdb/) gives information ranging from population distribution by age to local voting patterns.

- *Guerilla Marketing Online* (http://www.gmarketing.com) lets you review marketing tips and examine case studies.

- *Hoover's Online* (http://www.hoovers.com) provides a database of detailed profiles for publicly traded companies.
- *Market Research Center* (http://www.asiresearch.com) specializes in advertising, news media, and entertainment issues.
- *MediaInfo* (http://www.mediainfo.com/edpub/) offers news and commentary from *Editor & Publisher* magazine and maintains a comprehensive list of online newspapers.
- *Stat-USA* (http://www.stat-usa.gov) offers access to databases on business- and trade-related subjects.

Additionally, many business publications have electronic versions, including the following:

- *Advertising Age* (http://www.adage.com)
- *Adweek* (http://www.adweek.com)
- *American Demographics* (http://www.demographics.com)
- *Business Week* (http://www.businessweek.com)
- *Forbes* (http://www.forbes.com)
- *Fortune* (http://www.fortune.com)

● Step 3: Conduct Primary Research

Once you've exhausted the secondary sources, you may find you still have un-answered questions that warrant primary research. Here's where observation, focus groups, surveys, and experiments come in.

Firsthand Experience

Try it. Taste it. Touch it. Hear it. Smell it. What were your perceptions of the product before you used it? How about now that you've used it? Try the competition. What are the competitors' weaknesses? Your client's strengths? Why would you choose to buy your client's product?

Firsthand experience gives you important insights that may lead to the big idea. The idea for the memorable line "Two scoops of raisins in a box of Kellogg's Raisin Bran" came from an art director who emptied a box of the cereal onto his kitchen table and counted the raisins.

However, be careful not to assume that everyone thinks or behaves the same way you do. You may have a more sophisticated understanding of the product, or you may have a bias toward your client, or you may not be part of the target market. There-fore, other research methods are essential.

Observation

Watch your friends and family when they use your product. Go to a store and observe customers. How much time do they spend reading your product's label?

Looking at the price? Examining other products? If you have permission from the store manager, you may want to ask customers why they choose a particular product.

Jon Steel, director of account planning and vice chairman at Goodby, Silverstein & Partners, believes one of the best ways to understand people's behavior is to watch them in their natural setting. To get a true picture of how people use a product, GS&P tries to observe them in the environment in which they normally would use it. For example, GS&P employees have gone out with some families to Pizza Hut and stayed home with other families and ordered pizza in. In pitching Sega's video game business, almost all of GS&P's strategic development research took place in kids' bedrooms, where most kids play video games with their friends.

One of the more offbeat methods of observation came from an archaeologist who found that studying people's garbage may uncover hidden truths. Several marketing researchers have adopted this method and discovered some rather interesting things, such as the fact that cat owners read more than dog owners.

Focus Groups

Invite five to ten people who are typical of your target market to discuss their feelings about your product. You'll want to get permission to record the session, and you will need a moderator who encourages everyone to speak and who keeps the discussion on track. Because participants are urged to say what's on their minds, important issues may be uncovered. For example, when Arm & Hammer conducted focus groups to find ways to boost sales of their baking soda, they discovered that some participants used it to reduce odors in refrigerators. Seizing on this idea, Arm & Hammer ran an advertising campaign suggesting that the box be replaced every three months. The idea took off. And, thanks to Americans' dislike of offensive smells, Arm & Hammer has successfully developed flanker products including rug and carpet deodorizer, cat litter deodorizer, and underarm deodorant. Even Johnson's Odor-Eaters foot powder and insoles contain Arm & Hammer baking soda to battle sneaker odor. It almost makes you forget that you can also bake with the stuff.

Focus group participants for the California Fluid Milk Processors Advisory Board were asked to go without milk for a week before attending the focus group session. At first, the focus group participants didn't think it would be difficult, but the week without milk proved otherwise. The idea for the famous two-word line "Got Milk?" came out of the responses from the focus group participants who had been deprived of milk for a week.

Although focus groups can uncover some interesting attitudes, remember that this method of research reflects the opinions of only a few people. To determine whether you've really uncovered something important, you'll need to back up your findings with other research, such as surveys.

Surveys

Surveys, one of the most common primary-research methods, ask current or prospective customers questions about product usage, awareness of ad campaigns, attitudes toward competing brands, and so on. Surveys are conducted by mail, by telephone, or by personal interview.

Whichever method you use to conduct your survey, be certain to test the survey on a small sample to ascertain whether there are leading or ambiguous questions. When a team of advertising students wanted to determine people's awareness level of the American Red Cross slogan "Help Can't Wait," they tested a survey that asked respondents to match five not-for-profit organizations to five slogans. Almost all the slogans were correctly matched. But did this mean people really knew the "Help Can't Wait" slogan, or was it a fluke? To find out, the students conducted another test, using seven slogans and five organizations. The results were quite different. The fictitious slogan "The Life Blood of America" was matched to the Red Cross by 65 percent of respondents. Why the different results? In the first survey, respondents could guess the correct answer through the process of elimination. The second survey prevented the respondents from covering a genuine lack of awareness.

In addition to checking for ambiguous and misleading questions, keep the following points in mind when you design a survey:

1. Keep the survey short.

2. Use simple language.

3. Include complete instructions.

4. Put easy-to-answer questions first.

5. Ask general questions before detailed ones.

6. Save potentially embarrassing questions, such as about income, for the end.

Experiments

This research method compares results from a test group that receives a stimulus and a control group that does not receive the stimulus. Suppose you want to compare the attitudes of a group of people who saw your ad with a group who didn't. Did the people who saw your ad have a more favorable impression of your client? Were they more knowledgeable about the product? And so on.

Projective Techniques

Using projective techniques, researchers ask respondents to sketch drawings, tell tales, finish sentences, and match companies with animals, colors, places, and types of music in order to understand consumers' subconscious attitudes toward products. These techniques sometimes uncover surprising motives for behavior.

When Grey Advertising asked a group of consumers to imagine long-distance carriers as animals, AT&T was described as a lion, MCI as a snake, and Sprint as a puma. Grey used these insights to position Sprint as the one that could "help you do more business," rather than mimicking the savings approach of the competition.

Goodby, Silverstein & Partners asked luxury car owners to draw the way they feel about their cars. Most of the drivers of the BMW, Mercedes, Infiniti, and Lexus drew the outside of the cars. Porsche owners, by contrast, rarely drew the car. Instead, the point of view was from the driver's seat, showing winding roads. This exercise gave the agency the idea to emphasize the fun you'll have while driving a Porsche.

● FIGURE 3-2

Scatter some birdseed in your backyard or patio, and before you know it, you're captivated. You find yourself wondering, "What are they saying?" and "Why does the little brown speckled one do so-and-so?" Wild Birds Unlimited provides the answers in clever small-space ads such as these.

Although projective techniques may uncover information that would be missed with other research methods, it's important to keep in mind that they are expensive to use on a per-respondent basis and require the expertise of trained psychologists.

Psychographic Research Firms

Psychographic research firms such as SRI International and Yankelovich collect data from a sample of product users and determine the values, attitudes, personalities, and lifestyles of the individuals most likely to use the product.

SRI developed the Values and Lifestyles Program, VALS 2, which groups consumers into one of eight categories: (1) *actualizers* are successful, sophisticated, active, take-charge people who have high self-esteem; (2) *experiencers* are young, vital, impulsive, and rebellious and seek variety, excitement, the offbeat, and the risky; (3) *strivers* seek motivation, self-definition, and approval from others; (4) *fulfilleds* are mature, satisfied, comfortable, well-educated professionals; (5) *achievers* are successful, work-

oriented, in control of their lives, and respectful of authority and the status quo; (6) *believers* are conservative, have deeply rooted moral codes, and have modest income, and education; (7) *makers* are suspicious of new ideas and unimpressed by physical possessions; and (8) *strugglers* are poor, ill-educated, and low-skilled. As you can imagine, makers and stugglers aren't of much interest to advertisers.

Using Several Research Approaches

Each research method has its unique advantages and disadvantages. Therefore, researchers will often use more than one approach to find the answers to their questions. Kraft, the makers of DiGiorno Pizza, used seven research firms to conduct surveys, focus groups, taste tests, and copy tests to learn the best way to position their brand. Surveys and focus groups found that people wanted a frozen pizza with a fresh-baked taste but so far hadn't found one in the stores. In blind taste tests, DiGiorno scored highest among frozen brands and placed second only to one carry-out pizza. With this information, the creative team came up with the theme "It's not delivery . . . It's DiGiorno."

The ads creatively addressed the research findings, but still a question remained: Were the spots effective? To find out, Kraft ran a quantitative copy test to measure the effectiveness of the spots. Roughly 64 percent of the respondents recalled the spot's main message of "fresh-baked taste" while an average commercial scored about 24 percent. The ad also generated strong brand identification, with 52 percent recalling the DiGiorno name. And finally, one other set of figures proved the success of the big idea: Three years after its introduction, it's the second-best-selling frozen pizza.[1]

Step 4: Interpret the Data

You can collect mountains of data, but it's useless if you don't know how to interpret your findings. For example, your research may uncover some negative opinions about your client. An almost immediate reaction would be to try and change these perceptions. However, this may not be the best move. For example, Sabena Qualitative Research developed a perceptional map whereby customers evaluated stores on best/worst value and most/least up-to-date in fashions. Talbots was placed in the best value/least up-to-date quadrant. At first glance, you might be tempted to do something to make Talbots seem more up-to-date. In fact, the company tried that a number of years ago, introducing flashier colors and more current styles. Guess what? Sales dropped because the store's customers wanted classics, not the latest fashions. Talbots quickly went back to what it does best, and its loyal customers are happy once again.

Common Mistakes in Research

Research is a valuable tool, but it's not foolproof, as the Talbots example illustrates. Here are some common mistakes:

- *Going overboard with research.* Not every question deserves a lengthy, costly research project. Dave Thomas, founder of Wendy's, tells an interesting story in his book *Well Done!* He was considering whether to add taco salad to the menu and, rather than "spend $62,000 to bring in a crack squad of Harvard M.B.A. consultants to try out this idea in three restaurants and to measure it to death with computers, legal pads, and graph paper over three weeks," he decided to put it on the menu in three stores and ask customers what they thought of the salad. After all, his restaurants already had most of the ingredients and equipment to serve the salads—all they needed were a ladle to scoop out the chili and some taco chips. So, for an investment of $751.17, he learned what a $62,000 study would have told him: Customers liked the salad.

- *Asking the wrong questions.* Before Coca-Cola introduced New Coke in 1985, it conducted numerous focus groups, which showed people preferred the taste of the

---

[1]Adapted from Sara Eckel and Jennifer Lach, "Intelligence Agents," *American Demographics,* March 1999, p. 58.

new soft drink to the old one. The research led the company to change its 100-year-old formula. However, consumers revolted, and Coca-Cola had to reintroduce its old flavor. The problem was that consumers were not told that the original Coca-Cola might be eliminated.

- *Believing everything people tell you.* Jon Steel, director of account planning and vice chairman at Goodby, Silverstein & Partners, points to the problem of people saying the "right" thing: "To hear people talk in focus groups, and indeed to believe the answers they give in larger, more reliable quantitative surveys, one would think that Americans are the cleanest living, healthiest race on the planet. They all eat well, they work out, and cholesterol levels are universally low."[2]

- *Not testing to see if the data is relevant to your client's problem.* Sales of Jell-O were declining in the 1970s. To reverse the situation, the agency collected data which showed that consumers were interested in lighter desserts, so it positioned Jell-O as a light, tasty dessert that won't fill you up. Sales continued to decline. The problem wasn't that the data were erroneous. It was that the data didn't apply to Jell-O's core consumer, who thought of desserts as the fun part of the meal. Sales increased when the agency repositioned the brand as fun: "Make Jell-O gelatin, and make some fun."

- *Biasing the results.* To be reliable, your research must be repeatable. That is, the same questions or research techniques must produce similar results, regardless of who conducts the study. However, a variety of factors can bias results. For example, with interviewer bias, the person interviewing respondents gives cues (smiles, frowns) that suggest one answer is better than another. With sample bias, the sample doesn't represent a good cross-section of the target audience. Thus, if you wanted to investigate whether teenagers like an advertising campaign, you wouldn't test it on a weekday morning at a shopping mall because the target market would be (or at least should be!) in school, not at the local mall. With source bias, the source of the research message influences the answer. People aim to please, so they may say only nice things about company XYZ if they know the person asking the questions works for XYZ. And with nonresponse bias, questions aren't answered because they're too difficult, confusing, personal, and so on.

● Suggested Activities

1. Select two cities from different parts of the country (for example, New York and New Orleans), and prepare a report of their similarities and differences in shopping habits, food preferences, income levels, home ownership, number of children in the family, and so on.

[2]Jon Steel, *Truth, Lies & Advertising: The Art of Account Planning* (New York: Wiley, 1998), p. 83.

2. Observe how your target audience uses the product you're about to advertise. If you're selling golf balls, go to a golf course and watch players in action. If you're selling a detergent, go to a laudromat and observe how the people load their machines. If you're selling dog food, watch friends feeding their pets. What did you notice? Were there any surprises? Any common rituals? What insights can help direct your advertising?

3. Play a game with friends. Choose a product category (such as cars, jeans, or perfume), and write the names of different brands within the product category on index cards (each index card will have a different brand name). Distribute a card to each player, and ask them to describe their brand as if it were a person, without revealing the brand name. (To get them started, you might give them some questions to answer, such as, What would the brand do for a living? Where would it live? What kind of movies does it like? What kind of books? Magazines? TV shows? Who's their best friend? How would they dress? What kind of hairstyle would they have?) Then ask other players to guess the brand name that's being described. What did you discover?

4. Choose one of the following categories, which were taken from MRI data. Look under the appropriate product first; then use your campus library to assemble as much information as you can find about the product category: who uses it, what industry trends are, which are the top brands in the market, how products differ, how the product is used and for what, and where the category is headed in the future.

Adult Personal Care
Toothpaste
Mouthwash
Shampoo
Personal-care soaps
Hand and body cream
Deodorants/anti-perspirants
Electric shavers

Remedies
Athlete's foot remedies
Indigestion aids

Household Supplies
Cleaners
Glass cleaners
Fabric softeners
Charcoal
Air freshener sprays

Baked Goods, Snacks, Desserts
Frozen yogurt
Frozen desserts
Cookies
Crackers

Meat and Prepared Meals
Frozen pizza
Mexican foods
Prepared dinners

Beverages
Instant iced tea
Energy drinks
Bottled water and seltzer

Soup, Fruit, Vegetables
Canned or jarred soup
Flavored/seasoned rice

Search Online! Discovering More About Fact-Finding for Creative Excellence

Using InfoTrac® College Edition, try these phrases and others for Key Words and Subject Guide searches: *market research, creative research, advertising research, secondary research + advertising, advertising resources + Internet, marketing resources + Internet, focus group, marketing survey, projective techniques + research.*

BriefCase

Diabetics Discover the Joy of Eating Well

BY ROBERT BUTT

The mission of the American Diabetes Association is to prevent and cure diabetes and improve the lives of those affected by diabetes. And as the pile on my desk grew higher with focus group and public perception surveys, my hunt for the so-far elusive "unique marketing proposition" that would propel the American Diabetes Association into the marketplace remained just that—elusive. I needed a BIG idea.

Just when I thought I had exhausted my last avenue of thought, it happened. Our program director, Elizabeth Todd, who happens to be diabetic, dropped by my office one day. We were discussing the reams of paper piled on my desk when a response on a questionnaire caught her eye. A survey respondent had written, "Everyone knows that when you have diabetes, you can't eat sugar." "Wow!" Elizabeth exclaimed, "You know that's not true. Where do people get these ideas?" A misconception had just given birth to the big idea for which I had been searching!

The unique marketing proposition wasn't a health issue at all, but a lifestyle issue—food! Elizabeth and I combed through the surveys. What we discovered, and what I had missed all along, was that diabetes, in the minds of the public, was not about health issues or later complications, but about one basic emotional issue, one that we take for granted—eating. The fear of what one can and cannot eat. Socially, our lives are centered around food; holidays such as Christmas and Thanksgiving, large family gatherings on Sundays, weddings, funerals, business lunches, intimate dinners for two, and so on. When we delved further, we discovered that this "fear of loss" can be so great, food issues are avoided all together, and denial prevents healthy and "tasteful" lifestyle changes.

While campaign goals were always present, having the big idea helped clarify our objectives. They were:

- Address the "fear of food" issue that people with diabetes face on a daily basis by providing encouraging information on the joy of healthy eating.

COURTESY AMERICAN DIABETIC ASSOCIATION.

- Position the American Diabetes Association as the source for solutions to diet challenges.

- Use the response vehicle "call for recipes" to provide additional information on diabetes and our association.

- Create a "core" program that would be simple to replicate in all 50 states after our initial implementation and evaluation period.

Our campaign, appropriately entitled *Recipes,* contained these major program components:

- Two 30-second television Public Service Announcements showing beautifully prepared foods and urging a call to action by calling 1-800-DIABETES. The tag line: "There may be reasons you can't eat this well everyday, but diabetes isn't one of them."

- Visually stimulating outdoor advertising using the same call to action.

- Newspaper advertising modules for stand-alone PSAs or for inclusion in a sponsor's ad.

- A direct-mail piece featuring the recipes of the dishes shown in the television commercials as a teaser for the purchase of cookbooks.

- Cents-off coupons tied to sponsor food products.

Our strategy was a six-month marketing "flight" period followed by a complete review, analysis, and evaluation period that would allow sufficient time to retool needed areas. Our goals in the evaluation period were to assess:

- The effectiveness of the overall campaign
- The perception of the program by various groups in terms of strengths and weaknesses
- Similarities in the minds of our constituents between the American Diabetes Association and other national diabetes groups

As it turned out, the overall effectiveness of the campaign needed no questioning. As the television spots began a rotation on our local market stations, our calls picked up rapidly. Then, a few days later, our first newspaper release ran. Over the next two days, in combination with the television spots, we took 212 "Recipes" calls. During the course of the marketing flight period, our average calls rose to nearly 500 per month, compared to 200–300 for the same period of the prior year. Our preliminary evaluation found not only that we were on the right track but that we were having a significant impact as well. My new problem became not whether the campaign was good or not or needed anything additional—it became order fulfillment.

Any marketing professional will tell you that a business is the product of its environment. I spent too much time initially looking at the healthcare issues of diabetes because we are a voluntary healthcare agency. My big idea was waiting for me all the time, on the fringe of my environment. Elizabeth and I often have very different goals considering we are in the same business—hers are qualitative and educational while mine are quantitative and based on bottom-line dollars. And while I know she's wanted to whack me in the head many times over the years, this particular "whack" gave us both everything we needed to accomplish our dual sets of goals.

CHAPTER 4

Strategy: The Creative Before the Creative

John Lyons talks about strategy as

a carefully designed plan to murder the competition. Any premise that lacks a killer instinct is not a strategy. Any premise that doesn't reflect or include a consumer's crying need is not a strategy. Any premise embalmed in stiff, predictable language is not a strategy. Any premise that addresses the whole world, women 3 to 93, is not a strategy. Any premise interchangeable with that of another product is not a strategy. The true test of an advertising strategy is to let another human being read it. If that person can't say yes, that's me, or yes, I need that, or yes, that's my problem—throw it away.[1]

Strategy is the way you plan to sell the product, not the words and images you use to do so. Strategy consists of identifying what you need to say even before you've found the right way to say it. But mere facts do not a strategy make. To the facts you must add your insight—you must see connections that no one else has noticed. Strategic planning is the stage between fact gathering and the big idea. Think of your strategy as a road map for the client and creative team—it will map out the direction the advertising campaign should take. But it'll be the job of the creative team to describe the scenery.

For example, farming is more than a job or even a profession. It is a way of life. Farmers will tell you they farm because they love working outdoors, because they relish being their own boss, because they can raise their families in a good environment, and because they get deep satisfaction from making things grow, from being a part of "God's miracle."

At the same time, they are, of course, businesspeople. Managing millions of dollars in assets and making a profit is no easy task. So, in addition to loving the life they

[1]John Lyons, *Guts: Advertising from the Inside Out* (New York: AMACOM, 1987), p. 124.

lead, farmers are intensely interested in practical solutions to problems associated with farming.

What this all boils down to is that farmers are "spiritual pragmatists." And it was this insight that became the basis of the print campaign shown in Figure 4-3 on page 78. By sharing the farmers' values and positioning DuPont agricultural products as an extension of them, the agency sought to promote the DuPont brand through trust and empathy and to create preference for DuPont products in an area in which true functional competitive advantages are difficult to achieve or discern.

● O'Toole's Three-Point Approach to Strategy

John O'Toole of the American Association of Advertising Agencies says you should consider three things when determining a strategy:

1. *Who or what is the competition?* To set your brand apart, you need to know what other brands are saying. You also need to be aware that your competition may go beyond the product category. For example, the competition for home exercise machines includes diet supplements and health clubs, and not just other machines. It probably also reflects a preference for running or swimming and any number of other related things. For Sunkist, increased sales of its frozen and concentrated juices resulted only when the company realized it had to compete against both snack foods and other brands of similar products.

2. *Who are you talking to?* Are you targeting users of another brand? Consumers who've never used any brand in our category? Or consumers who use a related product but might be persuaded to switch to ours? The answers are rarely simple. Kleenex Facial Tissues were developed over a century ago as a replacement for the cloth towels used to remove a woman's makeup. Then someone had the urge to sneeze with one in hand—and the rest is history. Much of your audience information will be demographic: age, sex, marital status, income, occupation, owner or renter, user or nonuser of product category, and so on.

But demographics alone cannot help the creative team of copywriter and art director really see the person they're trying to reach. To illustrate the point, Jon Steel, director of account planning and vice chairman at Goodby, Silverstein & Partners, reminds us that the group of "men aged 35 and over with large household incomes" includes Bill Clinton, Billy Graham, Michael Jackson, Donald Trump, Bob Dole, and a large number of drug dealers. Much more meaningful is a profile of that person's lifestyle including values, leisure-time activities, attitudes toward work and family, and the stresses of everyday life. Steel describes the demographic information as the "skeleton" and the lifestyles and values as the "body and soul."[2]

[2] Jon Steel, *Truth, Lies & Advertising: The Art of Account Planning* (New York: Wiley, 1998).

Another important consideration are the gatekeepers, the people who influence the purchasing decision for your target audience. Ally & Gargano targeted many audiences in its campaign for Federal Express. As agency president Amil Gargano explained, "We focused on expanding the market with the target moving from management to every department of American business including secretaries, mailroom personnel and trainees. No one was spared."[3]

3. *What do you want them to know, to understand, and to feel?* Emotional benefits are almost always stronger than rational benefits. Remember "You deserve a break today"? Those five words revolutionized perceptions of fast-food restaurants. According to Kevin Fisher of Fisher Communications, effective advertising is all about evoking emotion: "I think it's all about making people feel something. If a picture is worth a thousand words, then a feeling is worth a billion."[4]

Ann Hayden believes that all advertising should make a human connection:

> I'm convinced that people—all people—want to buy from people. Customers want to know who you are, your habits, your values. They want to be able to predict you. They need to trust you. If they connect with you on some kind of human basis, and believe they have something in common with you, they will give you vast permission to sell them things that make them happy.[5]

● DDB Needham's Focus on One or More of the Basic Human Needs

Check your strategy to see whether it touches one or more of the basic human needs: to be popular, to feel attractive, and wanted, to obtain material things, to enjoy life through comfort and convenience, to create a happy family situation, to have love and sex, to wield power, to avoid fear, to emulate those you admire, to have new experiences, or to protect and maintain health.

The DDB Needham agency explores the emotional and rational rewards of using products in the process of defining its strategy. Cheese, for example, offers the following rewards:

- *In-use rewards:* is convenient (practical), offers a new taste (sensory), earns the gratitude of the family (social), and contributes to the belief that you're a good cook (ego-satisfaction)

- *Results-of-use rewards:* helps build strong bones (practical), makes you feel better (sensory), makes you look good to others (social), and contributes to the belief that you're a good parent (ego-satisfaction)

[3]Bernice Kanner, *The 100 Best TV Commercials . . . and Why They Worked* (New York: Times Books, 1999), p. 35.

[4]Anna Velasco, "Swimming with the Big Fish, Fisher Communications Makes It Big, but Stays Small," *The State,* 29 Aug. 1999, p. G6.

[5]From the Saatchi & Saatchi Business Communications Web site, 1999.

Figure 4-1

Style. Power. Performance. Luxury. Ads for Lincoln say all these things—and more. Notice how the ad copy is placed in a way that enhances the communication and involves the reader. The body copy of the first Lincoln LS ad shown here is set along the curve of the road.

The body copy of the second Lincoln LS ad shown on page 71 is positioned in a way that mimicks a motorist shifting from first gear to overdrive.

Copy reads, *"Look what fell out of the family tree. Introducing the new LS, a performance car according to Lincoln. Somewhere in the lineage, there was a wild gene. For more information, visit www.lincolnvehicles.com or call toll-free 877 2DriveLS (237-4835)."*

Copy reads, *"As a kid, you never acted out the sounds of an automatic transmission. 'Air shifting' through imaginary gears prepared you for the moment when you would have a car like this. The new Lincoln LS. With a close-ratio five-speed gearbox and lively DOHC V-6. It's not make believe anymore. Visit www.lincolnvehicles.com or call toll-free 877 2DriveLS (237-4835)."*

practical
sensory
social
ego-satisfaction

- *Incidental-to-use rewards:* provides low-cost nutrition (practical), makes no mess (sensory), adds variety to party refreshments (social), and makes you feel like a smart shopper (ego-satisfaction)

Which benefits do you think are the most important to mothers? To single people? To people living on Social Security?

● McCann–Erickson's Role-Playing Approach

The McCann–Erickson agency suggests that you get inside the head of your consumer by acting as if you were that person, writing your responses to the first six questions here in the consumer's "voice" and the final question in your own voice.

1. Who is our target?

2. Where are we now in the mind of this person?

3. Where is our competition in the mind of this person?

4. Where would we like to be in the mind of this person?

5. What is the consumer promise, the "big idea"?

6. What is the supporting evidence?

7. What is the tone of voice for the advertising?

Writing partially in the first person to arrive at a strategy for reaching parents, the initial thinking for Bell Helmets (see the BriefCase in Chapter 1) probably went something like this:

1. *Who is our target?*

"Hi. I'm Lena Emoto. I work full-time as an accountant, and my husband, Ray, is a mechanical engineer. We have two growing children: Michelle, 9, and Bobby, 12. And are they busy kids! Dropping in at their friends' houses practically every day. Biking up to the corner convenience store to buy a slush drink. I'm lucky they can take care of themselves after school and that their bikes allow them some mobility. But I sometimes worry about that. After all, the streets can be dangerous. Thank goodness I've convinced them to wear helmets, even though they originally fought me on it."

2. *Where are we now in the mind of this person?*

"Sure, there are lots of brands of helmets. I didn't spend much on theirs because they all looked pretty much alike to me. They also looked like they'd protect their heads in case they fell or hit something. So while we almost shelled out big bucks for a higher-priced brand, Ray's car needed a major repair job, and with all we spent for school supplies and clothing, we decided it wasn't necessary to buy an expensive helmet just for riding in the neighborhood."

3. *Where is our competition in the mind of this person?*

"As I said, most brands look about the same. We found two great-looking helmets for about thirteen bucks each. So far, they've been okay. Why spend more than you need? Clothes and shoes cost enough as it is."

4. *Where would we like to be in the mind of this person?*

"At first I thought it was dumb to spend more on a bicycle helmet. Then I heard about Bell Helmets, how they make them with such care, how they test them, how they're practically indestructible, and how they've saved the lives of professional and amateur racers."

5. *What is the consumer promise, the "big idea"?*

"They say Bell Helmets are thoroughly tested for safety. So when my kids wear one, they can enjoy biking, and I don't have to worry so much about them getting a bad head injury."

6. *What is the supporting evidence?*

"Bell pioneered the field of helmet safety. They're first with race car helmets, and now with bike helmets, too. They invented their own safety tests, which they still conduct in their own labs. They sell more helmets than any other company, and Bell is the helmet of choice for more race car drivers and pro cyclists than any other brand. I discovered that by reading their ad."

7. *What is the tone of voice for the advertising?*

Make parents think about spending money on a helmet in terms of safety, not status. Use humor to make a sobering statement.

● Stating the Strategy

Each agency approaches strategy from its own unique perspective. Whichever approach is used, the strategy must be carefully stated so it gives the creative team direction and inspiration. Although you may have gathered reams of data, only include what's relevant to solving the advertising problem in your strategy statement. Kevin Dundas, executive vice president and director of account planning at Foote, Cone & Belding, describes two opposite extremes:

> The urge to fill that piece of paper with detail, data, fact, and hearsay is unbelievably tempting. I recall a senior planner handing me a brief for sign-off and proudly stating, "Let's see the creatives get out of that one." It was a great piece of strategic thinking, but as a stepping-off point to a creative team it was DOA.

> Equally, I have had planners shuffle into my office embarrassed to reveal the one-page summation of a mountain of strategizing and positioning work for their brand. "It's too

simple and obvious; it is what the brand has always stood for." More than likely this is a good position to take; why challenge or rewrite a position like refreshment or performance or safety? The genius, of course, lies in how the planner has configured or retextured the brand proposition for today's target audience.[6]

● Choosing a Strategy Type Based on Your Goals

Depending on your goals, you have a number of strategy options, including the following:

- *Generic approach.* This approach works best when your brand dominates category. It does not acknowledge competition, but instead implies that this is the one and only brand in the category. This approach can also be used when a brand creates a new category, before competitors rush in. Such exclusivity is naturally short-lived.

- *Preemptive claim.* This refers to a claim that is not unique but as yet is unexploited by the competition, although other brands may be able to claim the same thing. This approach works best with products that have little to distinguish them within their category. You can compare brand claims, find a claim that isn't promoted, assess its importance, and consider featuring it. While you can't claim you're exclusive, you can sound as if you are.

- *Unique selling proposition (USP).* Popularized in the 1950s, this approach is based on a true competitive advantage or a unique characteristic or benefit. Since most brands in a category have much in common, USP strategies are rare. Choose this approach only if what you have to claim can't be claimed by your competitors.

- *Brand image.* Superiority is based on factors that are extrinsic to the product or service. In other words, product features may be undistinguishable from other brands, so the only way to make your brand stand out is to create an emotional framework, or personality, for it. This is the approach Bell Helmets took in its "Courage for your head" campaign (see the BriefCase in Chapter 1).

- *Positioning.* Most strategies employ the concept of positioning, but some strategies are pure positioning, an approach that places the product in a hierarchy of competing products in the consumer's mind. Pure positioning strategies stress how your brand is different from, and superior to, the competition. This strategy is useful for new products introduced in a crowded product category or for brands with small market shares that want to challenge leaders. Perhaps the classic case of positioning was the Avis's "We're only #2. We try harder," a direct hit at industry leader Hertz. This campaign not only put Avis in the big leagues but also expanded the target market for auto rentals overall.

- *Resonance.* Even though we live in a diverse society, we share certain fundamental experiences: birthdays, anniversaries, holidays, homecomings, family get-togethers, marriages, and so on. The essence of the resonance strategy is to link

[6]Kevin Dundas, "A Passion for Advertising," *Agency,* Summer 1998, p. 38.

the product or service with one or more of these universal experiences. You'll find it in practically every Hallmark greeting card commercial, in any number of soft drink and insurance company commercials, and, generally speaking, in ads and commercials for products and services with broad appeal and little or no product differentiation.

- *Affective.* This strategy is the most emotion-based. Its intent is to make contact on a purely emotional level. The idea is to crack consumer indifference and change the target market's perception of a product or service.

● Linking Strategy with the Thinking/Feeling and High/Low-Importance Scales

Advertising agency Foote Cone & Belding has created a strategy model based on two basic facts: (1) Some purchasing decisions are based more on logic while others are based more on emotions, and (2) some purchasing decisions may involve extensive deliberation, while others are made with little or no thought. Visualize this model as a grid with four quadrants (see Figure 4-2).

- *Quadrant 1: thinking/high importance.* Also called the informative model, this approach assumes that the consumer needs a great deal of information because of the importance of the product and logical issues concerning it. Many campaigns for autos, home furnishings, cameras, computers, new products, and home furnishings fit this category. Long copy, specific information, and perhaps a demonstration might be used to reinforce the selling argument.

- *Quadrant 2: feeling/high importance.* Also called the affective model, this approach views the consumer as an individual who relies less on specific information and more on attitudes and feelings about the product, because the purchase decision is related to one's self-esteem. Products for which this strategy works include jewelry, cosmetics, fashion apparel, and motorcycles. Image advertising, which communicates with dramatic visuals and emotional statements as opposed to logic, is the rule of thumb here.

- *Quadrant 3: thinking/low importance.* Also called the habit-formation model, this approach views the consumer as one who makes purchasing decisions with minimal thought. Simply inducing a trial purchase, as with a coupon, may generate subsequent purchases more readily than pounding home undifferentiated points in the copy. Campaigns for food and household items often use this approach; the messages always remind the consumer to choose the brand.

- *Quadrant 4: feeling/low importance.* Also called the self-satisfaction model, this approach sees the consumer as a reactor. It is reserved for products that satisfy personal tastes, such as smoking and consumption of alcoholic beverages, and that make the user feel "special" when using the brand in front of his or her peers. Messages are designed primarily to draw attention to the brand.

The Foote Cone & Belding strategy planning model ranks consumer purchasing decisions in terms of high versus low importance and thinking versus feeling.

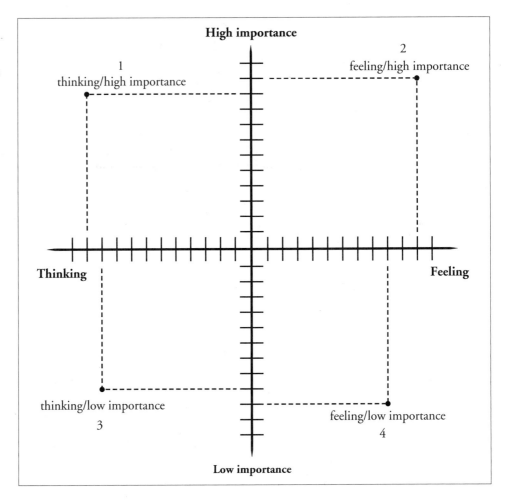

Note that, since consumers buy a variety of goods and services, they may fit any of the four quadrant profiles, depending on the specific purchasing decision.

● Think VIPS

David Bernstein, noted British advertising executive, claims that effective advertising can be summed up in four words: visibility, identity, promise, and simplicity (VIPS).[7]

- *Visibility.* A good ad must divert the casual reader, viewer, or listener who might be a target for the message. Something must make your message stand out from

[7]David Bernstein, *Creative Advertising* (London: The Creative Business Limited, 1974), pp. 155–202. Used by permission.

the clutter. Leo Burnett, founder of one of the most famous ad agencies in the world, writes:

> Best attention comes from the entirely natural interests of the reader, built around the results of the product advertised. Being different from others is not an asset if the others are right. An ad may get attention and fail completely in getting anything else. An able show window designer once said, "The thing to avoid is drawing a crowd. The hard thing is to catch the eye of every possible customer and keep the others walking past." It is better to attract the serious attention of possible buyers than, through an exaggerated and clever headline, to attract other possible readers who won't be interested in the message anyway.[8]

- *Identity.* In addition to being noticed, your message must register the brand name, the advertiser's identity. Feature the name on the package, use it in the headline if possible, mention it repeatedly in the copy, and use a prominent and distinctive logo or signature at the bottom of the ad or close of the commercial.

- *Promise.* Inherent in any ad is a promise to the consumer: Potatoes are low in calories and good for you; Lands' End clothing undergoes dozens of quality checks so you'll have few, if any, complaints; Bell Helmets protect your head better, so you have less to worry about; Carnival Cruise Lines offers something for everyone, even if all you want to do is relax, which means you'll love your cruise and come home feeling great.

- *Simplicity.* Make the point clearly. As in a good story with a beginning, middle, and end, the ad must stay on target, progressing logically from start to finish.

● Think ROI

Think about the return on investment (ROI) your client will receive from the advertising campaign. Be sure you answer the question "Why are we advertising?" After all, in this age of integrated marketing communications, a variety of other approaches might bring about similar—or even better—results than an advertising campaign. For example, if research shows that people aren't shopping at a store because they don't like the service they receive, an ad campaign probably won't help as much as improving employee morale at the store—something human resources or public relations could do far better than an ad agency.

There's another ROI that's important in testing your strategy. Doug Walker, managing partner at DDB Needham, defines it as "relevance, originality, and impact." Is your strategy relevant to the target audience? Is it original, or is it too similar to that of the other brands in your product category? And does it have an impact? Will it bring results?

---

[8]Leo Burnett, from a memorandum to his creative staff, 13 Nov. 1947. Reprinted in *Communications of an Advertising Man— Selections from Speeches, Articles, Memoranda, and Miscellaneous Writings of Leo Burnett,* Copyright 1961 by Leo Burnett Company, Inc., Chicago. For private distribution only. Used with permission.

● Figure 4-3

DuPont thinks of farmers as spiritual pragmatists. By sharing the farmers' values and positioning DuPont agricultural products as an extension of them, this campaign seeks to promote the DuPont brand through trust and empathy.

Checklist for Strategy

✓ Does your strategy have the potential for visibility, identity, promise, and simplicity?

✓ Does your strategy have the potential for relevant and unexpected connections that can build a relationship between the brand and the prospect?

✓ Did you use the best *type* of strategy for this task?

✓ Did you place the product at the appropriate point on the thinking/feeling and high/low-importance scales?

✓ Does your strategy address one or more of the basic human needs?

✓ Did you include emotional benefits as well as rational ones? Can the product and its advertising support these benefits?

✓ Did you consider what strategies the competition is using, as well as what they may have missed?

✓ Does your strategy address the target market in a tone appropriate to this market? (There's no excuse for errors in taste or tact here.)

"**I didn't** get into this business because I loved having people tell me what to do."

I know my fields better than anybody else. And I know that no one herbicide, not even Roundup[1], can get every weed out there. So next year, I'm going with that new program, Authority[2] followed by DuPont Synchrony® STS®. I'll get in early before that first flush gets out of hand. And I've still got more time at post, just in case bad weather sets in. For me, residual control of waterhemp and nightshade is a must. I also like using high-yielding STS® beans. I get the benefits of using a herbicide-tolerant seed without tech fees or hassles. It's all about having choices. Good choices.

THE HIGH-YIELDING, HERBICIDE-TOLERANT SYSTEM WITH SERIOUS CONTROL OF WATERHEMP AND NIGHTSHADE.

Authority followed by Synchrony® STS®
soybean herbicide program

Call toll free 1-888-6-DUPONT. Or visit us at www.dupont.com/ag/us Read and follow the label.

The seasons. The weather. Interest rates. Prices. **Everything changes.** Except what you're doing it for.

Living a life that's reserved for a very few. Doing what's right. That's why I farm. I'm always looking for flexible, new solutions. Like DuPont Basis Gold®. I can use it in a one-pass, total post, or as part of a two-pass program following a preemergence product like new LeadOff™ corn herbicide from DuPont. Either way, Basis Gold® controls emerged weeds and grasses even if it doesn't rain. And when it does, the residual protects me all the way to harvest. Plus, Basis Gold® can be used on virtually any corn, so I can plant whatever works best on my land. I like having these choices—especially the option to do it my way.

IN ANY KIND OF WEATHER, ON ANY KIND OF CORN, IT CONTROLS MY GRASS AND BROADLEAF WEEDS.

Basis Gold®
corn herbicide

Call toll free 1-888-6-DUPONT. Or visit us at www.dupont.com/ag/us Read and follow the label.

● The Strategy Statement

As you write your strategy statement for the product or service you have chosen to work on, use the outline in the box below to help you focus on the task. Ultimately, all parts of a campaign must reflect the final strategy. However, it's not unusual for the strategy to change as the creative work is being developed. The original strategy statement gets you going. Later, when you begin spinning creative

---

Strategy Statement for (name of product, service, etc.)

Give a brief description of the product or service to put the strategy in context—no more than one or two paragraphs, but enough to help the reader understand what is to be advertised.

1. *Who is our target?*
Give brief lifestyle/attitudinal descriptions. Include some demographics, but not as important for most products. Users, heavy users, nonusers, users of competitive brands? Relationship to other product/service usage?

2. *Where are we now in the mind of this person?*
They don't know us. They know us but don't use us. They prefer another brand because . . . They don't understand what we can do. They don't use us for enough things. And so on.

3. *Where is our competition in the mind of this person?*
Use the same approach as above, but focus on the competing brands.

4. *Where would we like to be in the mind of this person?*
Product is positioned as . . . Product is the best choice because . . . Now they know product will . . .

5. *What is the consumer promise, the "big idea"?*
State the major focus of your campaign. Not a slogan or tag line at this stage, but an idea in simple language that will serve as the basis for a tag line—a brief statement that sums up what the campaign is about.

6. *What is the supporting evidence?*
Draw on consumer benefits to strengthen and elaborate on what you chose in item 5. Build benefit after benefit in support of your big idea.

7. *What is the tone of voice for the advertising?*
Decide on the appropriate tone—warm, family values, startling, hi-tech, sobering fact, mild guilt, humor, and so on.

---

concepts from the strategy, those subsequent ideas may lead you to newer and better strategies. Don't worry about it. Your goal is to jump-start your thinking so that you will arrive at the best solution.

● Suggested Activities

1. Using the strategy statement form as shown in the box on the previous page, write a strategy for a product, service, or organization of your choosing or as assigned by your instructor.

2. Collect several advertisements for a single product, service, or organization. How much of the original strategy can you infer from what the ads say and how they say it? Is the target audience evident? What is the problem, and what is the ad's approach to solving it? What type of strategy is employed? Where are the relevant and unexpected connections? Which basic human needs are addressed? If you were in the target market for this ad, would you believe what it says? Why or why not? Strategically speaking, what might be another way to approach the problem?

3. Using this same campaign or another, do an Internet search for the product or service. What differences do you note in the strategic approach? For example, you might do a search for Bell Helmets and determine if their "Web strategy" is in keeping with the "Courage for your head" campaign.

Search Online! Discovering More About Strategy

Using InfoTrac® College Edition, try these phrases and others for Key Words and Subject Guide searches: *strategy, strategic planning, advertising strategy, creative strategy, target market, consumer as gatekeeper, advertising and trust, advertising and human contact, basic human needs, Bell Helmets, brand image, positioning.*

BriefCase

Barbed Advertising on a Limited Budget: The Success of Magic Ring© by Lovable

Just about every woman from the preteen years on wears a bra, and most women wear one every day. Most women in the United States wear a C cup or larger, which means most women are seeking support *and* comfort in their "everyday" bra. This basic insight became the impetus for a new bra from the Lovable Company. The challenge was to come up with an idea that would sell it that was dramatic and new. In other words, what was new about support with comfort? Everything, as it turned out. For this new bra was the Magic Ring©.

The Lovable Company is an international manufacturer of bras. It markets most of its products domestically at the mass-market level. With a 6.3 percent market share in the United States, the company is considered a second-tier player to megabrands such as Fruit of the Loom, Hanes, and Jockey. Lovable bras are distributed by retailers such as JC Penney, Wal-Mart, and Sears.

Consumer research indicated that a substantial number of women in the category were dissatisfied with most support bras. So the company developed and began selling to the retail trade a new bra called Magic Ring©.

The Magic Ring© is indeed different from anything that preceded it. Instead of wires, this bra uses a channel stitching that covers a soft fiber filling. The filling follows the same contour as an underwire, resulting in a bra that, while supportive and functional, is soft and comfortable as well.

With a national advertising budget of $1 million, much smaller than many other national brands, Lovable had only a limited number of insertions, or showings, with which to break away from the crowd. Discarding typical generic approaches (woman wearing bra, no specific benefits stressed except for, say, uplift) because these would get lost in the crowd, the company and its advertising agency developed this strategy: "The Magic Ring© bra offers comfortable support without the wire due to its patented 'comfort panels.' As such, it frees women from antiquated underwires and at last offers them the comfort they demand in a support bra."

GUYS SAY WE'RE MOODY AND EMOTIONAL. LET'S SEE HOW THEY FEEL AFTER 8 HOURS IN AN UNDERWIRE.

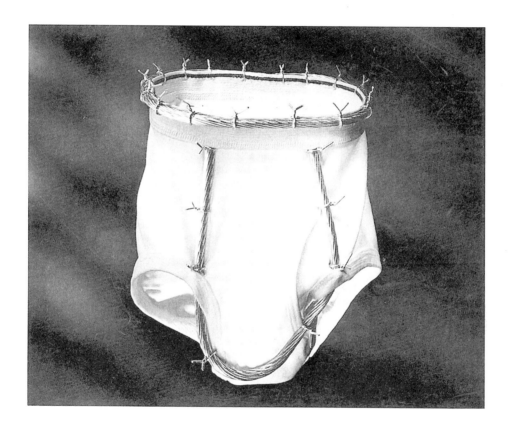

Chances are, few men would choose to wear a device that pokes, pinches and rides up into their delicate parts. So why should we? Introducing Magic Ring, the first true wireless support bra by Lovable. With unique

Magic Ring™
Wearing is believing.™

Comfort Panels™ stitched into the garment running from cup to shoulder, it cradles you in soft fabric. Instead of hard steel. Giving you the same shape and support as a wire. Without radically altering your state of mind.

by LOVABLE ♡

To find the Magic Ring bra in the store nearest you, call 1-800-822-9113. Original Magic Ring • Lace • Sports Bra • Body Briefers

SHORTLY AFTER THE INTRODUCTION OF THE FIRST UNDERWIRE BRA, VALIUM® WAS INVENTED. COINCIDENCE?

For as long as there have been underwire bras, there have been women trying to escape the pain they inflict. Finally, there's an over-the-counter remedy. Magic Ring, the first true wireless support bra by Lovable.

Magic Ring™

Wearing is believing.™

Comfort Panels™ stitched into the garment run from cup to shoulder. Embracing you in fabric. Instead of steel. So now you can get stylish support and elegant shaping. And safely operate heavy machinery, too.

by LOVABLE ♡

To find the Magic Ring bra in the store nearest you, call 1-800-822-9113. Original Magic Ring • Lace • Sports Bra • Body Briefers
Valium is a registered trademark.

LABOR. MENSTRUAL CRAMPS. AND TO ADD INSULT TO INJURY, THE UNDERWIRE BRA.

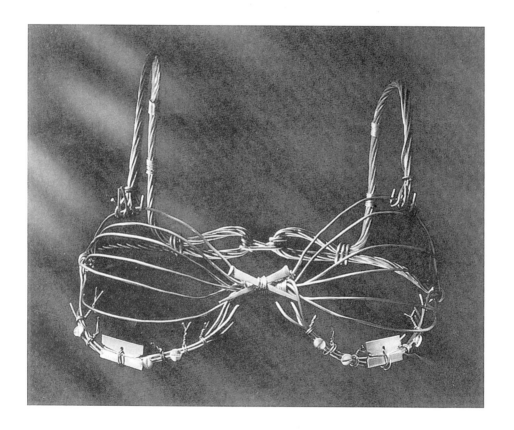

Among other things, you've had to put up with the constant pinching and poking of an underwire bra. In which case, you'll be delighted to learn about the Magic Ring by Lovable. It does everything a wire does. But it does it humanely.

Magic Ring™

Wearing is believing.™

By supporting and shaping you with Comfort Panels™ stitched into the garment that run from cup to shoulder. So you're surrounded by fabric. Instead of steel. How you survived this long without it is, quite frankly, beyond us.

by LOVABLE ♡

To find the Magic Ring bra in the store nearest you, call 1-800-822-9113. Original Magic Ring • Lace • Sports Bra • Body Briefers

The agency chose bold, unusual, and humorous themes for the tone of the advertising—a radical departure from the norm in this category. Using the tag line "Wearing is believing," magazine ads employed sarcasm and humor in depicting barbed-wire bra sculptures that resembled medieval torture devices. One accompanying headline read, "Labor. Menstrual cramps. And to add insult to injury, the underwire bra." A second headline, paired with another horrifying barbed-wire bra sculpture, announced, "Shortly after the introduction of the first underwire bra, Valium was invented. Coincidence?" And knowing that women like sly jokes about men, they showed a wired pair of men's briefs in a third ad, headlined "Guys say we're moody and emotional. Let's see how they feel after 8 hours in an underwire."

An 800-number used only in the magazine ads drew an average of 100 calls daily from women who wanted to know more about the Magic Ring© bras and where they could be bought. To stretch the small budget, media dollars were spent in short, concentrated bursts of national TV and magazine spots during the introductory phase of the product.

To introduce the Magic Ring© bra to the retail trade, ads were designed to sell the product to stores. This helped retailers grasp the significance of the product benefits and added sizzle to the sales process. For point-of-sale displays, Lovable employed posters, banners, header cards, and decorative shopping bags—all with a simple graphic of a bowling ball suspended by a feather. A folding collar tag on each bra told the engineering story to the consumer, and Lovable offered a $5 mail-in rebate for the first month to encourage trial purchases and to build a valuable database. Within six months, the company collected 50,000 names and was already seeing repeat purchases.

The result? The Magic Ring© was the single most successful product introduction in Lovable's 62-year history. The company's market share increased 50 percent in the first three months after the bra's introduction. And it's *still* a hot item.

CHAPTER 5

Finding the Big Idea

W e're in the idea business, because ideas will be the currency of the 21st century," Roy Spence, founder of Austin-based GSD&M, explained to *USA Today*. But Spence also observed, "The market is ad rich and idea poor."[1] George Lois of Lois/USA, another of the great minds in advertising, put it even more bluntly:

> If advertising is a science, I'm a girl. Eighty-five percent of all advertising is invisible. It's there but no one sees it. Then 14 percent of all advertising is terrible. It's ugly, stupid, pat. The remaining 1 percent is the great stuff, the advertising characterized by The Big Idea. The big idea can go further than you can imagine. It can save a business, start an enterprise, spark a revolution. If you're faced with an ad that doesn't have an idea that can be expressed in one sentence, save your money.

The key question becomes, How do you come up with the big idea?

● How Do You Come up with the Big Idea?

S ome writers and artists say their ideas come to them while they're taking a hot bath or a long walk. Others get ideas in the shower or while driving. And still others get ideas through free association with a colleague. Terence Poltrack describes the process of coming up with the big idea as "one man, one style. For every idea out there, there's a way to get to it. Ask advertising's creative thinkers about their personal road maps to The Answer, and you confront a mix of fear and bravado, chilly logic

---

[1]Bill Meyers, "He's in the Idea Business," *USA Today*, 29 April 1999, p. B1.

and warm emotion. The process is one part reason, one part heart, and one (big) part pure, simple intuition."[2]

James Webb Young, a former creative vice president at J. Walter Thompson, described a five-step process in his book *A Technique for Producing Ideas:*[3]

- Step 1: *Immersion.* Totally immerse yourself in background research.
- Step 2: *Digestion.* Play with the information. Look at it from different angles. Make lists of features. Draw doodles. Write down phrases.
- Step 3: *Incubation.* Put the advertising assignment aside. Go for a walk. Go out with friends. See a movie.
- Step 4: *Illumination.* Let the brainstorm happen. When you least expect it, your brain spurts out an idea. It can happen anywhere, any time.
- Step 5: *Reality testing.* Ask yourself, Is the idea really good? Does it solve the problem? Is it on strategy?

Other advertising pros have their own variations on the process. Alex Osborn, former president of BBDO (the "O" in BBDO), offered this approach: (1) Specify the problem, (2) gather information, (3) generate possible solutions, (4) evaluate the solutions, and (5) select the best one. And, as early as 1926, Graham Wallas proposed a four-step approach in his book *The Art of Thought:* preparation, incubation, illumination, and verification.

● Considerations in Brainstorming

As Poltrack said, there's no one right way to come up with a big idea, but here are some things to think about as you're brainstorming.

Strategy

The foundation for ideas are found in the strategy statement you learned to write in the previous chapter. This statement tells you who your customers are, what they think about your product, and what you would like them to think. It tells you about your competition and about what differentiates your brand from the others. It even tells you the main idea that needs to come across in your ads and the tone you should use.

Your strategy tells you a lot, but it doesn't tell you the exact words or images you need to use. Instead, strategy is a springboard for ideas. For example, Maytag didn't become known as a dependable brand by saying, "Maytag: the dependable brand." Instead, the creative team developed the lonely repairman, who is far more interesting and convincing than a simple slogan.

---

[2]Terence Poltrack, "Stalking the Big Idea," *Agency,* May/June 1991, p. 26.

[3]James Webb Young, *A Technique for Producing Ideas,* 3rd ed. (Chicago: Crain Books, 1975).

Target Audience

Jot down words, phrases, and images that come to mind when you visualize your customers. Don't think in terms of a large group of people. Think of it as an audience of one. Visualize the one person who's typical of the target audience and answer the following questions: What does she do for a living? For fun? What makes her laugh? What makes her worried? Where does she live? Where does she go on vacation? What does she hope to be doing in five years? And so on. Now take those thoughts and expand upon them. How do they relate to your client?

But what can you do if you have a target audience with varied backgrounds, interests, and tastes? Consider visualizing the typical person who represents the audience of the medium in which your ad will run. The milk "mustache" campaign was adapted to suit the interests of its magazine readers. Two ads in the campaign featured Tyra Banks and appealed to two entirely different audiences. In the ad that appeared in *Seventeen* magazine, she wears a white tank top, blue jeans, and a milk mustache. The copy reads:

> Girls, here's today's beauty tip. Think about you and your 10 best friends. Chances are 9 of you aren't getting enough calcium. So what? So milk. 3 glasses of milk a day give you the calcium your growing bones need. Tomorrow—what to do when you're taller than your date.

In *Sports Illustrated*'s swimsuit issue, Tyra sports a gold string bikini and a milk mustache. The copy reads:

> Stop drooling and listen. One in five victims of osteoporosis is male. Don't worry. Calcium can help prevent it. And ice cold, lowfat milk is a great source of calcium. So don't sit there gawking at me. Go drink some milk.

The Media as Part of the Creative Process

As the milk examples illustrate, the media can inspire creative ideas. And no wonder. Just look at the word *media,* and what do you find? Jack Arogeti, senior vice president and media director at McCann-Erickson/Atlanta, discovered the word *idea.*

MEDIA

IDEA

Arogeti believes that the media department should be involved in the creative process. Other agencies agree, including Kirshenbaum Bond & Partners. One of KB&P's most famous advertising messages was for Bamboo Lingerie. To break through the clutter of media-saturated New York, the agency stenciled the sidewalks with the message "From here, it looks like you could use some new underwear. Bamboo Lingerie." And to promote Jump sneakers, KB&P purchased space on an inner-city billboard and attached an actual basketball hoop to the board with the message "If you were wearing Jumps, this wouldn't seem so impossible."

Crispin & Porter Advertising used unconventional media to promote the Miami Rescue Mission and to describe what it's like to be homeless. Ads for the mission ran on shopping carts, bus shelters, park benches, and trash dumpsters. Each had the following copy: "When you're homeless, you see the world differently. To help call

● FIGURE 5-1

Truly there is nothing
standard about this ad.
The headline certainly
might make you curious,
but nothing about it will
confuse you, mainly
because the headline bears
a direct relationship to
the product. Remember
the difference; it's an
important one.

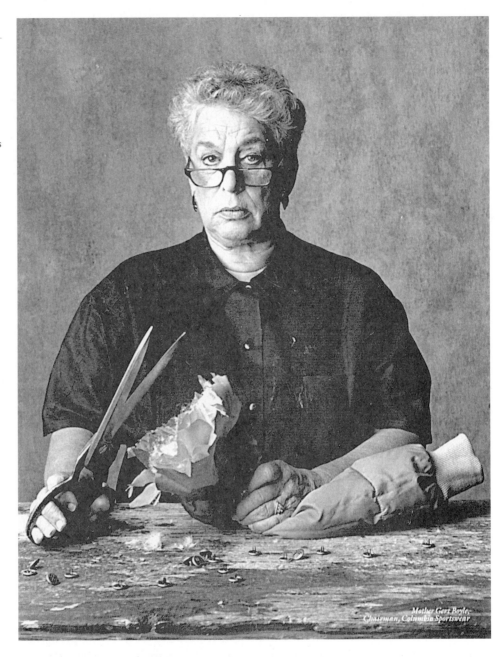

571-2273." What made the ads so powerful was how the headlines and media
choices related to the overall message:

● The ad on the park benches was headlined "Bed."

● The message on the dumpsters read "Kitchen."

● The poster inside the bus shelter was labeled "House."

● The sign on the grocery carts described it as a "Closet."

"SHE SNAPS NECKS AND HACKS OFF ARMS."

–By Tim Boyle, President, Columbia Sportswear

My Mother, Columbia Sportswear's chairman, will stop at nothing to get what she wants–superior outerwear.

In fact, the mountains around Portland, Oregon, frequently echo her sharply barked commands. "When I say a snap closed neck and storm front, that's what I expect to see!" Or, as she hacks away at an inappropriately attached sleeve, "All seams are to be double sewn!"

What, you may ask, is the end result of having such a, uh, vociferous chairman? The Columbia Interchange System,™ for one. It lets you brave multiple weather conditions with one jacket by matching a zip-in, zip-out liner to a weatherproof shell. They may be worn separately, or together. Take our Ponderosa Parka™ pictured here. The outer shell is 100% Technicloth II™–a soft blend of cotton and nylon woven into a durable rib fabric, oiled to keep water out. To hold warmth in, the bomber-style Zap Fleece™ liner is quilted with Thermoloft™ insulation.

All in all, it's easy to see why not just any parka can survive Mother's rather pointed demands.

Columbia Sportswear Company

6600 N. Baltimore, Portland, Oregon 97203. For the dealer nearest you in the U.S. and Canada, call 1-800-MA-BOYLE.

Traditional media can also inspire creative ideas. For example, Green Giant used magazines as creative inspiration:

"I've been digging up dirt for years."
(In the *National Enquirer*)

"When you dress like this, you better eat your vegetables."
(In *People's* "best dressed" issue)

"Eat your vegetables and you'll grow up big and strong like me (actual results may vary)"
(In *New Woman*)

"I have very good taste in vegetables."
(In *Southern Living*)

Minute Maid bought the back page of each section of the *New York Times* to introduce its Premium Choice juice. The ad in the Business section included a coupon for 35¢ savings along with some financial advice: "This might be the only sure thing you'll ever find in the business section." The ad in the Living section played off of the fact that so many New Yorkers become snowbirds when they retire: "Today, the metropolitan section also has important news from New York's sixth borough, Florida."

Context   Where will your customer see your message? When does your customer use your product? Noxema wanted a fresh approach to its advertising, so its agency, Leo Burnett, bought ad space in women's restrooms throughout Manhattan. The ads grabbed your attention because they were printed in reverse—you needed a mirror to read them. Appropriately, the ads were hung in frames on the walls across the mirrors so that, when a woman checked her makeup in the mirror, she was greeted with messages such as these:

"Look as good as the woman your date is hitting on."

"Did someone miss her beauty sleep?"

"He must really love you for your inner beauty."

Here are other clever messages that make a relevant connection to what consumers are doing when they see the message:

"Slow down. Our news isn't on yet."
(Outdoor board for Fox 32 news program)

"Ref, you need glasses."
(Outdoor board for an optician, placed at a sports stadium)

"Obviously, if you're reading Playbill,
you're fashionable, elegant and cultured.
Just like our pearls."
(*Playbill* magazine ad for Fortunoff's jewelry store)

"Hello to all our readers in high office."
(Message for *The Economist* magazine, painted on the roof of a bus)

Current Events   Did something major just happen in the news? Is something about to happen? Ads that tap into current events reflect what's on people's minds, and this approach is great if you have the resources to constantly change your ads. In 1999, Polaroid captured the Y2K frenzy in a commercial that shows a young man on New Year's Eve photographing his balance at an ATM, just in case the Y2K bug eats into his account when the clock struck midnight. The commercial shows him photographing his $342.63 balance before midnight and quickly snapping a second shot after midnight when the machine indicates his account holds millions. However, the American Bankers Association was not amused, and Polaroid pulled the ad.

When Kenneth Cole needed a device to appeal to cynical trendsetters and opinion leaders, he turned to two young freelancers, Jonathan Bond and Richard Kirshenbaum. They understood that they needed to position the Kenneth Cole brand of shoes as being chic and fashionable without resorting to something as lame as "chic and fashionable." To do this, they tied the brand into current events, using famous—and infamous—personalities. The first ad read, "Imelda Marcos bought 2,700 pairs of shoes. She could've at least had the courtesy to buy a pair of ours." A follow-up ad read, "Dear Mr. President: If you choose to pardon Imelda, please do so in time for our Semi-Annual Sale." When the Berlin Wall came down, an ad told customers,

● Figure 5-2

Creative media placement can make your message more powerful. The ad at the left was designed to be placed inside a taxi. The ad at the right was designed to be placed inside an elevator.

"Now there's nothing to keep people from coming to our Semi-Annual Sale." When the media reported that Nancy Reagan had booked White House events based upon astrology, the ad showed a visual of a constellation of stars in the shape of a shoe; the headline read, "According to Nancy Reagan's advisor, there's never been a better time to buy shoes." And when Ellen DeGeneres came out of the closet, the message was, "If a TV show can get people to come out, imagine what a sale can do." The Kenneth Cole campaign was so successful that it inspired other businesses to see what the two freelancers could do for them. Thus the agency Kirshenbaum Bond & Partners was born.

Timing

When will your ad run? Is the timing significant to your customers? For example, Pepto-Bismol ran an ad in April issues of magazines. What's significant about April? How does it relate to queazy stomachs? April 15 is tax day, a day that can make some taxpayers sick to their stomachs. That's why Pepto-Bismol ran a full-page copy of a 1040 form, with a corner rolled up to reveal a bottle of Pepto-Bismol.

Wild Turkey Kentucky Straight Bourbon Whiskey made an unexpected but relevant suggestion for people who were expecting company for the holidays: "This Thanksgiving serve Turkey *before* dinner." Vick's NyQuil promised a good night's sleep without a hacking cough. The ad ran during the holiday season, when many people seem to catch colds, with this message: "Silent night." And Saatchi & Saatchi used holidays as a source of inspiration for Tide laundry detergent ads:

"The only way to wear white after Labor Day."
(Ran on Labor Day)

"It takes a wee bit more than luck to get green beer out of your clothes."
(Ran on St. Patrick's Day)

"Removes alien goo, fake blood and, oh yeah, chocolate."
(Ran on Halloween)

"Recess. Gym class. Food fights. Any questions?"
(Ran in early September)

"This coupon entitles you to sit back while someone else attempts to do the laundry."
(Ran around Mother's Day)

Negative Thoughts

What negative thoughts do your potential customers have about your client? What negative thoughts do *you* have about your client? Don't try to cover up a negative—embrace it. After the media reported that Leona Helmsley was a tyrannical boss, ads for Helmsley Hotels read, "Say what you will, she runs a helluva hotel." Volkswagen didn't try to hide the fact that its car wasn't as fancy as other cars. Instead, one ad boasted, " It's ugly but it gets you there."

Analogies

Make an analogy. If your product was a person, what kind of person would it be? Would it be young? Old? Carefree? Uptight? If it were a tree, what kind of tree would it be? How about if it were a dog or plant? Visualize your product in a different way. What if it were bigger? Smaller? What if it could talk? How would someone else solve the same problem?

Crate & Barrel described its "Sonoma" collection of furniture as if it were a fashion model: "Shapely legs. French looks. Mildly distressed. Available for dinner." *Good Housekeeping* touted the virtues of its Seal of Approval to advertisers: "The seal is like your therapist: It assures you everything will be alright," and "The seal is like a mattress tag: It contains specific instructions for not getting ripped off."

Culture

It can be the high-brow variety or the pop culture variety. Just make sure it's relevant to your target audience.

A scene from the film *When Harry Met Sally* inspired the idea behind the Clairol Herbal Essences campaign. In the movie, Meg Ryan fakes an orgasm in the middle of a restaurant. She moans, "It's so goooood. Ohhhhh. Ohhhhh. Yes! Yes! YES!!!!" The movie camera pans to a middle-aged woman who tells the waiter, "I'll have what she's having." This scene inspired the idea of the totally organic experience offered to people who wash their hair with Clairol Herbal Essences shampoo, complete with a TV viewer who tells her husband she wants to try that shampoo!

Titles of books, movies, and plays can also serve as inspiration. To promote the fact that their business-class seats could fully recline, Air France described the experience as "180 degrees of separation." The ad ran in the *New York Times Magazine* and reached an audience who would appreciate the play on the movie title *Six Degrees of Separation*. Absolut uses literary references in some of its ads. While headlines for Absolut vodka are usually set in all caps, the headline "absolut cummings" was appropriately set in lowercase to reflect the poet's unique style of writing. And British Airways exchanged partners of famous couples in literature to communicate that companions fly free. One ad read, "Romeo & Delilah"; another, "Jekyll & Gretel"; and another, "Hansel & Juliet." All ran with the tag line "Who you bring is up to you."

Shape

Perhaps you put two things with similar shape together that at first glance seem unrelated. For example, the traditional way to advertise silverware is to show a beautiful table setting. But Oneida ads show close-ups of utensils being used in unexpected ways. In one ad, a boy is poised to shoot a pea out of a spoon; the tag line read, "The gentlemen's way to be sent to bed without dessert." In another ad, a little girl is blowing bubbles out of a pierced serving spoon; the tag line reads, "No wand. No problem."

In an effort to influence behavior, Allstate Insurance illustrated how drinking and driving don't mix. No, they didn't show a car wreck. Instead, they invented a "killer cocktail"—a martini with a car key jabbing the olive as if it were a toothpick.

Location

Where is the product made? What regions of the country (or the world) will see your ad? Can you customize it in any way?

Pace Picante Sauce promoted its authentic Tex-Mex heritage by poking fun of other brands that were "made in New York City!" A billboard for Zamboli's Italian restaurant (located in South Carolina) told drivers the mileage to the closest good Italian food:

Great Italian Food Ahead

Rome 4,574 Mi.

Venice 4,634 Mi.

Zamboli's Next Right

Some ads have fun with regional accents. An ad promoting a concert by a southern choir read, "Hallaluy'all." And an ad in a tourist magazine invited people to visit "The Boston Museum of Fine Ahht."

Pictures and Words

Think of a solution with just pictures. Then think of a solution with just words. For example, Target wanted to communicate that their stores sell a wide variety of merchandise. Billboards listed series of three things you could find at their store. Here are some of our favorites:

"Twinkies. Cheetos. Wide Aisles."

"VCRs. Barney Tapes. Aspirin."

"Bras. Binoculars. Mini-blinds."

"Candles. Barry White CDs. Baby Clothes."

"Aquariums. Fish Food. Toilet Plungers."

Target used a visual approach in its magazine campaign. One ad shows a woman jumping in the air as she twirls a lug wrench as if she were a cheerleader. Another shows a woman wearing a black top and what looks like curlers—only on closer examination they turn out to be paint rollers. Still another shows a woman wearing a car's air filter as a necklace. And another shows a woman wearing a backpack and a lampshade as a skirt.

● Guidelines for Brainstorming

When brainstorming, keep these guidelines in mind:

1. *Don't think you must come up with the big idea all by yourself.* Steve Hayden, one of the creators of the famous 1984 commercial for Apple Computers, puts it all in perspective: "It's better to own 20% of a great idea than 100% of a so-so idea."[4]

---

[4]Laurence Minsky and Emily Thornton Calvo, *How to Succeed in Advertising When All You Have Is Talent* (Lincolnwood, IL: NTC Business Books, 1995), p. 99.

● Figure 5-3

Outdoor billboards used icons to introduce the Lincoln LS as something new and dynamic.

A great visual idea can come from a writer. The perfect headline can come from an artist. And, as we saw earlier, creative solutions can come from media experts. You may want to work independently at first and then bounce ideas off your creative partner. Or you may want to start out by doing free association with one or two colleagues. Or perhaps you want to brainstorm with a group of six to twelve people. When you brainstorm in a group, be sure to designate a leader who will keep the session going and record the ideas. Also, be sure that every person participates and that no idea is considered stupid. After the session, there will be time to sort quality from quantity.

2. *Start a swipe file.* Fill a folder or file cabinet or wallpaper an entire room with work you consider outstanding. You shouldn't "swipe" ideas, but you can use them as a springboard. The legendary Leo Burnett used to rip out ads that struck him as being effective communications. About twice a year he'd riffle through that file—not with the idea of copying anything, but in the hope that it would trigger an idea that could apply to something else he was doing. Burnett also kept a folder of phrases he liked. "Whenever I hear a phrase in conversation or any place which strikes me as being particularly apt in expressing an idea or bringing it to life or accentuating the

smell of it, the looks of it or anything else—or expressing any kind of an idea—I scribble it down and stick it in there."[5] Burnett made that comment back in the 1960s, but the advice is still appropriate today.

3. *Exercise your creative mind regularly.* Rick Silver and Jeff Tobin of Chernoff/Silver and Associates believe it's important to expose yourself to other creative endeavors. Go to the ballet. Visit a museum. See a play. Silver and Tobin call these experiences "grease for your creative engine. They free up your thinking process and often trigger new combinations of ideas."[6]

4. *Come up with a lot of ideas.* The more ideas, the better. Consider these two sets of instructions:

> *Instruction 1:* "Come up with a good idea that will solve the problem of declining student enrollment at XYZ University. Your name and idea will be forwarded to the president of the university."

> *Instruction 2:* "Come up with as many ideas as possible to help solve the problem of declining student enrollment at XYZ University. Jot down as many ideas as possible. Try to come up with at least 25 ideas . . . or even more. Don't judge the merits of your ideas. Write every idea you have."

What would happen if you got the first set of instructions? You'd probably freeze up because you'd place unnecessary pressure on yourself. You'd second-guess the thoughts that came into your head and would automatically dismiss any that you felt weren't "good." The idea you finally put on paper would most likely be a safe approach because you knew others—including the president of the university— would be evaluating it.

Now what would happen if you got the second set of instructions? Well, you'd probably come up with some pretty dumb ideas. But you'd also probably come up with some pretty good ones. In fact, you might even come up with a great idea. Idea 23 might be the winner. But if you only came up with one idea, idea 23 would never occur to you. And who knows what would happen if you came up with 100 ideas!

Keep the second set of instructions in mind in the idea generation stage. Give yourself total freedom to come up with bad ideas. Who knows? Those bad ideas may spark great ideas when someone else hears them. And if the idea is a real dud, you can always drop it later in the process.

5. *Be ready for an idea to pop into your head when you least expect it.* Ideas will often strike you in the most unlikely places. Be ready to write them down because, as quickly as an idea pops into your head, it can pop out of it. Forever. Be sure to keep a pad of paper on your nightstand just in case a brilliant idea comes to you at 3 A.M.

---

[5]Denis Higgins, *Conversations with William Bernbach, Leo Burnett, George Gribbin, David Ogilvy, Rosser Reeves* (Lincolnwood, IL: NTC Business Books, 1989), p. 47.

[6]Rick Silver and Jeff Tobin, "Keys to Stimulating the Creative Process," *The State, Special section: Columbia Business Journal,* 4 Oct. 1999, p. 6.

6. *Set your ideas aside.* As you gather ideas, put them inside an envelope or folder, and don't look at them right away. If you evaluate early on, you may settle for an idea that's just so-so. Or you may never allow a gem of an idea to develop. Luke Sullivan, an award-winning copywriter at Fallon McElligott, warns, "As a creative person, you will discover your brain has a built-in tendency to want to reach closure, even rush to it. . . . But in order to get to a great idea, which is usually about the 500th one to come along, you'll need to resist the temptation to give in to the anxiety and sign off on the first passable idea that shows up."[7]

7. *Be sure to test your idea on others.* Ogilvy & Mather tells its account people to ask the following questions when evaluating creative work: Is it on strategy? What did you get from the advertising? Was that net impression a good or bad one? Why? Did you remember to react to this ad as a consumer, not as an advertising person? Does the ad address the right group of people? Is the tone consistent with the strategy? Is it a good execution? Is the promise visualized effectively? How? Is the brand name up front enough? Is the core selling idea clear? Does the execution lend itself to a total campaign? If so, what might be some other executions? Does something make you stop, look, listen quickly? What is it?

Using Criticism to Improve Your Creativity

A critical part of the creative process involves working in teams and checking your work by asking others to react to it. The other person can see your idea with a clear and unbiased mind. Second, if your evaluator knows advertising, chances are he or she can judge your work both as a consumer and as a professional. The key to a good critique is objectivity. This means you critique the work, not the person. Look for positive things, and then question things that may not seem clear or strong or that simply don't work for you.

Here are some additional pointers to help you make criticism palatable: [8]

1. Make "I" statements. Own your criticism by saying "I'm confused by this sentence," not "You confused me."

2. Be clear and specific, commenting on the work, not the person. Instead of "Why do you always make the same mistake?" try "This should be written as two separate sentences. Do you remember doing that before?"

3. Never say, "This is great, BUT . . ." Eliminate the threatening "but" and get to the point: "I think the opening is fine. Here in the middle, I don't know if you're stressing the right benefits."

4. Control your emotions, and speak in a normal tone of voice.

---

[7]Luke Sullivan, *Hey Whipple, Squeeze This: A Guide to Creating Great Ads* (New York: Wiley, 1998) p. 72.

[8]Compliments of Dr. Serge Piccinin, director of the Teaching Centre at the University of Ottawa.

● Figure 5-4

These ads use clean bathroom humor to sell you on American Standard products. Each ad has an offer for a free guidebook "overflowing with products, ideas and inspiration."

5. Show some empathy and understanding: "I wonder if you didn't hear me when I gave directions for this assignment."

6. Offer practical suggestions. Without suggestions on how the work might be improved, criticism is generally useless. Surprisingly, students seem to have a greater knack for offering suggestions to their peers than for figuring out how to fix their own work. Try it; pair up with someone in your class, and trade suggestions for improvement.

7. Be honest. If you don't like something, explain why. But begin with a positive comment, end on a positive note, and sandwich the negative comment in between. This helps the recipient to be more accepting of what you have to say.

Here are some guidelines for nonverbal behaviors:

1. Make eye contact with the person. Looking away diminishes the power of the communication.

IT'S SEEN YOU
NAKED
IT'S HEARD YOU
SING

Your bathroom probably knows more about you than your own mother. So it's only fitting you make it the most wonderful room in the house. Call us and we'll send you a free guidebook overflowing with products, ideas and inspiration. 1-800-524-9797. *American Standard*

{ *Dear Mom:* }
WARREN
AND I HAVE A
LITTLE
PROBLEM

The two of you may not always see eye-to-eye on every little issue in the bathroom. But we can help you agree on the stuff that really matters. Call and we'll send you a free guidebook overflowing with products, ideas and inspiration. 1-800-524-9797. *American Standard*

● FIGURE 5-5

What's that giant spot doing on this newspaper ad?! If you're a dog owner, you know. Good boy!

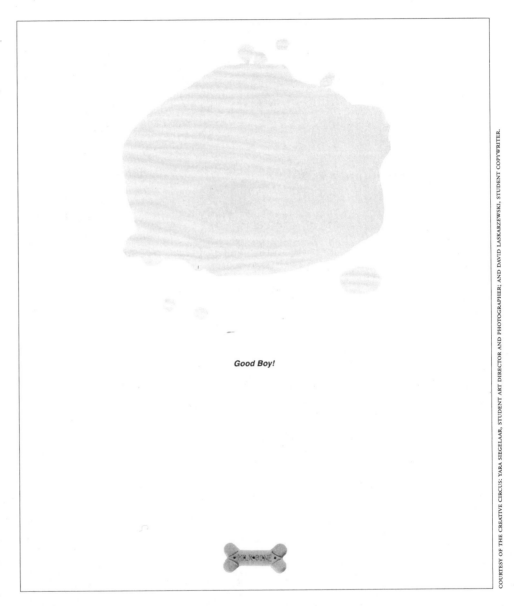

Good Boy!

2. Show your interest through a warm and expressive tone of voice.

3. Use facial expressions that are consistent with your message. Don't grin as you address deficiencies, and don't frown as you offer compliments.

4. Don't slouch or slump. This is important because these postures suggest either that you're uncomfortable with what you have to say or that you are not honoring the evaluator's effort.

5. Stand or sit an appropriate distance from the other person. Either both of you stand or both sit.

6. Choose an appropriate time and place for this discussion. As the recipient of the critique, you have both rights and obligations in this process. First, you have the right to ask for a later meeting if the time or place chosen is inconvenient or uncomfortable. And you have the right to terminate the critique if it is delivered in an offensive manner.

● Suggested Activities

1. Think of unconventional media to convince people to stop smoking, to drink responsibly, and to recycle. Now develop messages for each of these issues.

2. Create an ad that uses a headline and visual to communicate a selling point in an unexpected way. Next, create an ad that uses just a headline. And finally, create an ad that lets the visual stand on its own. Which approach works best? Why?

3. Develop 20 advertising ideas for a pawn shop. Here's some background information:

- Pawn shops date back to ancient times.

- Queen Isabella of Spain pawned her jewelry to finance Columbus on his voyage to America.

- The three gold balls in front of a pawn shop are derived from symbols used by Italian merchants.

- Pawnshops are the forerunner of modern banks. The pawnbroker loans money on personal property that his customers give him. The customer is issued a ticket, which is a contract stating the amount of the loan, the service charge, and the specific time the pawnbroker will hold the property. The process takes only a few minutes.

- All pawnbrokers are regulated by law, so the customers know they're not being "taken."

- Pawn shops offer values. Since pawnbrokers deal with people from all walks of life, they can offer for sale a vast array of merchandise: VCRs, color TVs, diamond rings, power tools, exercise equipment, and much more, at lower prices than just about any other place.

- All classes of people borrow and buy from pawnbrokers.

Search Online! Discovering More About Finding the Big Idea

Using InfoTrac® College Edition, try these phrases and others for Key Words and Subject Guide searches: *advertising ideas, exploring possibilities, lateral thinking, finding answers, finding solutions, brainstorming, visualization, analogies, metaphors, idea generation, criticism.*

BriefCase

Industry Cruising for First-Timers

From 1970 through 1993, the cruise ship industry enjoyed an average growth in business of 10 percent a year. But in 1994, the number of passengers fell 1 percent, and there was an even greater drop in 1995. To stem the tide, the 26-member Cruise Lines International Association made plans to spend at least $30 million over three years to tout the value of cruise ship vacations and to attract first-time passengers, since research shows that only 8 percent of Americans have ever been on a cruise. The three major players—Carnival Cruise Lines, Princess Cruises, and Royal Caribbean Cruise Lines—prepared for expansion by tapping into the 92 percent of Americans who've never enjoyed the pleasures of cruising. With intensive price promotions eroding existing consumer loyalty, cruise lines were determined to focus on product/image strategies to position their companies firmly in the consumers' minds.

Each cruise line endeavors to set itself apart from its rivals. Carnival's upscale subsidiary, Holland America Line, asks, "When was the last time?" Originally, Norwegian Cruise Lines used provocative poses and sexually alluring themes, tagging each message, "It's different out there."

The industry giant Carnival Cruise Lines struck gold with an innovative multimillion-dollar campaign that ran in *People* magazine. This was Carnival's first magazine ad purchase in years, as well as the biggest media buy ever placed exclusively in *People*. The campaign was created by HMS/McFarland & Drier of Miami, with nearly 20 different ad spreads asking, "What's *your* idea of fun?" Examine the campaign in detail, and you realize what Carnival had in mind—to counter the perception that (1) nothing much exciting happens once the ship leaves the shore, (2) that "cruising's not for me; I won't be able to do what I want," or (3) that programmed activities don't appeal to all age groups or lifestyles. The two-page color advertisements bring those attitudes to a screaming halt as they answer the question of what "fun" is in a number of ways, among them:

- A visual of a stylish young woman with a work of art in the background: "Looking at Art. And also at men with other names."

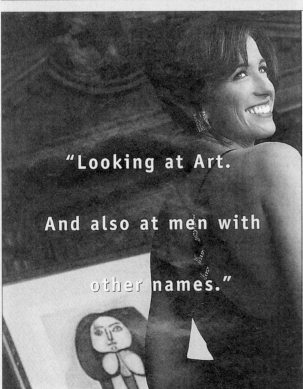

"Doing nothing.

All day.

Every day.

For as many days

as possible."

So you just want to lie there, huh? You're surrounded by dancing and music and casinos and shows, and you just want to lie there.

Toes in the pool. Face in the sun. Head in a book. Well, if that's your idea of fun, fine. Ignore the non-stop entertainment. The jogging track and fitness center. The shopping. The spa. The exotic ports of call. Ignore it all.

Just don't forget to eat. We prepare eight extraordinary meals and snacks a day. And

What's your idea of fun?

you'll want to get up for them, because they're all included in the price of your cruise, so there's never a bill.

Besides, if you don't eat, how will you have the energy to apply all that suntan lotion?

To book your Carnival "Fun Ship" cruise, call any travel agent. Or for more information and a free brochure, call 1-800-CARNIVAL. And have fun.

)|Carnival.
The most popular cruise line in the world.

"Not seeing my parents for

four whole days."

It's not that your kids don't love you. They do, they really do. They love that you want to take them on a great vacation. They love that you want them to have fun.

They just don't want to spend every single solitary second with you, okay? They're *way* too old for that. Just ask them.

That's why you should consider a Carnival cruise.

You see, included with every Carnival cruise, there's something called Camp Carnival. With swimming, and music, and arts and crafts, and scavenger hunts,

What's your idea of fun?

and basically, lots of ways for your kids to have fun. With kids their own ages. Away from you.

Which, when you stop to think about it, may be fun for more than just your kids.

To book your Carnival "Fun Ship" cruise, call any travel agent. Or for more information and a free brochure, call 1-800-CARNIVAL. And have fun.

)|Carnival.
The most popular cruise line in the world.

- A svelte young woman sipping a drink: "Dining. Munching. Nibbling. Noshing. And yes, slurping."
- A blissfully happy child in the ship's pool: "Not going home. Ever."
- Another child, arms raised in victory: "Not seeing my parents for four whole days" (the ad promotes a special supervised program for kids).
- A playful young couple in an embrace: "Licking the salt off my husband's margarita."
- A middle-aged man with a shrimp skewered on a cocktail fork and a look of pure bliss: "Eating a shrimp in its own neighborhood."
- A glamorous woman on a massage table: "Getting a massage after a grueling day of sunbathing."
- An older couple: "Getting lucky. In the casino, or course."
- A happy man in a tropical shirt: "Doing nothing. All day. Every day. For as many days as possible."

While not all companies can afford such a wealth of ads, Carnival—as the industry leader—can and does, using frequency to convince the diverse readers of *People* that a Carnival cruise promises enjoyment for all. The copy in each ad picks up where the headline and visual leave off, but it also promotes additional benefits of a Carnival cruise. And each ad uses totally original copy to match each headline and visual.

While you might view the campaign as a prime example of niche marketing, in reality it expands the target audience each time it asks, "What's *your* idea of fun?" Among the many answers, Carnival is counting on readers to identify with at least one or more. With its ample examples, each suggesting the excitement of a Carnival cruise, this campaign is quite an accomplishment.

CHAPTER 6

Working in Print

Print came first, and many creatives still view print as the ultimate challenge and the most fun. Print is what creative directors will want to see most when you make the rounds with your portfolio. As a copywriter or art director, your task is to turn a blank sheet of paper into something almost magical.

● A Quick Look at "the Look" of Print

We will be talking more specifically about the design process in the next chapter. For now, what's important to remember is that *how* an ad looks and *what* an ad says can contribute equally to the effectiveness of the message—and so should be agreed upon by both writer and artist.

If you're the art director, you'll be thinking about what the headline says, as well as how it looks and what the accompanying visual will be. If you're the copywriter, you'll be thinking about how the entire ad will look at the same time you're writing rough concepts for headlines.

How does it all begin? Like this: Using a soft lead pencil or a fine-to-medium black marker or roller-ball pen, draw a number of small horizontal rectangles (about 2 inches wide by 3 inches deep) to represent the general shape of a magazine page. Don't try to draw a straight line; just "freehand." Place your ideas for headlines and visuals within each rectangle. Scribble the words of the headline in the space, and use shapes and simple stick figures to represent the visuals. Indicate body copy with a series of lines, and place a rough logo at the bottom, probably in the right-hand corner. Congratulations! You have just done your first "thumbnail rough," the beginning stage of every print layout.

As you place other headlines in other rectangles, you'll probably think of still more ideas for words and pictures. Good! Don't stop until you've exhausted your topic, even if some of the ideas seem bizarre or ridiculous.

● Headlines and Visuals—Important Choices

Be honest. You don't usually pick up a magazine or newspaper and say, "I can't wait to see the ads." In fact, you probably just skim the ads unless something stands out from the clutter and captures your attention. It's the job of the copywriter and art director to create headlines that turn skimmers into readers.

Functions of Headlines

You can use headlines to accomplish a number of things, including the following:

1. *Capture the attention of your readers.* Imagine you're reading a food magazine filled with delicious recipes. You have a ravenous appetite when suddenly you read, "Start your next meal with Clorox bleach." The advertisement shows a fish with an eerie stare. It's disgusting. You don't want to look, but you can't help yourself. You read on and learn that Clorox bleach can sanitize your kitchen and prevent salmonella. You've lost your appetite, and you want to start cleaning. The ad has done its job.

2. *Lure readers into the body copy.* A good headline will make you think, "This is interesting. I want to know more." For example, who could resist wanting to know "What not to do in bed"? By the way, just in case you're interested, read on to find the answer later in this chapter.

3. *Communicate a benefit.* Tell readers what your product will do for them. Will it make them look better? Help them get ahead in their jobs? Make their children smarter? Protect their home? Check out the following headlines for various brands of cars:

33% OF ALL CAR ACCIDENTS ARE SIDE-IMPACT COLLISIONS.
GOOD THING YOU RAN INTO THIS AD FIRST.

(Ad for Lexus)

WITH 190 HORSEPOWER, THERE'S A REASON
WE PUT SCOTCHGARD™ ON THE SEATS.

(Ad for Chevy S-10)

THE NEW TURBO DIESEL HUMMER
IS FASTER THAN THE FERRARI TESTAROSSA.
UNLESS YOU HAPPEN TO BE ON A PAVED ROAD.

(Ad for Hummer)

SO QUIET YOU CAN HEAR YOUR BLOOD PRESSURE DROP.

(Ad for Jeep Grand Cherokee)

Muscles. Brains. Looks. If It Were A Person,
You Would Have Hated It In High School.

(Ad for Audi)

4. *Reinforce the brand name.* Have you ever loved an ad but been unable to re-member the name of the product? While it's fine to entertain readers, don't sacrifice getting the product name across for the sake of creativity. Some of the most creative (and successful) campaigns use the product's name as the big idea. Here are some examples:

ABSOLUT L.A.

(Visual of a swimming pool in the shape of an Absolut vodka bottle)

INGLE ELLS
INGLE ELLS
The festive season isn't the same without **J&B**

(Ad for J&B Scotch)

5. *Make a connection to the customer.* Most people are suspicious of advertising claims. Therefore, you must make your message believable. Avis won a spot in peo-ple's hearts with the line "We're #2. We try harder." This is much more convincing than boasting, "We're one of the nation's leading car rental companies." Some people are even suspicious of warning labels. For years, ads have been trying to convince smokers to kick the habit by pointing out the health hazards. However, diehard smokers ignore the warnings. The following headlines take a more personal approach to break the barrier:

SMOKING IS A COLORFUL HABIT.

(Drawing of a smile with stained teeth)

GET BAD BREATH IN TWO FLAVORS. REGULAR AND MENTHOL.

(All print ad)

6. *Enhance a visual.* If a picture is worth a thousand words, a picture and a headline are worth thousands more. Together, a headline and a visual create synergy, whereby the whole is greater than the sum of its parts. For example, how do you show that a

● FIGURE 6-1

Facts can be fun, particularly if they have an unexpected twist at the end.

ONE GOALIE.

TWO DEFENSEMEN.

THREE FORWARDS.

FOUR HUNDRED FIFTY-SIX STITCHES.

Hockey isn't complicated. There's no high math or complex equations. Just a few basic rules. So after only one game, you'll be an expert. And now you can come see for yourself right here in Columbia. Starting this October you can watch the Columbia Inferno rack up the numbers at the Carolina Coliseum. Call 1-800-4HOCKEY for tickets. Bring a friend, but leave your calculator at home.

THE HEAT IS ON
IN COLUMBIA

COURTESY OF BRIAN ZUFALL.

portable vacuum cleaner is really powerful? One solution is to run the warning "Be careful where you point it." This is a rather boring statement until you see the picture of a man's toupee flying toward the nozzle of the vacuum. Now that's picking up a rug!

Here are some other headlines and visuals that create synergy:

HTTP://WWW.JUANVALDEZ.COM

(Visual of a spiderweb woven in the shape of Juan Valdez Colombia Coffee logo)

REGULAR. (Visual of the Mona Lisa)

CHUNKY. (Visual of an overweight Mona Lisa)

(Ad for Prince Spaghetti Sauce)

*Checklist for
Headlines*

✓ Does your headline stop, intrigue, and involve the reader?

✓ Does your headline encourage readership of body copy?

✓ Does your headline offer a promise or benefit relevant to the selling idea?

✓ Does your headline make an emotional connection to the reader?

✓ Does your headline reinforce the brand name?

✓ Does your headline work with the visual to create synergy?

*Types
of Headlines*

Direct benefit These headlines offer readers a reason to use the product. For example, while it may be a bit of a fish story, Elmer's Sportsmen's Center catches the attention of fishermen with this direct-benefit headline:

MY MINNOWS ARE LIKE KAMIKAZES.
THEY'D RATHER COMMIT SUICIDE
THAN RETURN TO THE SHIP EMPTY HANDED.

Shore's Lures colorfully boasts:

IT'S LIKE TOSSING A TWINKIE
INTO A WEIGHT WATCHER'S MEETING.

Reverse benefit These headlines imply that consumers will be worse off without the advertised product or service. Some also imply, "You'll be sorry if you go with the competition." Here are some examples:

THE DIFFERENCE BETWEEN A BARBER NAMED MR. JOSEF
AND A BARBER NAMED JOE IS ABOUT 12 BUCKS.

(Ad for a Boston barber named Joe)

*No wonder they call it high fashion.
To dream up some of those prices you'd have to be high.*

(Ad for Daffy's clothing discounter)

If you use a reverse benefit, make sure you don't give your competition free advertising. Also, be careful that you don't make any remarks about your competition that aren't true.

Factual People love to read interesting pieces of trivia. This headline gives an interesting fact:

It takes 12 miles of cotton to
make a Lands' End® pinpoint oxford.
And that's just the beginning.

The Lands' End copy goes on to explain that the shirt is tailored with 69 different sewing steps and the buttonholes are edged with 120 lock stitches. How much will readers remember? If they recall only that Lands' End really cares about the quality of its clothing, they got the message.

The following headlines combine facts and a bit of whimsy:

The driveway is measured in miles.
The floor plan is measured in acres.

(Ad for the Biltmore Estate)

SIX RESTAURANTS IN THE WORLD
CAN PREPARE A PERFECT STEAK.
FOUR ARE IN ARGENTINA.

(Ad for Smith & Wollensky restaurant, New York City)

Selective To attract a specific audience, address them in the headline. Sometimes, the audience is directly identified. For example, a headline for Allstate Insurance asks, "Do you own a small business?" Other times, the tone and choice of the words and visual will identify your audience. As you read the following headlines, try to determine the target audience:

IF IT'S TOO LOUD, YOU'RE TOO OLD.

(Ad for Memorex audiotapes)

Michelin. Because so much is riding on your tires.

(Ad showing a baby sitting on a tire)

Curiosity Tempt your readers with just enough information to make them want to read more. "Ever wonder why most people make love in the dark?" entices readers to continue, especially when the only visual is a black rectangle where the picture should be. The ad, for a workout program, talks about getting in shape. "Why you should spend $250 for a pair of shoes you never heard of" is how J. M. Weston lures consumers into reading about the beautiful shoe in the ad, unless they don't *want* to pay $250 for them (in which case, they're not in the target market anyway). While curiosity headlines can pull readers into the copy, they should be designed to arouse curiosity, not to confuse. An impatient reader who turns the page after reading an incomplete thought will miss your message.

News Just as you want to know what's new with friends and family, you want to know what's new to eat, to wear, and to see. In fact, many advertising experts believe that the word *new* is one of the most powerful in a copywriter's vocabulary. Other powerful words include *introducing, now, finally, at last, today, presenting,* and *first.* Here are two examples:

> *Now you can do the wash without the wear.*
>
> (Ad for Tide detergent)

> **LIFE IN THE SOUTH**
> **JUST GOT A LITTLE SWEETER.**
>
> (Ad for Kellogg's Raisin Bran in *Southern Living* magazine)

Command Order the reader to do something. For years, Nike told sports fans, "Just do it." In the process, this simple phrase convinced people to just buy it (Nike, that is). Other persuasive command headlines include these:

> **REKINDLE YOUR LOVE AFFAIR WITH NEW YORK.**
>
> (Ad for New York City)

> *Hire us to paint your house*
> *and you won't need this newspaper.*
>
> (Ad for Merriam Park Painting with paint blotches on it)

Question A question piques our curiosity and involves us in the ad. The long-running question "Does she? Or doesn't she?" helped convince readers that Clairol's hair-coloring products produced natural-looking results.

A question headline should make readers want to stop, think, and read your ad for the answer, so be careful not to make the answer too obvious. For example, the question "Do you want more money?" is likely to provoke a response such as "Of course." Here is another question that grabs attention:

> IF YOU WERE TWO YEARS OLD,
> COULD YOU TELL THE DIFFERENCE?
>
> (Visual of a plastic jug of milk and a gallon of bleach)

Repetition Some lines are worth repeating. An ad for McGraw-Hill Magazines uses repetition to communicate the power of advertising:

> I DON'T KNOW WHO YOU ARE.
> I DON'T KNOW YOUR COMPANY.

When the school color is baby blue, you do whatever you can to intimidate the opponent.

COLUMBIA

RUGBY

To play, call Dan Wetmore at 212-853-6829.

Afraid to try

RUGBY

because you don't know how to play?

You go to Columbia. You can learn.

To play, call Dan Wetmore at 212-853-6829.

● Figure 6-2

Columbia University's rugby posters show that even smart, bookish guys can be jocks.

I DON'T KNOW WHAT YOUR COMPANY STANDS FOR.
I DON'T KNOW YOUR COMPANY'S CUSTOMERS.
I DON'T KNOW YOUR COMPANY'S RECORD.
I DON'T KNOW YOUR COMPANY'S REPUTATION.
NOW—WHAT WAS IT YOU WANTED TO SELL ME?

An advertisement for the seven-seat Nissan Quest van shows the roomy interior, and the headline reinforced the message:

LIVE IN THE LAP, LAP, LAP, LAP,
LAP, LAP, LAP OF LUXURY.

Puns   Writers love to play with words. However, be careful not to get caught up in the play and forget that you're selling a product. Beware, also, of overdosing on puns. Your readers won't appreciate it, nor will creative directors when you're showing your portfolio. The following pun headlines stay within bounds and drive the point home:

WHERE WOULD VAN GOGH FOR ART SUPPLIES?

(Coupon ad for Dutch Door arts and crafts supply store)

More experience than our name implies.

(Ad for Virgin Airlines)

AFTER JUST A FEW VISITS WITH ME,
MY CLIENTS DO THEIR BUSINESS ELSEWHERE.

(Ad for Luis Gomez, Master Dog Trainer)

HOLE SALE.

(Visual of a Life Savers candy, with a cents-off savings coupon)

Metaphors, similes, and analogies   One way to describe your product is to make a connection to another commonly known image. A metaphor takes the characteristics of one thing and associates it with something entirely different. During the gasoline shortage of the 1970s, Volkswagen used a drawing of a man holding a gas pump nozzle up to his head, as if it were a gun. The headline read, "Or buy a Volkswagen."

A simile states that one thing is "like" something else. For example, to dramatize the odor problem of litter boxes, an ad for Kitty Litter® Brand shows a skunk in a litter box. The headline reads, "Sometimes your cat can seem like a whole different animal."

An analogy compares two things on the basis of a similar feature. For example, an ad for Lubriderm lotion shows an alligator to communicate rough, scaly skin. The headline, "See you later, alligator," implies that the lotion will smooth and soften dry, flaky skin.

These headlines make unexpected, but relevant connections. They work because they use universal images everyone understands.

Think of us as an amusement park for readers.

(Ad for Books-A-Million)

Its mother was a mainframe.
Its father was a Maserati.

(Ad for IBM ThinkPad)

IMAGINE MICHAEL JORDAN WITH FUR.

(Ad for the Ashley Whippet Dog Frisbee Championships)

Parallel construction This headline repeats the structure of a phrase or sentence to emphasize a point. Simon David uses parallel construction in a single ad to sell variety:

The perfect place to shop when you're expecting a refund from the IRS.
(Visual of imported cheese, fine wine, roses)

The perfect place to shop when you're expecting a visit from the IRS.
(Visual of beer, American cheese slices, generic bread)

Target uses the technique to promote its practical Bridal Registry:

A typical wedding gift. (Visual of crystal salt shaker)
Atypical wedding gift. (Visual of vacuum cleaner)

Rhyme Rhyme headlines use the repetition of sound to make a point. Avoid the temptation to make a rhyme unless it helps to stress a selling point, as in these examples:

SAIL BY MAIL.

(Ad for Royal Caribbean inviting the reader to write for a brochure)

FLOPCORN VS. POPCORN.

(Ad for Pop Secret popcorn showing an unpopped kernel and a piece of popcorn)

*From Headline
to Visual*

If you know what to say, what do you show with it? Here are some possibilities:

1. *Show the product.* If it's boring by itself, set it in a context. Put the spray bottle of window cleaner beside a spanking clean picture window revealing a brilliant blue sky.

2. *Show only a part of the product.* If the interior of a car is what's going to grab attention, focus on that in the main visual. Then show the entire car near the logo.

3. *Show the product ready for use.* Instead of a frozen dinner in a cardboard box, show it on an elegant plate in a fancy setting.

4. *Compare the product with the competition.* An ad for Tilex mildew remover shows the results of cleaning bathroom tiles with Tilex versus the leading bathroom cleaner. The Tilex side is spotless; the other side is gross.

5. *Show the product being tested.* An ad for a nail polish shows a billiard ball, painted with the nail enamel, still wearing a perfect coat after hours of play.

6. *Show the product in use.* A child smiles as he plays a computer game. A woman looks excited as she uses a new shampoo. A dog wolfs down a bowl of the new chow.

7. *Show the happy results of using the product.* A woman who has exercised on her new machine shows off her trim body. A dog just groomed at the pet emporium stands tall and proud.

8. *Show the unhappy results of not using the product.* A commuter misses his train because his watch stopped running. A lawyer sports a bad haircut because he didn't use the right barber. An executive is drowning in paper because her office isn't using the latest communications system.

● Copy: Writing the Fine Print

While the headline piques the readers' attention, the body copy completes the story. Remember the headline "What not to do in bed"? As promised, here's the answer:

You can read.

You can rest.

You can sleep.

You can make phone calls.

You can eat breakfast.

You can watch television.

You can listen to music.

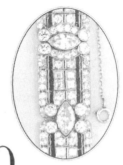

● Figure 6-3

You need to get into the mindset of your customers, as Windsor Jewelers does here. Notice that they didn't say something dumb like, "Trade in your treasured family heirlooms for cash." After all, they understood that people have a hard time parting with family treasures. These ads make it simple.

You can exercise.

You can snore.

You can even eat crackers—provided you're alone.

And, yes, you can snuggle.

But don't ever light up a cigarette when you're in bed.

Because if you doze off just once, all your dreams can go up in smoke.

While R. J. Reynolds could have run a public service ad with the simple headline "Don't smoke in bed," the combination of an intriguing headline and interesting copy gets readers involved and makes it more likely that they'll remember the message.

Before you begin writing ad copy, it's important to put advertising in perspective. You're not writing a letter to your mom who will still love you even if you run on a bit. You're not writing an essay for a professor who is paid to read your work. And

Y̶our grandmother gave it to you
so you'd always keep a warm spot
in your heart for her.

How about a condo in Boca?

Highest prices paid for your jewelry
Windsor Jewelers
581 Fifth Avenue, 3rd floor, between 47th and 48th Street, New York, NY
(212) 644-7900

Follow the simple Windsor method to get the most money for your jewelry:
1. See other jewelers.   2. Get your best offer.   3. Let the nice people
at Windsor make you an even better offer. It's that easy.
Licensed byConsumer Affairs #0817887

Y̶ou know that emerald bracelet
you were going to pass down to your
daughter?

Use it for her college education.
(And buy her the navel ring she really wants.)

Highest prices paid for your jewelry
Windsor Jewelers
581 Fifth Avenue, 3rd floor, between 47th and 48th Street, New York, NY
(212) 644-7900

Follow the simple Windsor method to get the most money for your jewelry:
1. See other jewelers.   2. Get your best offer.   3. Let the nice people
at Windsor make you an even better offer. It's that easy.
Licensed byConsumer Affairs #0817887

T̶he bad news is, he's the sole heir
to your jewelry collection.

The good news is,
there's still time to cash it in for
a round-the-world cruise.

Highest prices paid for your jewelry
Windsor Jewelers
581 Fifth Avenue, 3rd floor, between 47th and 48th Street, New York, NY
(212) 644-7900

Follow the simple Windsor method to get the most money for your jewelry:
1. See other jewelers.   2. Get your best offer.   3. Let the nice people
at Windsor make you an even better offer. It's that easy.
Licensed byConsumer Affairs #0817887

I̶f your Aunt Hedda
knew how much we'd pay for her
diamond earrings,
she wouldn't have given them to you
in the first place.

Highest prices paid for your jewelry
Windsor Jewelers
581 Fifth Avenue, 3rd floor, between 47th and 48th Street, New York, NY
(212) 644-7900

Follow the simple Windsor method to get the most money for your jewelry:
1. See other jewelers.   2. Get your best offer.   3. Let the nice people
at Windsor make you an even better offer. It's that easy.
Licensed byConsumer Affairs #0817887

you're not even writing a story for readers who have bought a newspaper or magazine to catch up on the news. You're writing for people who view advertising as an intrusion. Therefore, you've got to be interesting.

Guidelines for Writing Copy

Here are some guidelines that will make your copy enjoyable to read:

1. *Love your product.* David Ogilvy wrote that there are no dull products, just dull writers. Have you ever dreaded taking a required course and then loved it because the professor was so interesting? The professor's love of the subject made you want to go to class and learn more about it. It's the job of the writer to make people want to read about the product—and then go out and buy it.

2. *Don't try to do everything in one ad.* You should develop one theme and follow it through. When Stavros Cosmopulos, a famous creative director, speaks to advertising associations across the country, he slams a piece of cardboard against a "bed" of about 100 sharp nails. Nothing happens. Because the nails have formed a mass, they don't penetrate the cardboard. He then slams a piece of cardboard against a single nail and bam! One single point is more powerful than several.

3. *Write to one individual.* When consumers read or hear your copy, they should feel as if you're talking directly to them, not to a vague demographic profile. Use the word *you* liberally. Stick to singular nouns and verbs when possible.

4. *Translate business-speak into human-speak.* Many clients know their products so well that they begin to talk in jargon, which will be lost on the average reader. Your job is to listen, ask questions, and translate the jargon into tangible benefits your readers will understand. Edward T. Thompson of *Reader's Digest* poked fun at a scientist who wrote, "The biota exhibited a one hundred percent mortality response," instead of simply saying, "All the fish died."

5. *Avoid catchall phrases.* If a dress is "perfect for any occasion," does that mean you'd wear it to the opera after you've worn it while gardening or cleaning the house?

6. *Be specific.* Avoid vague generalities, such as "Save on a vast collection of beautiful tops in a variety of colors." What does this mean? Are they T-shirts? Turtlenecks? Scoop necks? Do they have long sleeves? Short sleeves? Cap sleeves? Are they tailored? Frilly? Sporty? Are they pastels? Brights? Neutrals? And, just what is a "vast" collection?

7. *Don't brag.* Instead of bragging about your product's features, tell your readers what your product will do for them. For example, compare the following sentences:

"We are pleased to announce our new flight schedule to New York."

"Now you can fly to New York five times a day."

Did you notice how the second sentence turns the airline's feature (the new schedule) into a traveler's advantage? The second sentence also gives more information in fewer words. That's good writing.

8. *Use the present tense and active voice whenever possible.* The present tense communicates a sense feeling of immediacy, and the active voice enlivens your copy. For example, "We try harder" sounds better than "We have tried harder."

9. *Use transitions to connect different thoughts and establish a relationship between them.* Here are some words that bridge thoughts:

So	On the other hand
Therefore	Furthermore
However	First
Additionally	Second
In fact	

10. *Avoid clichés.* Describe your product in a new, refreshing way; don't resort to overused clichés such as these:

Whose time has come	Early birds
For all seasons	Talk of the town
Age-old secret	Out of this world

11. *Vary the length and structure of sentences.* To highlight the importance of this, the International Newspaper Promotion Association printed the following statement in their *Copy Service Newsletter:* "The simple sentence starts with a subject. Then the simple sentence has an object. The simple sentence ends with a period. The simple sentence gets boring as hell after you've read three or four of them. And you just did!"

Doug Williams of the Capital Writers Group demonstrated this by writing the same message two different ways. Read the following paragraphs. Which one do you think is more engaging?

> The ear demands variety, so listen as I vary the sentence length, and create music that sings with a pleasant rhythm and harmony. I use short sentences, medium sentences and sometimes when I am certain the reader is rested, I will engage him in sentences of considerable length. These sentences burn with energy and build with the impetus of a crescendo. They have a roll of the drums and a crash of a cymbal. They have the kind of sound that urge a reader to listen because this is important.

> The ear demands variety. Now listen: I vary the sentence length, and create music. Music. The writing sings. It has a pleasant rhythm, a harmony. I use short sentences. And I use sentences of medium length. And sometimes when I am certain the reader is rested, I will engage him in sentences of considerable length—a sentence that burns with energy and builds with all the fire and impetus of a crescendo, the roll of the drums, the crash of a cymbal. Sounds that say, Listen to this. It's important.[1]

---

[1] From a lecture entitled "Mass Media Writing," given at the University of South Carolina, Columbia, March 1998.

● FIGURE 6-4

This innovative campaign uses personification to convince readers that it's okay to eat eggs again.

"At first you said you loved me,
you told me I was the only one.
You always had me around.
But then you turned,
because rumors were flying around
that I wasn't good for you anymore.

And now you want me back.
You've changed your mind and
realized I was the one after all.

And you think just because you said that
I'll come crawling back to you?
Well, I've got news for you . mister,
You're going to have to do better than that. "

"I'll wait for your skillet to get hot."

"Well..., ok."

 Eggs
They're more forgiving than you think.

12. *Don't overdo the brag.* Tell consumers what's in it for them, not how proud you are of your product. Use understatement, as Volkswagen did when it called its funny-looking car a "bug," told prospects to "think small," and broke new sales records for the German import.

13. *Make the strange familiar, the familiar strange.* Explain something complex in simple terms. Or take something simple and describe it in colorful language.

> *In the beginning*
> **you always had to have me.**
> *In the morning. The evening. Even at lunch.*
> *You couldn't get enough.*
> **But then you said I was fatty.**
> *That I wasn't good for you anymore.*
>
> **So you threw me out of the house,**
> *and tried to replace me with substitutes.*
>
> *And now you say you were wrong.*
> *That the things they said weren't true,*
> *and it was me you wanted all along.*
>
> *And now you want me to move back in?*
>
> ## *Who do you think I am?*
>
> *What could you possibly say*
> *to persuade me to come back?*

"You can be sunny-side up."

"Well..., ok."

Eggs

They're more forgiving than you think.

COURTESY OF JULIE EYERMAN.

14. *Write "out loud."* Imagine your customer is sitting in front of you. Talk to her. Convince her to buy your product. Zap the "uhs," "ums," and "ya knows," and you should have some convincing copy.

15. *Test your copy.* Be sure to read it out loud. If you find yourself cringing or saying, "That sounds stupid," ditch it and start again. Once you have copy you like, test it again on someone who represents your target audience.

Our Lab

Mt. Rainier

We don't test our shoes in a laboratory lined with concrete walls.

That's not where you'll be wearing them.

We go where the activity is.

We run up mountains, splash through creeks, trudge through mud, and well, you get the picture.

Take the Kuna Crest trail running shoe, for example. We know you don't want soggy socks after crossing The White River, so we designed a wicking lining to move moisture away from your foot.

Our designers were frustrated with the lack of support around their toes in ordinary trail running shoes.

The Kuna Krest has a reinforced box-toe with a rubberized cap.

Your toes will thank you for this little feature next time you're climbing Mt. Rainier.

Some designers might not think to include all of these features in a trail running shoe.

Unless, of course, they actually run trails. That's why The North Face believes in using real settings, not controlled settings.

Because where you're going, there is no concrete.

Double overlays in heel, side-guards and toe

Breathable dual-weave body mesh

All-terrain compound outsole with biting lug design

The Kuna Krest

Exploration gear for the feet.

16. *Revise your work.* Edit. Edit. Edit. Author Truman Capote once said of the revision process, "I know my book is done when the publisher grabs it out of my hands."

Approaches to Writing Copy

The standard approach   Most ads start with a lead-in paragraph that bridges the headline and the rest of the copy. Like the headline, this paragraph should pique the reader's curiosity and make him or her want to continue reading. The interior

Our Designers

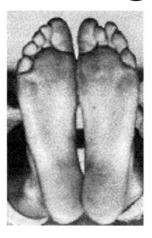

Most shoes are created in an artist's head. Then a designer tries to make their idea fit a foot.

We think there is a problem with this design policy. The shoe doesn't fit the foot.

It's no surprise that our hiking boot, The Palisade Crest GTX, was designed from the ground up. This boot features a dual density X-2 midsole engineered especially for cushion and support, which relieves stress from the arch of your foot.

As for the tops of your feet, the upper construction of The Palisade Crest GTX is created from one piece of Prime Weathertuff leather.

One piece construction insures a waterproof shoe.

Designs like this don't come from a sketch pad. They come from crossing a glacier on the Alaskan Range or scaling rocky trails in the Sierra Nevada Mountains.

And ideas like these don't come from a design team.

Unless of course, they happen to be your own two feet.

Gore-Tex membrane, durably waterproof and breathable

Aggressive multi-dimensional lugs designed for stability and durability with ascending and descending traction

One-piece vamp upper construction

The Palisade Crest GTX

Exploration gear for the feet.

paragraphs stress benefits as they elaborate on the selling premise. And the closing paragraph ties the ad together and often invites the reader to consider the product.

The ad for Columbia Sportswear Company (see Figure 5-1) follows a standard approach, although there's nothing standard about the ad—or the company or its chairman, for that matter. The headline grabs your attention: "She snaps necks and hacks off arms." You read on and learn in the first paragraph that "My Mother, Columbia Sportswear's chairman, will stop at nothing to get what she wants—superior outerwear." In the next few sentences, you learn about the demands of "Mother," the vociferous chairman; in the process, you learn about the construction of a Columbia Sportswear parka. The copy closes, "All in all, it's easy to see why not just any parka can survive Mother's rather pointed demands."

Copy as story   Narrative copy reads like a piece of fiction because it sets a scene and presents characters who get involved in some action.

Dialog copy   You know the routine "I said. She said." While you usually find this format in radio and television, it works in print, too. However, make certain your dialog sounds realistic by reading your copy out loud.

Bulleted copy/listings   An ad for the Massachusetts Society for the Prevention of Cruelty to Animals was headlined, "Get the best of everything. Adopt a mutt." The picture shows an adorable mutt looking straight into the reader's eyes, and bulleted copy points addresses the advantages of adopting a mutt: "The smarts of a Lassie. The spots of a Dalmatian. The bark of a Shepherd. The friendliness of a Beagle. The heart of a St. Bernard. The paws of a Great Dane."

Poetic copy   Norwegian Cruise Lines used poetic images to sell its fantasy adventures:

It's different out here.

I will put first things last.

I will study a sunset.

I will be naked more.

I will discover a color.

I will memorize clouds.

I will be amphibious.

I will eat a mango.

I will get a really good tan.

● Other Considerations in Writing Copy

Is It Okay to Break the Rules?   Some people believe advertising has destroyed the dignity of our language. They are appalled when they read sentences such as "Winston tastes good like a cigarette should." Cringe when they read incomplete sentences (like this one). And they wince when a sentence starts with a conjunction. Others argue that advertising must sound like people talking, so it's okay to break the rules. However, most people agree that, before you break the rules, you'd better know them. See the box on page 130 for some copy mistakes.

Here are some headlines that break the rules intentionally:

The quick brown fox
jumps over the
the lazy dog.

This ad for Ginkoba vitamin supplements demonstrates the need to increase your concentration. The subhead asks, "Did you find the typo in the above headline? Congratulations. Guess what? You might have found it even sooner if you had been using Ginkoba." Here's another headline that breaks the rules:

I QUIT SKOOL WHEN I WERE SIXTEEN.
(A convincing message to stay in school)

What's the Best Headline Length?

Unless you're writing to a specific layout with a predetermined character count, there is no "best" length. One of the most famous headlines for a car was one simple word, "Lemon." This unexpected headline for Volkswagen motivated people to read the copy, which explained the auto manufacturer's rigorous quality standards. In contrast, another famous headline for a car contained eighteen words: "At 60 miles an hour, the loudest noise in the new Rolls Royce comes from the electric clock."

Which Is Better, Long or Short Copy?

Certain product categories, such as perfume and fashion, are sold primarily on the basis of image, so brief copy, along with a striking visual, is probably the best answer. Other products, such as cars and computers, require quite a bit of thought before the buyer takes the plunge; therefore, they warrant longer copy with specific details about the various features. However, even these rules are successfully broken from time to time. The best advice is to write as much as you need to accomplish your advertising objectives.

How Should Copy Be Formatted?

Figure 6-6 shows a suggested copy format. "Slug" the ad in the upper-left corner with the name of the company, size, and medium (full page, magazine), and a working title in quotes. Identify the visual idea, headline, copy, logo, and baseline, plus other elements when used. Double-space so that it's easy to read, easy to revise, and easy to sell.

Checklist for Print Copy

✔ Did you restate your strategy in one sentence?

✔ Does the visual relate to the copy?

✔ Does the headline work with the visual? Does it do some or all of the following: offer a benefit, announce something new, select the audience, arouse genuine curiosity, draw readers into the copy, mention brand name, and entertain readers?

✔ Does the body copy contain readable paragraphs, conversational language, use of "you," an enthusiastic but nonboastful tone, sufficient information presented in an entertaining manner, a reason for readers to take action, and frequent use of the brand name? Does it end with an urge to action, a summary of the main idea, or an open-ended statement designed to provoke readers to complete the thought?

Copy Mistakes

You must proofread your copy. While Spell-check is a big help, it can't find every type of error. Here are some mistakes from the classifieds:

"For sale: an antique desk suitable for lady with thick legs and large drawers."

"Four-poster bed, 101 years old. Perfect for antique lover."

"Now is your chance to have your ears pierced and get an extra pair to take home, too."

"Wanted: 50 girls for stripping machine operators in factory."

"Tired of cleaning yourself? Let me do it."

"Used cars: Why go elsewhere to be cheated? Come here first!"

Church bulletins have their share of gaffes. Here are a few of our favorites:

"Thursday, at 5 P.M., there will be a meeting of the Little Mothers Club. All those wishing to become little mothers, please meet the pastor in his study."

"The ladies of the church have cast off clothing of every kind and they may be seen in the basement on Friday afternoon."

"This being Easter Sunday, we will ask Mrs. Johnson to come forward and lay an egg on the alter."

But don't think it's just small-town classifieds and church bulletins that make mistakes. Consider the following:

A Mercedes-Benz accessories ad begins, "Her trademark has always been making art out of the everyday. First, she was taken with fruits and vegetables. Next, she was inspired by popcorn, footballs and sharks. Then one day, Nicole Miller was struck by a Mercedes-Benz."

Bruce Hardwood Floors insulted a few grandmothers with the line "Solid oak, just like your grandmothers."

✔ Is the logo prominent? Is the package clearly shown? Is the tone of ad appropriate for the product and target?

As a copywriter, you will live in a world of what might be, not what is. Just as Alka-Seltzer once transformed itself from a headache remedy to "a cure for the blahs," so your copy ideas must work to erase the blahs. Honest enthusiasm can be far more effective than another clever, try-it-today message.

SAAB

Full page, magazine

"Saabs listen better"

VISUAL: Saab from side/rear view on narrow, winding country road.

HEADLINE: Roads talk to all cars. Saabs just listen better.

COPY:

Roads speak a language of infinite subtlety. And few cars understand the dialects of curves, hills and asphalt better than the Saab 9000 CSE.

From the performance of its low-profile tires to the spring tension in its driver's seat, the 9000 CSE has been carefully tuned to connect, rather than separate, the driver and the road.

The chassis, for example, is 25% more rigid than ever before. An improvement that gives you a tactile sense of the car's progress through a tight turn.

And while you're in touch with the road, the Saab Traction Control System* monitors it for slippery conditions. The instant the drive wheels begin to spin, computers make split-second power adjustments to each wheel. So you get traction comparable to that of many four wheel-drive cars.

Of course, you'd expect a car preoccupied with holding the road to come with anti-lock brakes and nimble rack and pinion steering. The 9000 CSE does not disappoint.

But since it is a Saab, the 9000 CSE doesn't just listen to roads, it also speaks to the needs of drivers. Which is why it has one of the roomiest interiors of any imported sedan. And more safety features than any preceding 9000-Series Saab; cars routinely ranked among the safest in their class.**

To experience the sports sedan that offers not just higher horsepower, but a heightened awareness of the road, ask your Saab dealer for a 9000 CSE test drive. Or, for more information, call 1–800–582–SAAB.

LOGO: SAAB

BASELINE: (none)

MANDATORIES: *With available 2.3 liter turbocharged engine.

**Based upon studies of insurance injury claims conducted by the Highway Loss Data Institute.

© 1993 Saab Cars USA, Inc.

● FIGURE 6-6

In this sample copy draft, note the use of a working title, double-spacing, and adequate margins on all sides.

● Other Print Media: Outdoor, Transit, and Point-of-Purchase

Outdoor Advertising

If brevity is the soul of effective copy, the outdoor board is the final proving ground for that premise. How much time can people spend with your outdoor message? Mere seconds when they're cruising down the interstate, and little more on a city thoroughfare—all the more reason an outdoor message must be boldly designed and conceptually intrusive. All rules for creating effective advertising apply, only more so. Here's how to achieve an optimal reaction to your outdoor messages:

1. *Keep the graphics simple.* One large headline with one major visual is the rule. Some boards are all type, with no visual.

2. *Make the type bold and big.* Remember, it must be read quickly.

3. *Make the brand or company name prominent.* If it's not in the main headline, use a logo big enough to get noticed.

4. *Consider using your campaign theme/tag line as the headline.* This way, your outdoor ad also reminds viewers of the rest of your campaign.

In preparing your outdoor layout, follow the same procedures as for other print layouts. Standard outdoor posters (paper pasted to existing structures) are scaled to a proportion of 1 to 2¼. Outdoor bulletins, painted on boards, are usually scaled to a proportion of 1 to 3½. This translates to a 4-×-9-inch layout for the poster and a 4-×-14-inch layout for the painted bulletin.

Transit Advertising

Transit advertising appears on the inside and outside of public transportation vehicles, as well as in bus, rail, subway, and air terminals. Like outdoor advertising, it works best when the message is short. It differs from outdoor ads in that the audience can spend more time with the message. For this reason, many transit ads include "take-one" cards or other literature attached to the ad.

Point-of-Purchase (POP) Advertising

Advertising at the point of sale—in the store where the buyer is about to choose between one brand and another—represents the last chance the advertiser has to affect the purchasing decision. Common forms of POP include window posters, permanent signs inside and outside the store, special display racks and cases, wall posters and "shelf talkers" (those ubiquitous reminders popping from the place where the product is shelved), coupon dispensers at the point of sale and checkout, shopping cart signs, and even signs on aisle floors.

● Suggested Activities

1. Go through several recent magazines, and cut out advertisements that contain headlines and visuals that fall into at least six of the thirteen types listed in this chapter (news, benefit, selective, factual, metaphor, etc.). If the same headline accom-

plishes several things, list them all. As you complete your search, also note why some ads attract you and others do not. To accompany your ad collection, write a brief paper on their positive and negative qualities.

2. Do the same with the visuals in these ads. Refer to the visual choices on page 119 and identify each visual using those categories.

3. Using the strategy statement you developed in Chapter 4, write two pieces of print copy with headlines. Describe any visuals you plan to use, and include a rough layout of the ad along with your copy. *Note:* To do the layout, draw a rectangle on a standard sheet of paper, roughly letter in your headline in the size you think it should be, sketch your visual (stick figures are okay), use lines to indicate where copy goes, and place a logo somewhere near the bottom. Don't spend more than a few minutes on the layout. Instead, focus on the idea for the visual and the copy that will accompany it.

4. Present this ad to the class as if you were presenting it to the client. How will you explain your strategy, or your ad concept?

5. Find a national ad that has what you think is effective copy, as well as a headline and visual that catch your eye. State why you chose it and what you believe to be outstanding about it. How does it meet the VIPS criteria for success presented in Chapter 4?

6. With a classmate, work out a series of ads for a local business. Begin by gathering information about your "client," and then brainstorm before you try your ideas on each other. Once you've agreed on a solution, develop and present a series of at least three ads.

 # Search Online! Discovering More About Print Advertising

Using InfoTrac® College Edition, try these phrases and others for Key Words and Subject Guide searches: *newspaper advertising, magazine advertising, outdoor advertising, point-of-purchase advertising, advertising concept, advertising headline, advertising copy, advertising clutter, breaking grammar rules, product benefit.*

BriefCase

Avon Cleaners: High-Profile Advertising Reaches a High-Profile Clientele

BY DAVID SLAYDEN, A.K.A. ADVERTISING
(CAMPAIGN BY DAVID SLAYDEN AND BRETT GROSSMAN)

Avon Cleaners has a high-profile, demanding clientele in a city where image is both the mark and burden of success. Best-dressed lists here are taken seriously as indicators of status, and Avon's customers expect to appear on those lists. And because their clothes are expensive, Avon customers harbor a good deal of anxiety about them. Will my suit look as good after cleaning as it did before? How should my cocktail gown be cleaned? Will it be ready when I need it? Even what are often perceived as relatively small details, such as buttons, become magnified for such a clientele. Particularly when the buttons are made of pearl or other expensive materials.

Our task was to communicate an overall image of quality to this market within an environment in which most other cleaners discount services, offer coupons, and design advertising consisting of direct-mail special offers and videotaped TV spots—all of which scream discount. How should Avon communicate and maintain an image of quality service and expertise within a category dominated by deals, particularly when Avon refuses to discount because they feel this compromises quality? How could they compete without being forced to play by the rules of their competitors?

A tour of Avon's facilities began to supply some answers. We learned that Avon removes buttons before cleaning a shirt or blouse and then sews them back on after ironing. That all ironing is done by hand. That the majority of employees have been with Avon for many years and are well versed in the intricacies of fabric care. That Avon does all work on site rather than subcontracting. That Avon drivers are bonded for the security of its customers who request home pickup and delivery. Avon offers special services, too, such as off-season storage, expert stain removal of difficult fabrics, and same-day service. And we even heard stories of clients away on business who ship their clothes to Avon for cleaning and reshipping. Unusual for a cleaner? Absolutely.

Bring in your summer clothes to Avon now, and we'll have them ready for you next year.

Is that service or what?

Stacy Godo, owner

It's a simple concept, really. Bring your summer clothes to Avon now and, after we clean them, we'll store them for you for free, until next Spring. Pay for cleaning. Get the storage free. It's good for you. Good for your clothes. You get more space in your closet. And your clothes spend the winter hibernating safely with us. When the warm weather returns, so do your clothes–ready to wear. Any questions?

AVON
cleaners

4347 Lovers Lane   6301 Hillcrest Avenue
521-4803   521-9927

You see some guy in an old shirt.

We see a fine example of how proper care can keep most anything looking younger.

This is Stacy Godo. The owner of Avon cleaners. While we think he looks pretty good for his age, we're really talking about the shirt. Since the day he bought it, it's been cleaned, pressed, and stored (when we could get him to stop wearing it) at Avon. It's just one more example of the difference expert care can make in the life of your clothes. As Stacy likes to say, "we're committed to the longevity of your wardrobe." It's a personal commitment. Obviously.

So come in to Avon. Or call about our full line of services to keep your clothes in top shape–from formal wear to everyday favorites. And if you see Stacy, you might say, "Hey, Nice Shirt."

AVON
cleaners

4347 Lovers Lane   6301 Hillcrest Avenue
521-4803   521-9927

To all those who slavishly follow fashion, spend an inordinate amount of time and money on their appearance, and aspire to best-dressed lists, we have only one thing to say.

Cool.

Stacy Godo, owner

Call Avon. We've been caring for the clothes of the people who care about clothes for the past 26 years.

AVON
cleaners

4347 Lovers Lane
521-4803

6301 Hillcrest Avenue
521-9727

COURTESY OF AVON.

One of the benefits of developing advertising for a small business is that the owner's contact with customers is direct. They often know their clientele well. One of the limitations is budget. We understood that "quality" has become one of those invisible words, repeated so often it is relatively meaningless. No business, for example, would ever say they were *not* concerned with quality work! Yet quality is clearly the bedrock of both Avon's business philosophy and its customers' expectations. Our task was to communicate this on a limited budget without looking cheap.

We understood that we needed to establish a brand image in a category dominated by price and make it pay off with an increased market share. The ads you see here do just that. We used the owner because his customers know him and prospective customers would be drawn in by his involvement with his business. We used highbrow humor because we were reaching for an upscale audience. But even when the headlines are funny, the message is serious. Looking great is important to you? Cool. Your old, classically tailored shirt looks great? Congratulations. You've been using the right cleaner. You need your valuable clothing safely stored for the winter? You can trust us. Those are the relevant messages, expressed in unexpected ways that work.

And work they did. Avon's market share increased 8 percent, an accomplishment we attribute to a key consumer insight that anxiety about appearance resulted in a strong need for security about clothing care. We understood that such confidence was better addressed, not by stressing particular services, so much as by conveying an attitude about style and an understanding of what clothing means to these customers. We wanted customers and prospects to think of Avon, not as a cleaner, but as "one of them." We chose humor to suggest a relaxed confidence about Avon's capabilities to provide quality service, a tactic that reassures customers more effectively than merely saying that Avon does quality work.

While the increase in business is a tangible measure of the campaign's success, owner Stacy Godo figures there have been other qualitative indicators. He is now greeted regularly by customers, both in the store and socially, who approach him and say, "Hey. Nice shirt."

CHAPTER 7

Designing
to Communicate

BY RONALD J. ALLMAN II

A dvertising is a team sport. The copywriter and art director begin by exchanging ideas on content and approach, and then proceed to work out the problems. The design idea may come from the writer; the headline, from the art director. Such teamwork implies that each partner has some understanding of and appreciation for the other's talent. While we may not all be great artists, we should certainly be able to understand the principles involved in arriving at a graphic solution.

In fact, designing is like writing. You have to put your imagination to work to produce vibrant headlines and powerful text, just as you do when you come up with a traffic-stopping visual. You're thinking visually, whether you know it or not, when you attempt to find the right words to explain product benefits. So when you start to think about how you want the campaign to look, imagine that someone else will be doing the finished artwork and dig in—just start sketching. It's okay if it's rough. As you will see, the processes for these two endeavors are also similar. Each consists of finding a solution to a problem, and each begins with ideas. And the toughest part of each process is the beginning, when you've got to do some serious thinking.

● Functions of Design

In designing your advertisement, keep its purpose foremost in your mind. Remember that an ad must communicate quickly and effectively. The prettiest ad is worthless unless what you want to convey to your audience is clear, understandable, and useful to them. Good design makes your message easier to understand. In other words, your design needs to get as much information as possible to the audience in the shortest time possible. A thoughtful design helps you accomplish this.

Your design must attract your target audience. Thousands of media messages are competing for consumers' attention. A well-designed ad grabs their attention, at least momentarily. Since you have their attention only briefly, your design must help them remember the message. Good design not only commands attention, it holds it. If your audience is quickly bored with your ad, you're not going to communicate much of anything.

Design enables you to organize ideas. Information carefully placed breaks the facts into digestible messages—some visual, others textual; some large, others small. This helps product facts stick in consumers' minds. Good design makes information easier to remember.

Good design emphasizes the most compelling information. Where you place information in the ad, how large you make that information, and how you display it in relation to other elements in the ad can strengthen or diminish its importance.

● Basics of Design

Before you organize information visually, it helps to know something about the basics. Do you know what negative or "white" space is? What do *gestalt, balance, contrast, harmony, proportion,* and *rhythm* mean in terms of design?

Negative or "White" Space

You can think of your layout as the "package" for your idea. How you use white space in your layout can determine how effective your package will be. By white space, we mean blank, or "negative," space. Always leave some white space on the outside of your layout. Allow white space to invade the center of your layout, and you are guaranteed to have a scattered, incohesive design. However, there is more to white space than simply including it on the outside of an ad. Use lots of white space, a great expanse of white space, and what's the result? Often, it's a feeling of exclusivity. This can be great for an upscale target audience but probably isn't appropriate for bargain hunters.

Gestalt

Put simply, gestalt is the idea that the whole is greater than the sum of its parts. Although the parts can be—and should be—observed and analyzed on their own, the whole of a design should strike you first. When you first see a painting, you take it in as a whole. Only later do you look at the individual parts. Similarly, a designer uses to advantage the mind's tendency to group things together and see them as a whole.

If two objects are similar and are near each other, we mentally close the distance between them and see them as whole. Imagine a flock of geese flying overhead— we first see the wedge shape they form rather than the individual birds. When flowers are arranged a certain way, they can spell out words—we see the words, not the individual flowers. Our eyes are drawn more to groups than to things spaced widely apart. And because we are drawn to such patterns, we respond to them in predictable ways.

● FIGURE 7-1

Gestalt principles remind us that elements of design should be integrated so that the design, not the elements, is the first thing the viewer observes. The design principles of contrast, harmony, rhythm, and proportion are other ways to focus attention, hold various elements together, and present elements in ways that please the eye.

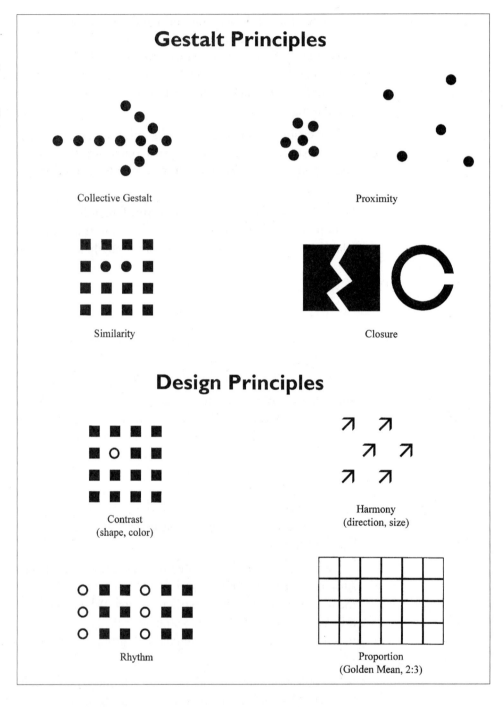

Conversely, when an item is dissimilar to the objects around it, it commands attention. At a baseball game, the person in a rainbow-colored wig is definitely going to stand out. When a car is going the wrong way on a one-way street, we notice it at once. (Thank goodness!) People notice and react to items that stand out.

Balance

Balance can be symmetrical or asymmetrical. When both sides of an advertisement are equal, the design is symmetrical. So, if there is a picture on the left, symmetrical balance requires that there be a picture on the right that is similar in size, shape, and placement. Think of two kids on a seesaw—if they are the same size and you place them the same distance apart, they will balance each other.

Asymmetrical balance depends on the weight of the items on a page. Imagine our seesaw again, only this time with a large child on one end and a much smaller child on the other end. To balance the seesaw, the larger child moves closer to the center, the smaller child moves farther away from the center, or more small children join the smaller child. Although symmetrical balance is fine, it can also be static—something advertisers usually wish to avoid. So we see more ads with asymmetrical balance because the advertisers are striving for a dynamic look.

Knowing what is "heavier" or "lighter" in a layout takes some practice, but you probably already have an intuitive feel for the concept of weight. A darker item is heavier than a lighter item. A bigger item is heavier than a smaller item. Thick is heavier than thin. It is when you combine layout elements that their weights become less clear. Photos and headlines are usually seen as heavier than text or logos. Text usually is the lightest item on a page.

Imagine the pieces of your design as little weights on a page. To balance this design asymmetrically, you must arrange the pieces in such a way that the balance is in the center of the page. You need to balance not only left with right but top with bottom. A bottom-heavy design will tempt the reader to turn the page. A top-heavy design will discourage the reader from reading the rest of the ad.

Contrast

We encounter contrast everywhere. A white circle stands out among black squares and thus attracts and keeps our attention. But contrast is not limited to color or shape. Contrast can be effectively used in type size, slant, font, and weight. Texture—in both images and text—is another way to use contrast. A feather on a piece of sandpaper will stand out even if the feather and sandpaper are similar colors. Too much contrast, however, and your design can lose its cohesiveness.

Harmony

Harmony is the opposite of contrast. Using text that is all one font, even if the sizes are different, produces a harmonious layout. Harmony lets the viewer know that all elements are related. Using harmonious shades of one color brings a design together. Harmony, like contrast, can also be found in texture, direction, and weight. But remember, if things get too harmonious, people tend to fall asleep.

Proportion

We like things to be in proportion. We get a feeling of discomfort when one side of an item cannot be equally divided into the other side. We sense discordance—something is wrong even if we can't explain it. This feeling of discomfort we get when items are out of proportion or unbalanced is known as cognitive dissonance. Our minds reject these items. If your layout violates the rules of proportion, your consumer may reject the whole advertisement.

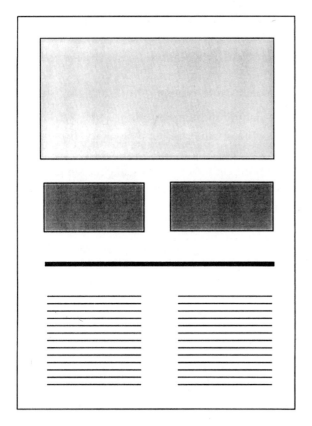
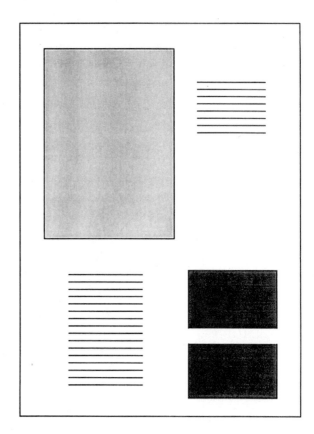

Symmetrical Balance   Asymmetrical Balance

● FIGURE 7-2

Asymmetrical balance is the dominant choice in advertising, because it allows one point of the design to "take over" and attract the eye to the rest of the ad. To achieve asymmetrical balance, just be certain there's a difference top to bottom or right to left in the ad, all the while arranging elements so the ad doesn't appear lopsided. Symmetrical balance suggests a static quality; asymmetrical balance suggests dynamism. Which is appropriate for your ad?

The "perfect" proportion is a 2-to-3 proportion, known as a "golden mean." Most photographs are designed to adhere to the golden mean. The Greeks used this proportion when they built the Parthenon.

Rhythm

Repetition creates rhythm. A layout in which photo is followed by text is followed by photo is followed by text creates rhythm. Rhythm lets us know when to expect text in this layout. We get used to the pattern. And when you use repetition to create direction, you create a sense of movement in your design. Dots placed horizontally across the page move the viewer's eyes across the page. But make sure that you place important information at the end of this movement.

● The Four R's of Design

You're ready to start designing an ad. How do you begin? Where do you go from there? All designers use the same process. They may have different names for it, but they all use it. We like to call this process the four R's: research, roughs, revise, and ready.

Research

You've been asked to design an ad for Acme Flakes. So where do you start? Remember Chapter 3? That's right—you start with research! You first need to know what Acme Flakes are. Are they soap flakes, instant potato flakes, or corn flakes? Or is it simply a cute name for an advertising design company? You find out all you can about the product, company, or service. Would you approach the design of an ad for Ben and Jerry's Ice Cream differently than you would one for Breyer's Ice Cream? They both sell the same product—premium ice cream—but everything about the two companies and their products is different. They offer different flavors, have different public images, attract different buyers, and are packaged in different ways. The more you know about your client, the more appropriate your design will be.

Not only do you need to research the product, company, or service, you must also know your target audience and your competition. How do your competitors advertise? What do their ads look like? What do you offer that they don't? How can you design an ad that will lure consumers away from their product to yours? What is your target audience like? What do they read? What kind of design catches their attention? Once again, the more research you do, the easier your designing job will be.

Another type of "research" is less project specific but still vital. This involves your "swipe file," a collection of advertisements and visuals (photos, illustrations, etc.) that you think are interesting, attractive, or just plain different. Ideas are not copyrighted. Good designers appreciate good design, so make a copy of a good idea for later reference. Who knows? It may be just the stimulus you need next week. What's important is to borrow the idea, not the ad itself. A swipe file is a great place to start when you need ideas. It's also a good way to see what sorts of designs, typefaces, and visuals are being used; what they look like; and how they work in layouts.

Roughs

Once you've completed your research, you're ready to start sketching. These early sketches are just rough versions. The important thing is to get your ideas on paper. There are as many ways to do roughs as there are people doing them. Whichever way works best for you, the idea behind the rough is the same. You want to put down on paper each and every idea you have about what your finished ad might look like. Don't be afraid—some of these ideas will be goofy. The best designs often start this way. What is important is that you get your ideas on paper before you forget them.

Many designers like to create little roughs called "thumbnails." Thumbnails are useful because you can sketch an idea quickly, without much detail, and you've got your concept in miniature form. There is no need for great artistic skill here. You just want to give yourself a lot of options.

Revise .

Once you've got your roughs, take a look at your ideas and pick the ones you like best. Let your knowledge of your client and of your target consumer guide you in deciding which ideas will work. Don't become too attached to one idea yet. Develop several ideas. Start making more elaborate sketches, and then revise them. And remember that revising is never a one-way street. You can always go back and do more roughs or more research. You may get lucky and have a couple of ideas that you can develop, but don't be afraid to backtrack if you get stuck.

The revision stage is often a good time to get some initial feedback from your client. But remember: Although your client is in business, his or her business isn't design. The client may not have the background to visualize your big idea from a thumbnail rough, so make certain your ideas are finished enough for him or her to visualize the end product. Also, listen carefully to the client's feedback, because he or she has to be happy with your efforts thus far. Get feedback from other designers, too. They might see ideas or mistakes that you've missed. Just remember that this is your design, not theirs. Keep revising until you create a couple of versions you're happy with. Then choose one and base your campaign on it.

Ready

Once you've got an ad with the copy and design elements in place, it's time to prepare a finished layout for your client's approval. Using a computer, you can produce a presentation ad that is nearly as finished as what will be submitted for publication.

After doing scores of thumbnails and choosing the one that best solves the advertising problem, it's time to use the rough to create the final layout. This layout should be "actual size." Since a majority of magazines use the following dimensions, this is a good size to start with:

Trim size: 8″ × 11″

Nonbleed and type area: 7″ × 10¼″

Bleed: 8¼″ × 11¼″

The trim size represents the finished size of the page after the magazine has been printed, bound, and trimmed. Your layout should be drawn to this size if you're designing a full-page ad. Be aware, however, that magazine sizes do vary, so always check the mechanical specifications for each magazine you plan to use. A bleed ad is one that runs all the way to the trim on at least one side. A nonbleed ad is contained within the nonbleed page limits, with a margin surrounding it on all sides. Whether your ad is designed for bleed or not, you should keep all type within the nonbleed limits. In setting type too close to the trim, you run the risk of having a letter or two trimmed off. You might want to draw the nonbleed limit as a second frame within the frame you draw to establish the trim. This will remind you to keep all type within the inner frame, or nonbleed area.

Type Categories

Serif Type	Sans Serif Type	Script	Novelty
Times Roman	Helvetica	Brush Script	Comic Sans
Garamond	Gill Sans	Lucia	CRACKLING
Goudy	**Impact**	Elegant	CRYPT
Bodoni	Eras		Saint Francis

Cursive

Coronet

Zapf Chancery

Text Letter

Old English

Lombardic

● FIGURE 7-3

Literally thousands of type fonts are at your disposal on computers. Unless you're a type expert, however, be wary of using most of them. Generally, stick to the serif and sans serif fonts, which contrast with each other nicely. Or use one font for all type in your ad, using a larger size for the headline and other display lines, and perhaps a bolder face than for the body copy. Script and cursive, while lovely on invitations, should be used cautiously, because they're harder to read. And for the same reason, avoid novelty and text letter fonts unless the concept calls for something unconventional. The body copy for this book is Adobe Garamond.

● Selecting Type

If you spend any time around designers, you'll hear them talk about type in such descriptive and affectionate terms that you might think designing causes brain damage! It doesn't, but if you work with type for awhile, you too may begin to fall in love with it. You will find that different fonts have totally different personalities. Zapf Chancery is an elegant but still very legible font. Helvetica is a workhorse as far as fonts go, but it's rather boring and plain. Gill Sans has the flair that Helvetica is missing. Before long, you may find yourself talking like those crazy designers.

Type can be divided into six groups: serif, sans serif, script, cursive, text letter, and novelty. Letters in a serif font have little horizontal strokes at the tops and bottoms of the letter. These serifs help draw the eye along a line of type. Most body text is in a serif font for this reason. The most common serif font is Times Roman. Other serif fonts are Palatino, Goudy, Bookman, Caslon, Bodoni, and Garamond. Serif fonts are sometimes called roman fonts.

Letters without serifs are called sans serif fonts. Sans serif fonts have a more modern and geometrical look than serif fonts. Sans serif fonts can be distinctive in headlines and logos. They are clean-looking fonts that communicate a sense of simplicity. Some common sans serif fonts are Helvetica, Futura, Gill Sans, Avant Garde, and Optima.

Fonts designed to look like handwriting are either script or cursive fonts. The difference between script and cursive fonts depends on whether the letters connect. If they connect, it's a script font; if they don't, it's a cursive font. These fonts add a sense of formality and elegance and so are popular for invitations and announcements. But their use in advertising is limited, perhaps because of their delicacy and the fact that they can be difficult to read. Park Avenue, Mistral, and Brush Script are common script fonts, while Zapf Chancery, Freestyle Script, and Reporter No. 2 are popular cursive fonts.

If the font was created to look like the hand-drawn letters of monks and scribes, it's a text letter font. These fonts, also known as black letter fonts, are usually found in newspaper nameplates and church logos. They are very hard to read and usable only in certain situations. The most common text letter font is Old English.

Novelty fonts are those that don't easily fit into the other categories because they are unusual or unconventional. Fonts that make type look like stenciled letters or Old West "wanted" posters are novelty fonts. Novelty fonts are good for display headlines and logos when you need a certain flair. Some of the more commonly used novelty fonts are Hobo, American Typewriter, and Stencil. Text letter fonts are sometimes considered to be novelty fonts.

Type is measured in points. There are 72 points to an inch. Body text is usually between 10 and 12 points. Type larger than 18 points is considered display type and is usually used for headlines. For advertisements, it's wise to consider 10 as the minimal point size, and 12-point type may be more legible in some fonts.

The space between lines of type is known as leading and is also measured in points. If you have 10-point type and want 2 points of space between the lines, you will specify 12 points of leading. In this case, to tell a designer what size type and leading you are using, you would say, "10 on 12." When you want the same font size and leading, you specify, "Set solid." For legibility, however, it's usually wise to have at least 2 points of leading between lines.

The space between letters is known as letter spacing. If you adjust the spacing between two letters, you are kerning the letters. For display lines such as headlines, subheads, and baselines, this is useful with certain letters that can be moved closer together because of their shapes, such as AV, To, AW, and Te. If you adjust the spacing between all letters, you are adjusting the type's tracking.

You can line up paragraphs of type in four different ways. If you want all your text lined up vertically on the left side, specify flush left. If you want it lined up only on the right side, specify flush right. If both sides are lined up, your text is justified. Of course, you can always center your type. Most advertisements are set flush left, ragged right. This is easier on the reader because the eye goes back to a consistent starting point and the ragged right allows for some "air" in the text, especially between columns if you use more than one column.

Type Alignment

Flush Left	*Centered*	*Flush Right*	*Justified*
Dolor in hendrerit in vulputate velit esse molestie consequat, vel illum dolore eu feugiat nulla facilisis at vero eros et accumsan et iusto odio dignissim qui blandit praesent luptatum zzril delenit augue duis dolore te feugait nulla facilisi. Soluta nobis eleifend option congue nihil imperdiet doming id quod mazim placerat facer possim assum. Lorem ipsum dolor sit amet, consectetuer adipiscing elit, sed diam nonummy nibh euismod tincidunt ut laoreet.	imperdiet doming id quod mazim placerat facer possim assum. Lorem ipsum dolor sit. Sit amet, consectetuer hendrerit in vulputate velit.	praesent luptatum zzril delenit augue duis dolore te feugait nulla facilisi. Soluta nobis eleifend option congue nihil imperdiet doming id quod mazim placerat facer possim assum.	Hendrereit in vulputate velit aliquip exea lorem ipsum minim.
	Hendrereit in vulputate velit aliquip exea lorem ipsum minim. Ut hendrerit in vulputate velit aliquip ex ea commodo minim hendrerit i vulputate velit veniam: Sed diam nonummy nibh tincidunt ut laoreet. Dolor in hendrerit in vulputate velit esse molestie consequat, vel illum dolore eu feugiat nulla facilisis at vero eros et accumsan et iusto odio dignissim qui blandit	Lorem ipsum dolor sit amet, consectetuer adipiscing elit, sed diam nonummy nibh euismod tincidunt ut laoreet. Soluta nobis eleifend option congue nihil imperdiet doming id quod mazim placerat facer possim assum. Lorem ipsum dolor sit.	Ut hendrerit in vulputate velit aliquip ex ea commodo minim hendrerit i vulputate velit veniam: Sed diam nonummy nibh tincidunt ut laoreet.
Soluta nobis eleifend option congue nihil		Sit amet, consectetuer hendrerit in vulputate velit:	Dolor in hendrerit in vulputate velit esse molestie consequat, vel illum dolore eu feugiat nulla.
			Facilisis at vero eros et accumsan et iusto odio dignissim qui blandit praesent luptatum zzril delenit augue duis dolore te feugait nulla facilisi.
			Soluta nobis eleifend option congue nihil imperdiet

● FIGURE 7-4

The majority of ads today have body copy set flush left, ragged right, as in the first column here. The ragged-right column provides "breathing space" between columns of type. Centered type must fit logically into the rest of the layout. Flush right might be used to offset a visual silhouette to the left of the type column. Justified type, while common in books, creates a formal look that also allows little white space between columns.

When choosing a font, keep in mind the message you want to convey. A headline that says "Welcome to the Electronic Age" in a script font sends a mixed message. A long paragraph in Old English would be tedious to read. Fonts send signals about your advertisement even if the viewer can't read, so choose carefully.

● Basic Ad Layouts

If you can't decide how to lay out your ad and your swipe file is no help, try some of these basic advertising layouts: Mondrian, grid, picture window, copy heavy, frame, silhouette, type specimen, color field, band, axial, or circus. (Figure 7-5 gives examples and descriptions of each.) Bear in mind that your ad concept affects the design choice, not the other way around.

● Inviting Readership

You have many options at your disposal for luring readers, including the following:

1. *Don't set type wider than 39 characters.* Any wider, and you discourage readership. Instead, break the space into two or more columns of equal width. The larger the type, of course, the wider it can be set.

2. *Avoid setting copy in less than 10-point type.* Smaller type is hard to read.

3. *Break up long copy blocks with subheads.* Careful paragraphing will also help you avoid the "gray mass" look.

4. *Avoid setting body copy in reverse (white on black).* This tends to cut down readership. Headlines may be reversed for impact, provided the type is large and bold enough.

5. *Take care when you print copy over tonal matter, such as photographs.* If you must do this, be certain there is enough contrast to make the type legible.

6. *Use lowercase when possible.* It tends to be more legible than all-capital letters, especially in smaller type sizes.

7. *Either capitalize the entire headline or capitalize only the first word of a sentence and any proper name.*

8. *End the headline with punctuation.* Use a period or a question mark. Save the exclamation point for the rare occasion when it is warranted.

9. *Align all copy elements to avoid a jumbled look.* This is easily done in an axial layout by aligning them on a common axis.

10. *Use normal punctuation throughout.* Avoid leaders (. . .), which look sloppy and uninviting.

11. *Use italics sparingly.* They are good for occasional emphasis, but too many italics make copy look pale and weak, just the opposite of what is intended.

● Creating the Finished Ad: Computers and Design

Using computers for design is fairly recent. In the early 1980s, the first personal computers merely replaced the typewriter, but computer technology advanced rapidly. It was not too long before computers were doing spreadsheets, graphics, and simple desktop publishing. Today, all a designer needs is a good computer, a few peripherals

● FIGURE 7-5

These thumbnail sketches show eleven approaches to selling wineglasses.

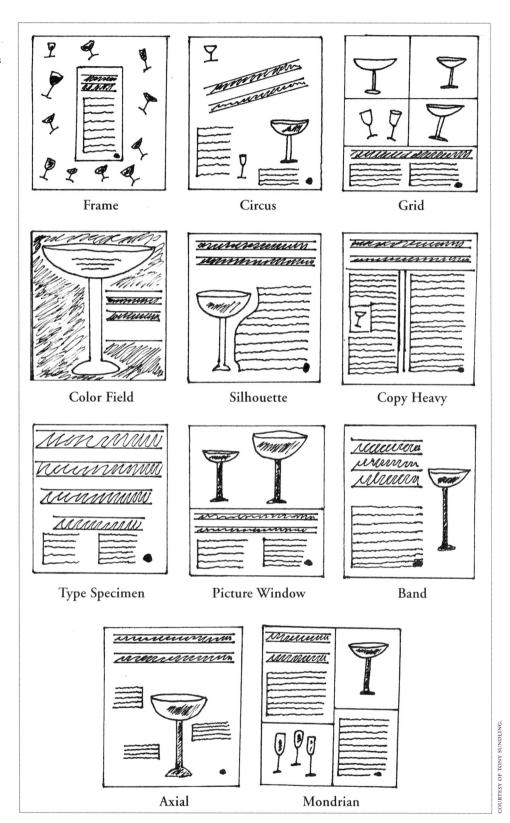

Frame

Circus

Grid

Color Field

Silhouette

Copy Heavy

Type Specimen

Picture Window

Band

Axial

Mondrian

(printer, scanner, design software), and a good eye to design and produce any type of advertisement.

An advertising designer might use four types of computer applications:

- *Photo manipulation software.* Software like Adobe Photoshop is mainly used for making changes to photographs and other images on the computer, but they can also be used to create images and text. Since these applications can manipulate images, you can create interesting, eye-catching text and visuals using these programs.

- *Presentation software.* Software like Lotus Freelance Graphics is mainly used for business presentations, but it is also useful in creating quick and easy advertisements. The idea behind business presentations and advertisements is basically the same—to present information in the most useful and interesting way.

- *Illustration software.* If you are looking for more control over image creation and special effects with text, an illustration program might be your design tool of choice. Software such as Adobe Illustrator and Macromedia Freehand allows you to create any type of image or text you can imagine. These applications are less friendly to images already created, such as scanned images, but if you are creating directly from your imagination, this type of software is best suited to your needs.

- *Desktop publishing software.* Perhaps the most useful application for advertising design is desktop publishing software such as QuarkXPress or Adobe Page-Maker. These programs were written specifically for designers who create pages for publication. Most newspapers and magazines use desktop publishing software in creating their pages.

● Suggested Activities

1. Find a black-and-white ad that presents strong possibilities for rearrangement; perhaps it can even be improved. Don't choose an ad with a simple picture window, in which the only possible change will be to transpose the picture and the headline. Challenge yourself! After looking long and hard at the original ad, sketch some thumbnails. How many different ways can you rearrange this ad? Choose your best arrangement. Now, tape the original ad to your drawing board. Draw the border on your layout paper, making certain it corresponds to the size of the original ad. Using your thumbnail as a guide, start moving your layout paper around to trace the various components from the original. Shade in dark values with the side of your No. 2 pencil. Compare the new ad to the original. What do you think?

2. Find a gestalt-type print ad or one with a silhouette design. With tracing paper, draw the positive shape and shade in the negative shape. This will produce a silhouette of the positive shape (the headline, copy, and illustration) while sharply empha-

sizing the negative space. The result will be quite abstract; this will force you to see the negative and positive shapes in the original design.

3. Collect several ads that you think are effective, and set the headlines in three other typefaces from samples you've collected. Lay the new type over the old. What effect does the change in type style have on the advertisement?

4. Take one of your ads, and enlarge and reduce elements to form a new design. Compare your design to the original.

5. Find eight ads with different typefaces, and defend or criticize the choices. Does the personality of the type fit the image of the ad? Does it work with the visuals? Does the type overpower everything else and undermine the effectiveness of the ad?

Search Online! Discovering More About Advertising Design

Using InfoTrac® College Edition, try these phrases and others for Key Words and Subject Guide searches: *copywriter + art + director, visual thinking, advertising design, negative space + design, gestalt + design, balance + design, contrast + design, typography, type fonts, reverse type + design, computer design, desktop publishing.*

BriefCase

Traveler Magazine Sends Their Minds—
Media Buyers Soon Follow

BY BRETT ROBBS,
UNIVERSITY OF COLORADO

When Arnold Advertising of McLean, Virginia, won *National Geographic Traveler*'s trade advertising account, the agency's challenge was clear. Its advertising would have to establish a strong image for the magazine and change the target's perception of *Traveler* readers. And with a target consisting of hard-nosed media buyers seeking the best vehicles for their clients' ad monies, the campaign had to get it right.

In the publishing industry, a primary goal of trade advertising is to convince media buyers to place their clients' advertising in particular periodicals. Obviously, a publication's readership is one of its key sales points. Reports from the *National Geographic Traveler* sales force indicated that, although research showed the magazine's readers to be relatively affluent, college-educated professionals who led active lives and who liked to travel, media buyers had quite a different view of these readers.

Media buyers saw *Traveler* readers as older, armchair travelers who were more likely to get in a car and visit a state park than to hop on a plane and fly to an international resort. For the magazine to meet its new advertising sales objectives, that perception would have to change—no easy task, given the magazine's relatively modest ad budget and the firmly established positions of its main competitors, *Travel and Leisure* and *Conde Nast Traveler*.

But according to Julie Leidy Bradsher, account supervisor at Arnold, the agency was confident it could meet the challenge because *National Geographic Traveler* has a number of unique assets. One of the most important is the heritage and credibility of the National Geographic Society itself. The Society's name is closely associated with international travel. Its reputation gives *National Geographic Traveler* strong credibil-

THE ISLAND IS ONLY a few miles in diameter, but after eight days I hadn't seen it all and wasn't ready to leave. Like a kaleidoscope, Mackinac can re-create itself in an endless array of dramatic designs.

WE SEND THEIR MINDS. THEIR BODIES SOON FOLLOW.

NATIONAL GEOGRAPHIC
Traveler

For more than a century, the National Geographic Society has inspired people to see the world. For more than a decade, National Geographic Traveler has shown them how.

Photographer: Declan Haun

ity, and that credibility is one of the primary reasons readers rely on the magazine's stories and maps to plan trips.

The agency realized that this heritage and the readers' subsequent belief in the magazine were the keys. The advertising would need to employ these keys to convince its target market, consisting of potential advertisers, that *Traveler* inspires its readers to travel abroad. If it could do that, the advertising would get *Traveler* on the media buyers' short list and open the door so that the magazine's sales force could complete the sale.

Knowing what to say is one thing. Giving the message impact is something else. As Francis Sullivan, a creative director at Arnold, noted: "One of the things most people immediately associate with the National Geographic Society is beautiful photography. Since we wanted to play on the Society's heritage and also suggest the quality of

I take one more look at my beat-up map of Barcelona, limp from use now, coming apart on the fold lines, full of notes and arrows and question marks and coffee stains—symbol of an intense, wonderful affair, a love letter I will read over and over.

WE SEND THEIR MINDS.   THEIR BODIES SOON FOLLOW.

NATIONAL GEOGRAPHIC
Traveler
For more than a century, the National Geographic Society has inspired people to see the world. For more than a decade, National Geographic Traveler has shown them how. Call (212) 398-2735 for information on advertising, subscriptions or Society membership.

the magazine, we knew great photography would be a dominant element in the campaign." But, as Sullivan pointed out, *Traveler* is also extremely well written, and the stories have a special flair. So he wanted the advertising to include a passage from an actual story to give the target a better sense of the magazine's editorial flavor.

While Sullivan and the art director, Nora Jaster, knew some of the elements they wanted to include in the advertising, they needed a memorable idea that would cut through the clutter and remind the target that *Traveler* inspires its readers to travel abroad. They tried a variety of approaches. Some ideas focused on the magazine's value to its advertisers. Other ideas attempted to project a more contemporary image for the magazine.

But Sullivan and Jaster knew they'd found the solution when they came up with the line "We send their minds. Their bodies soon follow." From there, it was simply a matter of developing the visuals. Placing a passage "torn" from the magazine near the headline "We send their minds" and a striking color photograph showing people in

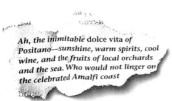

Ah, the inimitable dolce vita of Positano—sunshine, warm spirits, cool wine, and the fruits of local orchards and the sea. Who would not linger on the celebrated Amalfi coast

WE SEND THEIR MINDS.   THEIR BODIES SOON FOLLOW.

Photographer: Jonathan Blair

NATIONAL GEOGRAPHIC
Traveler

For more than a century, the National Geographic Society has inspired people to see the world.
For more than a decade, National Geographic Traveler has shown them how.

exotic locales next to "Their bodies soon follow" visually reinforced the message and suggested the very process *Traveler* readers go through: They read a story in the magazine; then they decide to travel to see the place for themselves. Jaster subtly enhanced this message, Sullivan says, by taking a color from the photograph and adding it to the type. "It's a way of visually saying that the words transport you there."

The body copy cements the magazine's image to the National Geographic Society's proud travel heritage. Interestingly, to create the copy, Sullivan drew on a headline idea he had developed for another *Traveler* campaign.

Because the campaign had to deliver its message with a limited number of media insertions, consistency of theme and design was of special importance. To firmly establish *Traveler's* position, the theme line became the headline for every ad. Theme and look were carried over to the magazine's collateral pieces and sales presentation materials aimed at prospective advertisers.

Jurassic desert some years ago—now lie etched by wind and water into delicate swirls of geologic time. Rococo formations and cool, deep, narrow slot canyons characterize the Paria Canyon

WE SEND THEIR MINDS.

THEIR BODIES SOON FOLLOW.

NATIONAL GEOGRAPHIC
Traveler

For more than a century, the National Geographic Society has inspired people to see the world.
For more than a decade, National Geographic Traveler has shown them how.

And the target is definitely getting the message, says Pandora Todd, the magazine's director of promotions. The campaign has helped the sales force attract not only new advertisers but new categories of advertisers. The ad series has also been recognized for its creative excellence—two Gold Clios and a first place in the London International Advertising Awards.

CHAPTER 8

Writing for Radio—
Can You See What I'm Saying?

Radio offers a format for every listener and for every advertiser: country, adult contemporary, news, talk, sports, business, oldies, religion, adult standards, Spanish, soft adult contemporary, alternative rock, classic rock, ethnic, classical, jazz, and new age. You name it; radio has it.

● Why Advertise on Radio?

Radio reaches everyone (well established)

Radio is everywhere—at home, in cars, at places of business. And radio reaches *everyone,* from teens to seniors. While the proliferation of cable and satellite dishes has transformed television into a segmented medium within the last decade, radio has held this distinction almost since the birth of TV in the late 1940s.

Radio is both a great stand-alone medium and a great support for other media. Airing commercials for its Bubble Jet printer on radio allowed Canon USA to create awareness among a specific audience, the ones ready to buy a printer. Spots were aired in thirteen large markets on news, talk, sports, and classical music stations. In each market, the radio ads were supported by newspaper ads on the "best computer day," including a Tuesday "Science Times" section in one market and a Monday business section in another.

Snapple Natural Beverages claims it chose radio because of the medium's special ability to target specific markets, along with its cost-effectiveness and the power of radio personalities to move products. Macy's used radio to advertise job opening at their new stores. Why choose radio and not just stick to the classified ads section of a newspaper? Simple. Macy's wanted to find people who *weren't* job hunting. Other leading advertisers, such as Philip Morris, Anheuser-Busch, Kmart, General Motors, PepsiCo, and Delta Air Lines, find spot radio an effective way to target and localize their advertising dollars.

● Radio: A Writer's Medium

And what do radio commercial writers love about this medium? One calls writing for radio a unique adventure that transcends the limitations and the costliness of the camera lens and the shooting schedule. Others say radio is "a lot sexier than sex" and must touch our hearts to work effectively. Seasoned radio writers will remind you that radio is a visual medium, in which the audience sees whatever the writer makes them see. The better the writer knows radio, the more the audience will see. To see how this medium works, consider how you would "show" the ad's location on a radio spot. You could simply have a voice say, "Now when you're walking the streets of Manhattan as I am" or "So I'm sitting here staring at a sink full of dirty dishes." Or you could use sounds to provide the location: stalled traffic in New York City with a few well-chosen taxi driver groans or car horns thrown in for good measure, or clanking dishes. Music can locate the ad; think about what you "see" when you hear a Bavarian band, the stirring finale of the 1812 overture by Tchaikovsky, or Scottish bagpipes. And even a single voice can call up a locale—can you "see" the location in an exaggerated Southern drawl, a West Indies clipped English, or a New England twang?

As you start to conceive your radio commercial, think about the one big idea you need to communicate. In 60 or 30 seconds, you can't expect listeners to remember a series of benefits. They can't go back and reread what interests them as they can in a print ad, so take your big idea and play it for all it's worth for the length of the commercial.

Think of the voice or voices that can best command the attention of your audience. You want to use not specific personalities, but voice types: skeptical young woman, trustworthy older woman, genius child, conservative Vermonter, gushy Southern belle, or thickheaded caveman. Be sure to offer directions on the script in parentheses as to delivery: angry, sarcastic, dopey, heavy British accent, or snobbish.

Imagine sounds and music. Or no sounds. And no music. Sound effects should further the message, not be the ends in themselves. They shouldn't attempt to duplicate reality; calling for footstep sounds serves little purpose unless it helps make the point. Unexpected sounds may be more compelling. One public service announcement on child abuse uses the violent sound of doors slamming as the narrator talks about how some people hide such abuse behind closed doors. A spot urging older people to remain active uses a constant background sound of rocking chairs squeaking on a wooden porch as the narrator tells listeners to do quite the opposite.

Be aware that sounds can save words and dramatize situations. Here's a spot that used sound effects very effectively:

ANNCR:	Some of the fastest automobiles in the world take their names from some of the fastest animals in the world. Ford Mustang. 0 to 45 . . .
<u>SFX:</u>	<u>CAR SPEEDS BY</u>
ANNCR:	6.9 seconds. Volkswagen Rabbit. 0 to 45 . . .
<u>SFX:</u>	<u>CAR SPEEDS BY</u>
ANNCR:	6.4 seconds. Jaguar XKE. 0 to 45 . . .
<u>SFX:</u>	<u>CAR SPEEDS BY</u>
ANNCR:	4.3 seconds. But even the fastest animals on four wheels can't catch the fastest animal on four feet. The African cheetah. 0 to 45 miles per hour in 2.0 seconds.
<u>SFX:</u>	<u>THE ROAR OF A JET</u>
ANNCR:	Catch the cheetahs if you can. Now through Labor Day at the Minnesota Zoo.

This clever spot encouraged fathers to take their children to the Minnesota Zoo. Had the ad taken a traditional approach, it probably wouldn't have been as effective.

Don't be afraid to use music. Or to leave it out. If the tune has a life of its own, it may detract from what you are trying to say. Frequently, silence can be more powerful than sound, as long as it doesn't overstay its welcome. Of course, music can also enhance a mood, but never plug music in for its own sake. And remember that obtaining commercial rights to copyrighted music and music performances can be extremely costly.

Begin with something relevant yet unexpected to gain the listener's attention. End with something as memorable to drive home your point. Since you can't see the product on radio, be certain its name is mentioned several times, but never so intrusively that it smacks of "commercialism."

Radio's a great way to take a small budget and do big things with it. Exciting things. Creative things. And funny things. Production budgets are tiny compared to television. But you don't have to be able to draw a straight—or crooked—line, and you won't be agonizing over typefaces and design. More than most media, radio demands that your writing be given free rein, because if you don't choose unusual techniques to break through typical listening habits, the radio audience won't "hear" you.

● The Theater of the Mind

Think of a great radio commercial you've heard. It probably wasn't read in a monotone. It probably wasn't rushed through because the script wasn't timed properly. Instead, you were entertained in some way—whether it was humor or drama or pathos—and you probably still remember the brand name and the key selling idea. Radio has been called, appropriately, "the theater of the mind," and those who grew up with radio (before TV!) know what this means. Without pictures, radio writers had to work hard to deliver visual impressions through voices, sounds, and music emanating from a tiny speaker—and they succeeded. Today, you must create the same impact with cerebral pictures to overcome the indifferent listening habits of many radio listeners.

For example, a commercial for Aztec suntan lotion uses a character called the Aztec Sun God, who speaks as if he's just earned an Ivy League degree. (Nothing like unexpected connections to hold interest, remember?) As he converses with a store manager, he mentions that most customers won't recognize him in his suit and wing-tip shoes. Then he begins to strip down to his bronzed body as the store manager expresses understandable anxiety. That's not only funny and involving, it reinforces the point of the spot: Aztec suntan lotion can make your body look like a sun god's body.

● Live Versus Produced

A radio commercial arriving at a station on tape, ready to air, is called a "produced" commercial. But some commercials are sent in script form, in which case they are either read live or recorded for airplay by a staff announcer. Other advertisers don't even furnish a script; instead, they send a fact sheet describing the major selling points and benefits of their product, service, or place of business. Which should you choose? Here's a general guide to what works and when:

1. Use a fact sheet when the radio station has a popular on-air personality. Number the facts in descending order of importance, and you may get more than your paid minute's worth if the personality is having fun chatting about your product or place. A donut shop did just that. The shop sent a dozen donuts each morning to a local announcer who was known to love his food. Each morning, the announcer would lovingly describe every bite and rhapsodize on the flavor, texture, and so on. The spots ran during morning drive time, when people are most likely to buy donuts. The campaign was a tremendous success.

2. Use a script read live only if you're using straight copy with no sound effects, music, or multiple speaking parts. A problem with this approach is that many radio personalities are flippant by nature and can have too much fun being cynical or sarcastic with live copy. Therefore, use this approach primarily when you must make last-minute changes to your advertising: a store announcing a fire sale or a promotion that changes daily.

3. Use a produced commercial when your script calls for multiple speaking parts, sound effects, music, or any combination of these, and when you want assurance

that the quality of the spot will never waver. Most local radio stations provide basic production for free, but you may prefer to use a production house that specializes in a particular style.

4. Use a live-taped commercial when you want to be able to update copy on a regular basis. The advertiser produces a tape with a musical introduction. At some point, the music "fades under" or is reduced in volume so that a local announcer can read copy over the music. At the end, the music swells to its conclusion, usually with a taped closing line. Since the middle of the spot contains this "hole," this format is called a "live donut." While the music provides continuity for the entire campaign, the scripted inserts keep the ad up-to-date. Obviously, the inserts must be timed so that they fit the hole in the music.

Most national radio spots and a growing number of local spots are produced commercials. You can imagine why many advertisers prefer this approach. Like a print ad that arrives ready to run, the produced radio commercial allows little room for human error once it leaves the advertiser. Some produced commercials allow a 5-second space at the end for the local announcer to voice a local tag (where to buy it, when it goes on sale, etc.).

● Writing for Radio

Effective radio ads result when the writer understands how to use the power of the medium, when the client grants the writer freedom to do so, and when the production company delivers the perfect combination of performers, music, and sound effects.

During production, the writer should be present to review and approve script adjustments and to work with the production staff on ways to enhance the spot. Some of the best commercials result from last-minute ideas in the studio. That's fine, as long as the essential message and strategy remain unchanged. For example, the slogan for Motel 6 came about through a fortuitous accident. After Tom Bodett finished his folksy monolog, there was still a smidgen of time left on the tape, so he ad-libbed, "We'll leave the light on for you."

Guidelines for Writing Effective Radio Spots

Peter Hochstein of Ogilvy & Mather offers these rules for making better radio commercials:[1]

1. *Identify your sound effects.* Unless you do, you may confuse listeners. The sound of rain falling in a forest is the same as the sound of bacon sizzling. Let the context of the spot remind listeners what they're hearing or even have someone voice an

---

[1] Peter Hochstein, "Ten Rules for Making Better Radio Commercials," *Viewpoint III,* 1981. Used by permission of Ogilvy & Mather, New York.

explanation. ("Another day in the rain forest, where the waters feed lush tropical plants.")

2. *Use music as a sound effect.* A brokerage house created an image of financial power with the same sounds of kettledrums Prokofiev used in his classic symphony *Peter and the Wolf* to conjure up hunters. Another commercial depicted a German neighborhood by playing a few bars of oompah band music.

3. *Build your commercial around a sound.* The sound of a crisp new cracker. Thunder to represent the power of a sound investment. Animal voices to make you want to come to the local zoo.

4. *Give yourself time.* Fight for 60-second spots. You need time in radio to set up a scene and establish a premise. You also need time for voices to speak lines properly.

5. *Consider using no sound effects.* A distinctive voice, a powerful message straightforwardly delivered, can be extremely powerful. People love a good story. If it can stand alone, be conservative in your use of other sounds.

6. *Be careful of comedy.* Although well-written and relevant humor is powerful on radio, be certain it's really funny to someone besides you and your friends, and that the humor has fun with the product but doesn't make fun of the product.

7. *If you're going to be funny, begin with an outrageous premise.* The customers at the film store are goblins who want to take their own Halloween pictures. Lake Michigan will be drained of water and filled with whipped cream. A man puts on his wife's nightgown at 4 A.M. and goes out to purchase *Time* magazine—and the police pick him up. Weird premises, but the events that grow from them are perfectly rational, given the circumstances. And they make a selling point. For *Time*, the point is the guy can't wait for the new issue.

8. *Keep it simple.* Radio is a wonderful medium for building brand awareness. It's not so good for spewing out a long list of benefits or making complex arguments.

9. *Tailor your commercial to time, place, and a specific audience.* If it's running in morning drive time, remember that most people tuned in may be on their way to work. If it runs in Milwaukee, tailor it for Milwaukee. Talk breakfast at 8 A.M. or offer a commuter taxi service during rush hour.

10. *Present your commercial idea to the client on tape if possible.* Dialog, timing, vocal quirks, and sound effects come alive when you can hear them. And most recording studios will produce a "demo" at a reduced cost if you promise to let them produce the approved script. If you can't get it on tape for presentation, have a person or persons on hand who can act out voices and sounds and indicate music.

Other Considerations in Writing Radio Spots

Here are some additional tips for writing radio ads:

1. *Make every word count.* As Hochstein suggests, fight for 60-second spots if you need them. However, if you can say it in 30 seconds, all the better. By writing a 30-second spot, you can run the spot more often and maximize your client's budget.

2. *Write for the ear, not the eye.* As producer Jeffrey Hedquist emphasizes, you should write for the ear. Don't read a print ad into a microphone and expect it to work as a radio commercial. And don't just run the soundtrack from a TV

● FIGURE 8-1

Here's what an actual radio script looks like. This one also provides a wonderful example of how sounds can be used to bring an idea to life. Notice how the sound effects are capitalized and underscored for quick identification. And as in all ads in all media, notice how the spot wraps with a restatement of the theme line.

RENT.NET
:60 Radio
"Vampires"

SFX: COFFIN CREAKS OPEN. SPOOKY MUSIC BEGINS TO PLAY, THEN FADES UNDER.

VAMPIRE 1: Hey! What are ya doing?! You know we can't go out in the daylight! Vampire Code 6!

VAMPIRE 2: Relax! I'm just trying to find us a new apartment . . . Maybe a *nicer* one?!

SFX:DRIPPING FAUCET

VAMPIRE 1: I'm tellin' ya—this is the only place where the landlady would meet us *after dark!*

VAMPIRE 2 (sarcastically): Yeah! Crazy ol' bat!

VAMPIRE 1 (nervously): But anyway, you can't do this NOW! I mean, how you gonna get a newspaper out there in the sunlight! You can't go out there, man!

VAMPIRE 2: Relax! I'm using rent.net!

SFX: MODEM DIALING IN

VAMPIRE 1: What?!

VAMPIRE 2 (exasperated): Have you been living in a cave? Rent.net! It's the most comprehensive rental guide on the net! We can search for an apartment right here online by city, number of bedrooms—we can even choose our price range and view photos and check out the apartment's amenities!

VAMPIRE 1: Oh! Hey—do a search for a place that allows pets—you know those juicy little, uh, I mean cute little puppies!

VAMPIRE 2 (typing): You're sick man, really sick . . .

VAMPIRE 1: Hey a vampire's gotta eat!

ANNCR: Rent.net—the easiest way to find a new apartment in any city. Find your new home without leaving the . . . (SFX: CREEPY APARTMENT NOISES) . . . *comfort* of yours.

commercial on the radio. Remember, radio is unique. Your eyes don't see the message; your mind does.

Some copy that works in print sounds absolutely dreadful when read out loud. For example, a radio commercial sent a powerful message about the problem of child abuse. The sound of an abused child's blood-curdling scream sent chills down listeners' spines. But the mood was blown when the announcer read the line; "Kids. You can't beat them." While the line may have worked as part of the logo in a print ad, it was too cute when read out loud.

3. *Make sure you're really funny if you use humor.* Humor is one of the most effective and popular devices in radio commercials, yet it's also one of the hardest things to do well. (Refer to Chapter 1 for guidelines for using humor.) The following commercial for Ant-Stop Orthene Fire-Ant Killer from Ortho used an announcer with a serious voice:

ANNCR:	Fire ants are not lovable.
	People do no want fire-ant plush toys.
	They aren't cuddly; they don't do little tricks. They just bite you and leave red, stinging welts that make you want to cry.
	That's why they have to die.
	And they have to die right now.
	You don't want them to have a long, lingering illness. You want death. A quick, excruciating, see-you-in-hell kind of death.
	You don't want to lug a bag of chemicals and a garden hose around the yard; it takes too long. And baits can take up to a week.
	No, my friend, what you want is Ant-Stop Orthene Fire-Ant Killer from Ortho.
	You put two teaspoons of Ant-Stop around the house and you're done. You don't even water it in. The scout ants bring it back into the mound.
	And this is the really good part. Everybody dies. Even the queen; it's that fast.
	And that's good. Because killing fire ants shouldn't be a full-time job—even if it is pretty fun.
	Ant-Stop Orthene Fire-Ant Killer from Ortho. Kick fire-ant butt!

4. *Repeat the name of your client.* You can't show the product's package or product logo as you can in print and television. Instead, you need to incorporate it into your overall message. As a general rule, try to state your client's name at least three times. The trick, of course, is to do it without being obnoxious.

5. *Avoid numbers.* Very few people (if any) are sitting next to the radio with a pen and pad in hand, just waiting for you to give them an important number. So avoid numbers if you can. If you have to give a phone number, spell it out as a word. It's

much easier to remember the American Red Cross's phone number as "1-800-HELP-NOW" than it is to remember a bunch of numbers. And if you need to include a street address, put it in terms your listeners can visualize. Instead of "17349 Main Street," say, "On the corner of Main and Green Street" or "On Main Street, across from City Hall."

6. *Make it simple and direct.* A commercial that tries to do too much is confusing. A good spot must capture and hold attention, develop and resolve the concept, and also sell the product.

7. *Give your campaign variety.* A commercial can become familiar very quickly, so it's important to develop a number of spots for the campaign.

8. *Be aware of time considerations.* As a rule of thumb, about two words per second is a good place to start when timing your script. You can go as high as 135 words in a 60-second commercial and 75 words in a 30-second commercial. Adding more words can work against you by forcing performers to rush through your lines with little time for those pauses and special inflections that add color, clarity, and depth to the spoken word. Also, you should come to the studio prepared to cut and revise if the spot runs long. Mark potential cuts beforehand to save time and money.

● Approaches to Radio Commercials

However you structure your radio script, remember to begin with an attention-getting opening. The lead-in must lure the listener into hearing what follows. Generally, it's a good idea to have an announcer drive home the key selling idea at the end. Think of the announcer as the voice of the advertiser, while character voices in the rest of the spot should sound like genuine people, or exaggerations of them.

One Voice

Make the voice interesting and relevant. Make the words exceptional. You might add music or sounds, or you might choose to let the voice "speak for itself." The following spot for Ricoh cameras demonstrates how effective one voice can be. It was written by Jackie Eng of Chiat/Day, New York, and produced by Pat Faw at Doppler Recording, Atlanta:

ANNCR: A couple of weeks ago I bought myself a Ricoh 35mm Auto-Focus camera.

And I take out the instruction folder and it says, "It's the camera that thinks."

So I think about this, you know, and I realize it's true. When you're taking a picture with a Ricoh, it's thinking about the right exposure; it's thinking about the right focus, thinking about the film speed. It's thinking about all the things that give you a terrific picture.

But let me ask you this . . .

What do you think a Ricoh camera thinks about when it isn't taking pictures? Does it wonder if you're gonna keep it for yourself or give it away for Christmas? Does it believe in Santa Claus? Does it think you believe in Santa Claus? Do you? When it thinks, does it think in Japanese?

Does it dream? And, if so, does it dream in color or black and white? Or does that depend on the film you're using? Does it worry about being dropped? I would.

Does it think you've got a screw loose thinking about all this? Think about it. . . .

The previous spot is an example of one-voice exposition, in which the announcer speaks directly to the listener. Another approach is one-voice internal dialog, which sounds like we're listening in on someone's private thoughts. Here's an example:

SFX:	SOUND OF WRITING
WOMAN:	Dear Tom. I completely understand why you stood me up last night. You're too good for me. How could I ever expect to hang on to a guy like you? After all, those hair transplants are really starting to take hold, and the dime size bulbs on your forehead are barely noticeable now. You're quite a catch. So what if you're 36 and still live with your mom. I was just lucky you asked me out in the first place. Well, I could write a lot more, but I'm running out of lipstick and there's no more room left on your windshield.
ANNCR:	If you ever need a squeegee, remember at Unocal 76 you can always find one waiting in clean, soapy water. 76. We get it.

Dialog

Two people talking. Sounds simple, doesn't it? But be careful. It's easy to fall into the trap of putting dull words into the mouths of dull characters, especially when you introduce product features into the conversation. Never say anything like, "Edna, this new detergent has a water-soluble bleaching agent that seeps through dirt to render fabrics brighter than ever!" That isn't Edna talking—that's the advertiser putting words in her mouth, and everyone will know it.

How do you make the dialog sound real while still getting across a selling message? Use the dialog to set the stage, and let the announcer do the selling. Try this one from TBWA, New York, written for Carlsberg beer by Jeff Epstein and produced by Ed Pollack at 12 East Recording, New York:

SHE:	Honey?
HE:	Yes, Precious.
SHE:	I have a confession, Dearest.
HE:	What, Buttercup?
SHE:	You know the clock in the hall?
HE:	The 17th-century fruitwood grandfather clock?

SHE: I knocked it over.

HE: Not to worry, Lambykins.

SHE: Oh, Porkchop, you're so understanding.

HE: It's only money.

SHE: Sweet Pea?

HE: Yes.

SHE: You know the rug in the den?

HE: The leopard skin throw in my study?

SHE: Well, when I shampooed it, the spots came out.

HE: Don't worry your pretty little head.

SHE: I'm so relieved.

HE: What's mine is yours.

SHE: Cream Puff?

HE: Yes, Marshmallow?

SHE: You know those cigars in the fridge?

HE: The hand-rolled Hondurans?

SHE: They got wet.

HE: Pray tell how, Carrot Stick?

SHE: Well, when I moved the Carlsberg beer in the . . .

HE   (interrupting): I told you not to touch my Carlsberg.

SHE: Cucumber.

HE: Just have your lawyer call my lawyer in the morning . . .
            Sugar . . . Plum.

ANNCR: Carlsberg beer. The imported taste that can't be touched.

            Carlsberg Breweries, Copenhagen, Denmark.

Multivoice   A number of voices speak, not to one another but to the listener. A commercial for AIDS awareness used a variety of voices to make young people aware of the number of misconceptions about the disease and its victims. For this spot, college students were asked to speak candidly about their chances of getting AIDS. The producers edited small sound bites from each of the participants:

VOICE 1: It can't happen to me . . .

VOICE 2: There's *no way* he's got it.

VOICE 3: You can't get it from a girl . . .

VOICE 4: Isn't there already a cure?

VOICE 5: I know *she* doesn't have it . . .

VOICE 6: I just want to have fun.

VOICE 7:   But I'm not gay.

VOICE 8:   I hope it doesn't happen to me.

A message about AIDS was read by an announcer and appeared within the commercial.

Dramatization   A dramatization uses the structure of a play, with a beginning, a conflict, and a resolution. You can use sound effects and several voices to act out the story. Or you can use a narrator to tell the entire story.

Sound Device   With this approach, a sound or sounds are used repeatedly or intermittently to make the main point. For example, in one ad you can hear someone trying to start a car. The engine goes, "EEEERRRRR . . . EEEERRRRR . . . EEEERRRRR." As the person continues to try to start the car, it sounds weaker and weaker. "Eeeerrrrr . . . eeeerrrrr . . . eeeerrrrr." The sound of military taps fades in as the sound of the engine fades out. The battery finally dies. A voice-over announces that Sears is having a sale on DieHard batteries.

Sometimes music is used as a sound effect. For example, one spot opens to the sound of a man singing in the shower. His voice is dreadful—but he keeps on singing, and singing. You can't imagine what's going on until an announcer interrupts and asks, "Think this has gone on long enough? So do we. Take shorter showers and save water."

Vignette   A vignette is a series of short situations linked by a repeated device (announcer line, musical bridge, sound effect, etc.). After the first vignette makes the point, the ensuing situations need not be as long. An announcer usually wraps up the spot near the end, followed by a quick closing vignette. To illustrate, here's a portion of the commercial for George Schlatter's Comedy Club:

ANNCR: Number 17. The chuckle.

SFX: <u>MAN CHUCKLING.</u>

ANNCR: Number 22. The giggle.

SFX: <u>WOMAN GIGGLING.</u>

ANNCR: Number 56. The snort.

SFX: <u>WOMAN SNORTING WHILE LAUGHING</u>

ANNCR: Number 61. The nasal burst.

SFX: <u>MAN LAUGHING THROUGH HIS NOSE.</u>

Interviews   With this approach, someone is interviewing someone, or groups of people, somewhere—on a busy street, at the North Pole, in outer space. In one spot, the interview takes place under a house where the interviewer talks to two termites as they casually chew up the wood subflooring.

Jingles   David Ogilvy said, "When you have nothing to say, sing it." Not everyone agrees with that, however. A catchy jingle can make a lasting impression in our minds. For example, there's a good chance you can sing the lyrics to "Oh, I wish I were an Oscar Mayer weiner . . ." and "Hot dogs, Armour hot dogs, what kind of kids eat Armour hot dogs?"

Most copywriters are not lyricists or composers, so you'll probably want a professional songwriter to develop the jingle. But you'll need to supply the songwriter with your key selling point and the attitude you want to convey (upbeat, sexy, whimsical, etc.).

● Radio Script Format

Like all copy, a radio script begins with a tag in the upper left-hand corner (see Figure 8-1). In this instance, you should indicate on the second line, after the timing, whether the spot is a fact sheet or live announcer copy, or if it is to be produced.

Notice the designation for a sound effect: SFX. This is capitalized and underscored, along with the entire sound-effect direction, to alert the producer to the effect and its position within the script. For the same reason, all effects are entered on a separate line. If the effect should come in the middle of a line of dialog, use ellipses (. . .) to break from the first part of the line, drop to a new line for the SFX, and then continue the dialog on the following line with additional ellipses at the beginning to indicate resumption of the dialog. All radio copy should be double-spaced to facilitate reading and should leave room for notes and alterations during production. The names of speakers should be typed in capital letters and followed by a colon. Any directions to the speaker should be enclosed in parentheses after the speaker's name.

Music is simply another type of sound effect and should be treated as such. If a commercial is to begin with music, which is then to fade under the speakers (play softly in the background), a direction might read like this:

SFX: HARP INSTRUMENTAL (5 SEC) AND FADE UNDER.

TIM: Sometimes late at night, when you wish you could talk to a special voice far away, it's nice to know long distance rates are lower after 11 P.M.

If the music is to disappear at some point, you should indicate this through another sound-effect cue.

SFX: MUSIC OUT.

TIM: Because when you can pick up the phone . . .

SFX: CLICK OF RECEIVER.

TIM: . . . and dial your favorite person thousands of miles away. . . .

Often, especially if your commercial consists of a conversation between two or more people, you may want to wrap up the message by bringing in an authoritative announcer (ANNCR) at the very end. This is a good way to bring your audience back to earth (especially if you've been treating the subject with humor) and to reinforce what you want remembered about your message.

Checklist for
Radio Copy

✓ Did you restate your strategy in one sentence?

✓ Is the major premise repeated? Does the spot end with it?

✓ Is the structure appropriate for the message?

✓ Does humor detract from the product message?

✓ Are voices, music, and sounds described clearly?

✓ If you used copyrighted music, is it essential, affordable, and available?

✓ Do music or sound effects drown out the selling message?

✓ Is there sufficient time for comfortable, believable delivery of the lines?

✓ Is there time for all sound effects and musical bridges?

✓ Does the commercial time correctly?

✓ Is brand recognition achieved through mention of the brand, music, or sounds that trigger awareness?

Radio is fun and challenging at the same time. As with all advertising copy, it isn't always easy to find the best solution. But when you hear your commercial in finished form, you'll know if it's right. A well-written, well-produced radio spot can have a tremendous impact on its target audience.

● Suggested Activities

1. Using the campaign theme from your print ads, write a radio commercial for the same product or service. Write it as if it were to be produced. Note as you are doing this that merely paraphrasing the text from a print ad may not work because of the essential differences between the media. What sort of voices will work best for your message? What will be the appropriate tone? These are but a few of the new issues you need to consider.

2. Visit a local business establishment and interview the person in charge. Devise a creative strategy for this business, indicating how radio might be used. Cover approaches, target audience, mood, and expected results. Then write two or three radio spots based on your strategy, and tie them together using a specific theme or device.

3. Listen to a different radio station every day for the next week. Make mental notes of the types of commercials you hear on each station. Did you learn anything? What did you learn?

4. Practice your editing skills. Take the following print copy for the Mitsubishi Home Theater, and rewrite it so it makes a powerful 60-second radio commercial:

The insane laughter faded away behind me. To one side of the clearing sat a deserted house, as decomposed and forgotten as the people who once lived there. The door opened, and I was in the front room, a room so dark I felt I could reach out and run my fingers through its inky stillness.

From outside the window came the sounds of the night. Owls. Crickets. And from across the room . . . drip, drip, drip. My eyes, adjusting to the light, made out what appeared to be a coat hanging from a hat rack, but as the haze dissolved from my sight I saw that from the neck of the coat stared the lifeless face of Kuperman, his eyes frozen in horror. A shrieking laugh, as inescapable as a nightmare, rang out around me.

My heart, already shaking at the cage of my chest, exploded as a hand fell upon my shoulder. "So how do you like the Mitsubishi Home Theater's surround sound?" asked the sales guy. "Uhhh, great," I said as I stumbled to the door of the showroom for a breath of fresh air.

 Search Online! Discovering More About Radio Commercials

Using InfoTrac® College Edition, try these phrases and others for Key Words and Subject Guide searches: *radio commercials, radio commercial format, radio audiences, radio + visuals, theater of the mind, sound effects, mood music, writing for the ear, humor + radio, vignette, classic radio commercials.*

BriefCase

Seeing the Light: Tom Bodett Sells
Affordability and Comfort for Motel 6

Motel 6 helped define the budget motel sector when it opened its first property in Santa Barbara, California, in 1962. Its "no-frills" concept (no telephone, no television, just a clean, comfortable room) offered a cheap alternative to the pricey full-service hotels that then dominated the market.

In 1986, to avoid getting lost in the clutter of low-budget motels and to stay within a limited advertising budget, the chain's advertising agency recommended radio as the exclusive medium for its relatively low cost and potential reach.

Then came two happy accidents.

As Tom Bodett tells it, David Fowler, a creative director from the Richards Group advertising agency in Dallas was driving down the Dallas Parkway in his pickup truck listening to public radio. Suddenly, a down-home monolog emerged from his dusty dashboard. He heard the name Tom Bodett and thought, "If only I had an account for a national budget motel with a sense of humor and humility. I could make a heck of an advertising campaign with this guy."

Soon, Bodett was recording a series of commercials for Motel 6. When he finished his folksy monolog, there was still a smidgen of time left on the tape. So he smoothly chipped in, "We'll leave the light on for you."

And the rest is history. Bodett's laid-back style and sincere delivery have made him and Motel 6 household words. "Look for a Motel 6 wherever you're going," says Bodett, "unless it's in Pinball, Idaho. There's no Motel 6 there, so you may have to stay with relatives. If you're headed there, you're on the couch, pal."

In 1999, Bodett and the agency introduced a twist to the famous tag line. Bodett now asks visitors, "When did you first see the light?" The new campaign is designed to dispel any notion that economy-class Motel 6 attracts disreputable guests. "We're trying to portray that you won't just be comfortable in the rooms, you'll be comfortable with the people next door," said Rod Underhill, a principal at the Richards Group.

The Richards Group, Dallas, creators of the Motel 6 campaign, have won numerous awards for their work. But perhaps the most meaningful award is the dramatic rise in Motel 6 revenues, which grew 283 percent between 1986, the year the campaign began, and 1998.

Here is a small sample of how Bodett works his magic to create a warm, friendly image for Motel 6, and how the updated "see the light" theme becomes an integral part of each script. Each of the three scripts is 30 seconds long.

MUSIC:	(MOTEL 6 THEME UNDER THROUGHOUT)
TOM:	Hi, Tom Bodett for Motel 6. You know Blind Cave Salamanders never see the light. Course, they also end up with transparent skin and dark holes instead of eyeballs—plus they're kinda sticky. And you don't want that do ya? So c'mon and see the light, save your money and your skin. Call 1-800-4-MOTEL-6, and we'll leave the light on for you.
MUSIC:	(MOTEL 6 THEME UNDER THROUGHOUT)
TOM:	Hi, Tom Bodett for Motel 6. When you see the Northern Lights, you're witnessing the highly charged ionosphere being bombarded by solar winds. Boy it's pretty. But when you see the light at Motel 6, that means you won't ever be bombarded by highly charged room rates. Boy it's pretty too, pretty . . . smart. Call 1-800-4-MOTEL-6, and we'll leave the light on for you.
MUSIC:	(MOTEL 6 THEME UNDER THROUGHOUT)
TOM:	Hi, Tom Bodett for Motel 6. You know when you see that light that lingers in your eyeballs after somebody takes your picture? Well, that's bad. You know that money that lingers in your pocket after you see the light at Motel 6? Well, that's good. Be good. See the light. Let it linger. Call 1-800-4-MOTEL-6, and we'll leave the light on for you.

COURTESY TOM BODETT

CHAPTER 9

Working in Television

In Alfred Hitchcock's classic 1959 thriller, *North by Northwest,* there's a 14-minute scene that's a self-contained movie-within-a-movie. Using the barest amount of dialog, the 15 minutes elapse with a story made unmistakably clear through the careful actions, sounds, camera angles, and editing of the legendary director. It goes something like this:

1. We open on an extreme long shot, aerial view, of the middle of nowhere: a dusty crossroads on the prairie. A bus rolls into the frame, stops, deposits a passenger, and drives off.

2. We cut to a medium shot of our hero, Thornhill, who has just left the bus. In the previous scene, we learned he was to travel to this spot alone and wait for a man named Kaplan. He looks around.

3. Through a succession of crosscuts between Thornhill and point-of-view shots showing what he's seeing, we realize his frustration that no one is in sight.

4. We cut back and forth as he watches; then we see what he's watching: cars whizzing by. No Kaplan.

5. Soon he looks toward the camera. We cut to what he sees: a long shot of a car just coming out of a dirt road onto the main highway across from where he's standing.

6. The car drops a man off and heads back where it came from.

7. Thornhill stares at the man.

8. The man halfheartedly stares at Thornhill.

9. Thornhill begins crossing the road toward the man as the camera dollies to parallel his movement.

10. We cut to what Thornhill sees as he crosses: the camera moves closer and closer to the stranger.

Once Thornhill discovers the man isn't Kaplan, he's left alone again as the man boards an arriving bus. The rest of the scene takes us through a harrowing episode in which a crop-dusting airplane begins firing shots and spraying insecticide at Thornhill. The scene culminates in a fiery crash when the out-of-control plane smashes into an oil truck.

What has all this to do with writing television commercials? Everything. Although the scene runs for about 14 minutes, and your commercial will probably run no more than 30 seconds, one thing both have in common is the use of film "language" to tell a story. Rent the video *North by Northwest,* and watch the scene (watch the whole film; it's terrific!) after reading the visual description at the beginning of this chapter. You'll begin to see why the director chose those shots and how they are connected to one another to heighten the impact of the story. In a commercial, you can do the same.

● A Meaningful Message for Business Travelers[1]

In a United Airlines television commercial, a group of businesspeople are getting a pep talk from their supervisor about the way they've been doing business. "I got a phone call this morning from one of our oldest customers," says the supervisor. "Over twenty years. He fired us. Said he didn't know us anymore. We used to do business face-to-face. Now it's a phone call and a fax and get back to you later. Probably with another phone call or fax."

Then he reveals that he's sending the entire sales force out for face-to-face chats with every customer they have. "But that's over 200 cities," whines one man. Then comes the clincher. The supervisor hands out United Airlines tickets to all and tells his crew that he's going to personally call on the guy who fired them that morning. Although the spot clearly shows the United logo on the ticket envelopes, this is one airline commercial that shows no planes, inside or out.

Bud Watts adds: The client said,

> "Demonstrate United's scope in a manner that will be meaningful to the business traveler."

[1]Thanks to Bud Watts, executive vice president, group creative director, Leo Burnett Company, Inc.

We said to ourselves, of course, fine. But just telling people United flies to a lot of places won't do the job. We need to cut through. Get people's attention. So, using modern-day business methods as the theme, an idea came: the growing popularity of doing business solely electronically and how that can fail you.

There will never be a substitute for a face-to-face with a client or business associate. That's the idea.

Face to face, that's real solid ground—and it worked.

The story starts with a shocker, then empathetically drives home the idea and finishes with a real "Knute Rockne" tug.

The spot was a tremendous success for United. It demonstrated the airline's understanding of business fliers and the realities of business.

Visual storytelling began when silent movies were born. Though movies, TV shows, music videos, and commercials now "talk" and make sounds and music, it's what we see that we remember most. And when we have 30 seconds or less to leave a lasting visual impression, we must make every second count.

● Getting Ready to Write Ads for TV

For the copywriter–art director team, it's especially important to remember this: While the bag of computer-generated, interactive, digital tricks is growing almost daily, be careful. If it furthers the strategy, use it. If it doesn't, don't. When you have no more than 30 seconds to make an impression, strategy is where the television commercial begins.

If writing for television seems awkward to you, that's normal. All your life, you've learned to tell stories using words. Now you must shift to images, with the words emerging as a natural outgrowth of those images. Try writing the words first, and you may end up, not with a television commercial, but with a radio commercial with pictures. And there's a big difference.

Watching TV Commercials with a Critical Eye and Ear

If you think about it, you'll probably realize that the commercials you remember are few and far between. What makes you forget most commercials, and what makes you remember those rare gems? Sit down in front of the TV and start watching commercials. Watch at least ten. For each commercial, jot down answers to the following questions:

1. What was the single central message or idea?

2. What was the value of the opening shot with respect to that idea?

3. Did you get involved with the commercial? If so, at what point did it happen?

4. To what extent did the pictures, as opposed to the words, tell the story?

5. Were the words redundant, or did they add something? What did they add?

6. Were interesting, exciting, complicated, beautiful visuals on screen long enough for complete understanding or appreciation? Were dull, static visuals on too long? How would you make them better?

7. Was the story an irrelevant attention-getter, or was the product an integral part of the story?

8. Did you enjoy the story? Did you believe it or find some other value in it? Or was it unrelated to the product story and just there to make you watch?

9. Afterwards, could you say why you should care about the product or service in a sentence?

Questions to Ask Yourself Before You Write

Before you actually write a commercial, you need to answer these questions:

1. *What's the big idea you need to get across?* In 30 seconds, you'll barely have time to do much more than that. For Bell Helmets, everything in each commercial (sound-less shots of bikers flipping and crashing as a lone whistler is heard on the sound-track) suggests that when bikers' heads are protected they can be cool about riding.

2. *What's the benefit of that big idea, and whom does it benefit?* Now, in addition to thinking about what your target audience will want to hear, you need to think about what they'll be interested in seeing.

3. *How can you turn that benefit into a visual element that will stick in the viewer's mind?* The intrusive Bell Helmets signature at the end of each commercial merges movement, visuals, and sounds to deliver the main message. As a full-screen "Bell Helmets" tag line appears when the announcer voices the name, a huge helmet descends with a whoosh over a model of the human brain. The chin strap locks with a powerful click. The words "courage for your head" are voiced and seen at the same time. Prior footage includes pictures and full-screen titles that, in their whimsical way, take potentially disastrous situations, add self-deprecating humor, and make the whole thing work. You sweat, then you smile, and then you agree: With a Bell Helmet on your head, you can enjoy this sport to the fullest with fewer risks.

From Visual to Script

Now, taking that visual, how can you write a scenario that takes the story to its logical conclusion? Here are some tips:

1. *At this point, just use narrative to tell the story:* "We open with a guy flipping on his bike in grainy, slow motion. We follow with other shots of guys who look like they're hell-bent on a path of self-destruction. We intercut titles to let the viewer know there's something more here than meets the eye. Whatever we put on the titles tells a continuous story that leads to our tag, 'Bell Helmets. Courage for Your Head.'"

● FIGURE 9-1

Note that it's more what you see than what you hear in this script. And rightly so. This is television, where most good commercial ideas begin with the pictures, adding words and sounds to fortify the visual images. Each number on the left moves the visual story forward—title shots included. The audio on the right simply calls for a soft, easy whistling, which makes a surprising contrast to the mayhem on the screen. At the all-important close, the theme line literally wraps things up with a startling graphic along with sounds that bring the whole idea of "courage for your head" to a memorable finale.

Bell Helmets

:30 TV

"Reason"

1. (GRAINY FOOTAGE THROUGHOUT) LS CAR CRASHING ON TRACK.	SFX: SOFT WHISTLING THROUGHOUT. NO OTHER NOISES.
2. LS GUY WEARING HELMET FLIPPING OFF BIKE.	
3. TITLE (WHITE ON BLACK): "HUMANS ARE THE ONLY SPECIES"	
4. LS GUY IN HELMET FLYING THROUGH THE AIR AS HE LEAVES BIKE.	
5. TITLE (WHITE ON BLACK): "WITH THE ABILITY TO REASON"	
6. LS SHOTS OF VARIOUS OTHER CRASH SITUATIONS.	
7. TITLE (WHITE ON BLACK): "AND SOMETIMES"	
8. GUY CRASHES BIKE FLIPPING OVER IN MIDAIR IN THE PROCESS.	
9. TITLE (WHITE ON BLACK): "THEY EVEN USE IT."	
10. CUT TO FULL SCREEN BELL HELMETS LOGO.	ANNCR (VO): Bell Helmets.
11. CUT TO REVOLVING "BRAIN." HELMET WRAPS AROUND IT.	SFX: WHOOSH OF HELMET COVERING HEAD, CHIN STRAP LOCKING TIGHT
12. CUT TO TITLE: "COURAGE FOR YOUR HEAD."	ANNCR (VO): Courage for your head.

2. Once you're happy with the scenario, put it in script form. (See Figure 9-1 and the instructions later in this chapter.)

3. *Read the script out loud, and listen carefully.* Check for timing, clarity, and continuity. (Do the words and pictures follow a logical sequence?) Check for product identity. (Is the product "buried" by needless overproduction or story exposition?) Have you essentially confined your story to one major point? If not, try again.

4. *Revise. Revise. Revise.* Make sure it's not too long. Then ask yourself the following questions: How well does the opening shot command the attention of the viewer? How much does the opening relate to the main idea of the message? How well does the closing reinforce the main idea and drive home the point? How much time is spent on the product? How visual is the idea? Try telling the story in pictures only, leaving out the words, and see whether it still makes sense.

5. *Finalize.* Once you have a script, prepare your storyboard. (See Figures 9-2 and 9-3 and the accompanying instructions.)

● Formats for Television Commercials

As with other types of advertising, the best way to begin thinking about a television commercial is to immerse yourself in facts and ideas about the product. Only then do you start writing. If nothing happens, these suggestions can get you jump-started:

- *Demonstration.* Television can show what the product can do better than any other medium. Here are some examples:

  Product-in-use: A man swipes shoe polish on his handkerchief and cleans it by shaking it in a cocktail shaker filled with ice and a little bit of brand X laundry detergent.

  Before-and-after: A guy who looks to be about 100 years old shampoos some coloring into his hair. Presto! He's 35. (Okay, we admit we're exaggerating a bit, but you get the idea.)

  Side-by-side: Two identical battery-operated toys are entertaining the viewer. One of the toys dies, while the toy with brand X batteries keeps working.

- *Product as star.* A can of car wax dominates every scene, becoming a character in the commercial. The can is rained on, spattered with mud, frozen in snow and ice. At the end, the sun comes up, and a hand wipes the can shiny clean.

- *Speaker in an interesting location.* A narrator walks through a car factory as robots stamp out parts. A glamorous star tells us how to stay slim as she wanders past gorgeous bodies sunbathing by a pool.

- *Vignette.* Several brief episodes are threaded together to drive home the same point over and over. Each episode usually involves different people at different places, but they all say something relevant to the product story. For example, an ad for Viagra shows an older couple waltzing, a young woman sitting on the lap of her lover who's in a wheelchair, and a middle-aged woman embracing her husband.

- *Slice of life.* The star of the commercial has a problem, and brand X is the solution. For example, a Swedish commercial shows beautiful people at a wedding. The bride and groom walk up a staircase and wave goodbye to their wedding guests. The guests wave back, and some blow kisses. The groom lifts the bride to carry her over the threshold and . . . THUD! The bride's head hits the doorway as the groom tries to carry her through, and he drops her. The camera cuts to a close-up of two pills being plopped into water. The groom drinks the remedy, and a voice-over says, "Headaches can suddenly appear. Treo gives quick and effective relief."

- *Presenters.* Someone looks into the camera and tells you why you should buy the product. It could be an expert, such as a nurse who recommends a certain brand of painkiller. Or a person associated with the company, such as Dave Thomas from Wendy's. Or a made-up character, such as the "Where's the beef?" lady. Or an animated character, such as Charlie the Tuna or Tony the Tiger. Or a celebrity who looks cool using your product (or any product, for that matter—refer back to Chapter 1 for guidelines for using celebrities).

- *Testimonials.* "Hey, I use this product. So should you." Testimonials must be true. They must be based on real experiences of real people and be supported by facts. Remember, just because a person says something on camera doesn't make it true.

- *Stories.* Think of them as 30-second television shows. For example, in one ad, a boy spots an attractive girl in class. He passes her a note that says, "I love you. Do you love me?" There are two boxes ("Yes" and "No") for her to check off her answer. The girl looks at him, scribbles her answer, and passes the note back. He opens it. The answer is no! He hangs his head. When he looks up, he spots another cute girl. He erases the "no" and passes her the note. The tag line appears on the screen: "You're never too young to start recycling. Weyerhaeuser."

● Camera Shots, Camera Moves, and Transitions

Camera Shots

How many shots should you use in 30 seconds? It all depends on the story you want to tell and the best way to tell it. Each shot, however, should fulfill a specific need. Here are the basic shots to know.

ECU or extreme close-up In this shot, you get as close as you can and still show what needs showing: part of a face, a detail on a product. The ECU permits a bigger-than-life glimpse that can be used to dramatic advantage to further your story.

CU or close-up In this shot, a face fills the screen, or a product stands tall, commanding your attention. Early moviemakers such as D. W. Griffith invented this way of magnifying the emotional communication of the moving image, in part to compensate for the absence of sound. And it's still a powerful way to provide visual emphasis. The CU contains no distractions; it shows only what you want the viewer to see. When we're this close, however, we rarely know where the action is taking place. So the choice of a CU or a wider view depends on the purpose of the shot.

MS or medium shot In this shot, one can identify location to some degree, although the camera is focused on something more specific. A typical MS shows two people, from the waist up, engaged in dialog (also called a 2-shot, because it covers two people). Much action is shown in MS as an ideal compromise in framing action. When a CU reveals too little and a long shot (LS) is too unfocused, the answer usually lies somewhere in between.

LS or long shot Also known as an establishing shot, the LS broadly covers an area, revealing instantly where we are—flying in the clouds, working in the kitchen, exercising in the gym. Use an LS to open a commercial if your audience needs to know where it's taking place from the start. Or start with a CU to purposely hide the location until later. Again, it depends on the story you want to tell.

Camera Moves

Zoom in/out (dolly in/out) This involves a movement toward or away from the subject. In a zoom, the lens revolves to bring the image closer or to move it farther away. In a dolly, the camera actually moves forward or backward. A zoom is limited by the range of the lens, while a dolly is limited only by the imagination. Use either term in your script/storyboard, and allow the director to make the final decision.

Pan R/L (truck R/L) This involves a movement to the right or left. In a pan, the camera turns to one side or the other, or follows a moving object as it travels across the screen. In a trucking shot, the camera actually rolls sideways to follow, or keep alongside, the action—creating quite a different perspective than the pan.

Tilt U/D (boom or crane shot) In a tilt, the camera "looks" up or down—like a vertical version of the pan. In a boom or crane shot, the entire camera and cinematographer are hydraulically raised or lowered while film or tape rolls. A famous boom shot is *Gone with the Wind*'s dramatic pullback as Scarlett O'Hara wanders aimlessly through rows of wounded soldiers at the Atlanta train depot. The camera finds her, swoops majestically upward to suggest her insignificance amidst the thousands of casualties, and then comes to rest on a tattered Confederate flag. How many words do you think would be necessary to adequately relate what this single shot communicates?

Transitions

Like camera moves, transitions carry you from one point of action to another, but usually in less time. And when you have only 30 seconds, timing is critical.

Cut The cut is the most basic transition, and one you should rely on. A cut is an instantaneous change from one shot to another—for example, from a CU to an MS. One second we're seeing a CU, and then suddenly we "cut" to a MS. It's essential that the two shots make visual sense when run together and that they carry the action forward with purpose.

Dissolve The dissolve is a softer transition in which a second image slowly fades in and takes over as the original image fades away. A dissolve can suggest the passage of time, freeing the writer to skip chunks of time in a sequence to focus on the most important elements. You don't want to watch someone washing her hair for 5 minutes (impossible in 30 seconds!), so you dissolve from her shampooing to her putting the final touches on her hairdo. You can also use dissolves throughout a commercial to create a softer mood or to connect a series of shots unrelated in time and space, yet important in the telling of the story. (See the discussion of "compilation cutting" below.)

● Editing for Continuity

Editing, which should begin with the writing of the commercial script, can accomplish a number of things. It can condense time, extend time, or jumble time. To condense time, you might show a man unable to sleep at night, dissolve to him sleeping soundly, and then dissolve to the reason his sleep habits are better—the product, of course. To extend time, you might show a speeding train approaching a car, cut to the driver's frenzied expression, cut back to the train, cut back to the driver attempting to get out of the way, back to the train, and so on. Trains move fast, and people in the path of trains don't linger, but extending the action makes the sequence more dramatic and involving to viewers. To jumble time, you might cut from present to past in a flashback or even "flash forward" to an imagined scene in the future.

Methods of Cutting

Compilation cutting In this type of editing, the storytelling is dependent on the narration, usually voiced over the action, and each shot merely illustrates what is being said. The shots may be somewhat unrelated to each other, may occur in different places, or may consist of a series of different people or objects shot in similar fashion to one another.

Continuity cutting Here the storytelling depends on matching consecutive scenes without a narrator to explain what is happening. Action flows from one shot to the next. Various angles and cutaways may not even be part of the previous shot. For example, a conversation between two people may consist of a 2-shot, several close-ups of each speaker, another 2-shot, and a cutaway to something happening elsewhere in the building that is related to the action within the room.

Crosscutting Crosscutting combines two or more parallel actions in an alternating pattern. The actions may occur at the same time but in different places—as when we see a farmer driving a tractor, cut to his wife preparing dinner, cut back to the farmer, and cut again to the wife. The actions may also occur at different times in different places—as when scenes of a man enjoying a vigorous shower are intercut with shots of the same man at various times during the day to suggest that using the right soap helps him feel fresh for hours. (This was the idea behind a classic, long-running Dial Soap campaign.)

Crosscutting may also be used to suggest details of an action that occurs at one time in one place. For example, he runs toward her, she runs toward him, again he runs toward her, again she runs toward him, until—at last—we see both of them in one shot about to run into each other's arms. Their embrace is somehow more personal to us precisely because we've been watching their longing gazes for most of the commercial.

In one beer commercial, crosscutting makes us as thirsty as the man in the story. A bartender reaches for a frosty mug. A man leaves his office. The bartender begins to draw a draft. The man steps out of his building onto a busy street. The bartender has the mug almost topped off. The man walks down the street. The mug is filled. The man enters the bar. The bartender slides the draft down the polished bartop. The man reaches out and catches it just in time.

Point of View

Subjective versus objective While you won't always have to specify point of view, doing so often helps others understand your idea. Essentially, point of view is either objective or subjective. In the objective point of view (objective camera), the camera records the action from the viewpoint of an observer not involved in the action. Those on camera never look directly into the lens, as this would destroy the objective relationship between them and the viewer.

In the subjective point of view (subjective camera), the camera involves the viewer in the action by representing the point of view of a person in the scene. An actor rages at the camera, but we know he's angry, not with us, but at the guy who just punched him out in the previous shot. The camera itself becomes the punch-happy guy. In an experiment in subjective camera, a late 1940s feature film used this point of view exclusively. The main character was rarely seen, unless he happened to walk by a mirror. Punches were thrown at the camera and were usually followed by a blackout. A hand would reach from the camera to grab someone. The film was probably too odd for most tastes, but it did show the power of subjective camera. Note Ray Tom's storyboard in Figure 9-2 to see how subjective camera is used briefly.

Camera angle An eye-level camera angle presents a view as seen by most of us. A high-angle shot, looking down on the action, may be chosen because (1) it's the best way to say we're on, say, a football field; (2) it's a way to see something you couldn't see yourself, such as overhead shots of dance formations; or (3) it adds a psychological dimension to the story (looking down on something means we think little of it while looking up means we are in awe of it). Low-angle shots can add importance to a product. High-angle shots can make competitors seem somehow diminished.

Other Considerations

Here are some more guidelines for combining text and visuals:

1. *Specify voice-over (VO) prior to dialog when the words are to be "voiced over" as opposed to spoken on camera.* VO lines are usually recorded after footage is shot. They can also help others understand your concept in script/storyboard form.

2. *Use split screen sparingly.* It's been done before. But if you can use it imaginatively, by all means do so.

Abalone Vintage Guitars
:30 TV
"Rock the Cradle"

VIDEO:
OPEN ON LS BABY'S NURSERY

SFX: SOFT, SOOTHING LULLABY MUSIC IN BACKGROUND

VIDEO:
CUT TO CU DOORKNOB. IT SLOWLY BEGINS TO TURN.

SFX: SOUND OF KNOB TURNING QUIETLY.

VIDEO:
SLOW ZOOM OUT TO MS AS DOOR GENTLY OPENS. ATTRACTIVE YOUNG MOTHER PEERS IN ADORINGLY.

AUDIO:
ANNCR (VO): Some things in life are just more precious than others.

VIDEO:
CUT TO LS WOMAN WALKING ACROSS ROOM TO CRIB. PAN L TO FOLLOW HER.

AUDIO:
ANNCR (VO): And those things are worth all of your attention, every single moment . . .

● FIGURE 9-2

Raymond Tom's storyboard for Abalone Guitars not only uses an unexpected analogy but also explains what he plans to shoot. Here the right column is used for video and audio, with space between so there's no confusion. As in all good commercials, it's best to stick to one big idea. Thirty seconds doesn't give you enough time to do much more.

Abalone Vintage Guitars
:30 TV
"Rock the Cradle"

VIDEO:
CUT TO LOW ANGLE CU WOMAN FROM POV INSIDE CRIB. SHE SMILES ADORINGLY.

AUDIO:
ANNCR (VO): . . . 'cause it's one of a kind, and there's not another one like it in the whole wide world.

VIDEO:
CUT TO CU ELECTRIC GUITAR RESTING INSIDE CRIB. STUFFED TOYS SURROUND IT.

AUDIO:
SFX: ELECTRIC GUITAR JOINS LULLABY MUSIC.

VIDEO:
DISS TO LS WOMAN SITTING IN ROCKING CHAIR, PLAYING GUITAR WITH WILD ABANDON.

AUDIO:
ANNCR (VO): We've always been there for top recording artists . . . and we'll always be there for you, too.

VIDEO:
SUPER TITLE: ABALONE VINTAGE GUITARS. THE GUITAR AUTHORITY (ADDRESS/PHONE)

AUDIO:
ANNCR (VO): Abalone Vintage Guitars. The Guitar Authority.

3. *Use an "insert" or "matte" to place one image into another.* A tiny man walks on a giant menu, pointing out the special entrees. A product is inserted over action in the closing shot to help you remember what it looks like.

4. *Use a supertitle to place words over the action on a screen.* Supertitles are most effective when they are also voiced, with the oral message matching the written words exactly.

Getting It on Paper: The TV Script

Look at the script for the Bell Helmets commercial in Figure 9-1. The idea behind the whole campaign (see the BriefCase in Chapter 1), remember, was to show that a quality helmet like Bell gives you more courage to enjoy your sport. Here's how the TV script guides readers through the idea.

First, "scenes" are numbered down the left side of the page to guide us through the action. Scene 3 is a title, as are scenes 5, 7, 9, and 12. The words of the titles appear exactly as they will in the finished commercial, so we know and understand the point of the whole thing. Everything on the left side is "video," or what we will see. Everything on the right side is "audio," or what we will hear. The audio and video are aligned so that we know how they relate to each other.

As in radio, we use "SFX" to denote music and other sounds. And we underline all SFX directions for clarity. Since all we hear in this commercial is that cool whistling, the right side is blank till we get to scene 10. Then the announcer voices the words "Bell Helmets" over a full-screen logo. The sound of a whoosh (more like the squish of a brain about to be protected), followed by a locking sound as the chin strap snaps together, is simultaneous with the action in scene 11. Finally, the announcer voices "Courage for your head" as the exact same words appear in the supertitle on the screen.

Making It Clear: The TV Storyboard

In Figure 9-2, notice how Ray Tom suggests that a certain guitar shop in town understands what your guitar means to you and how the frames help you understand more fully what the finished spot is meant to be. In storyboard format, the right-hand side contains both video and audio directions, with audio running beneath video. Leave space between the two to make things clear.

Tom opens with a LS to let us know we're in a nursery. He cuts to a CU of a doorknob turning. He's confident we'll know that it's in the same room (and that the baby isn't opening it!). He zooms in to an MS as a young mom peeks in adoringly. He cuts to a LS as she walks toward the crib, panning right to follow her. He cuts to a point-of-view (from baby's view) CU of the woman's face as she smiles with love and pride. Now comes the shock as we see what she's beaming at in a reverse point-of-view shot; it's not her baby, it's her guitar! A dissolve allows us to accept that she's been enjoying her performance for some time, while a supertitle reminds us where to go if we're hankering for a new guitar or a repair on our present one.

In sketching frames, indicate zooms, pans, and tilts, as well as the movement of things or people by using arrows (see Figure 9-3). To save frames, draw a smaller frame within the full frame to show zooms. Keep the number of frames conservative, but don't leave out important actions, transitions, or other significant moments.

● TV Production

Once the client approves a commercial for production, the agency normally seeks competitive bids from a number of sources. A copy of the storyboard is sent as the basis for the bid, along with production notes that cover all aspects of the commercial not specified in the storyboard. Production notes describe in detail casting preferences, wardrobe considerations, sets to be built, special effects needed, specific sizes and packages of the product to be photographed, and other aspects of production. It's also a good idea to discuss the strategy of the campaign with the production house to further clarify the purpose of the commercial.

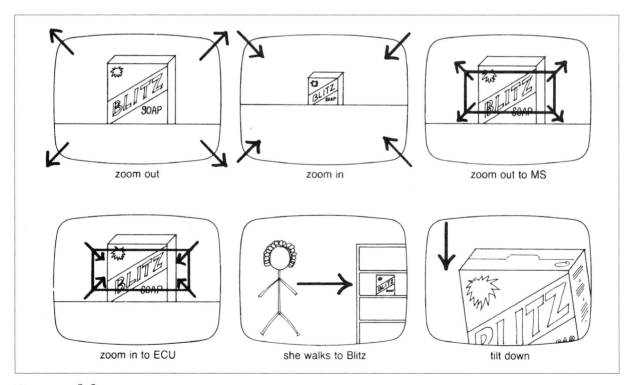

● FIGURE 9-3

Using arrows will help others understand what is happening in your storyboard.

Once the agency accepts a bid, production begins. Most commercials take several working days to shoot. Prior to actual shooting, agency personnel, along with the commercial director, audition actors for parts, agree on locations, and work with crews to locate props, products, and other necessities. After the shoot comes the post-production work of screening dailies or rushes (all the takes from production), choosing the best takes, and editing them down to the required time frame.

For local commercials, a local television station often serves as a production source. While videotape remains popular for locally produced commercials, many national and regional commercials are still shot on film. Despite the advantages of videotape, many directors prefer film because they feel it gives them more control over the quality of the finished product. Fans of film claim that it tends to be kinder to people, products, and settings, affording a richer palette of colors and a softer, more upscale texture than videotape. For cosmetics, foods, and automobiles, film seems a natural choice over videotape. But video is closing the quality gap as videographers create high-definition footage that, even when projected on a large screen, is virtually indistinguishable from film.

Checklist for Television Copy

✓ Did you think pictures first and add the words later?

✓ Did you choose a format that best expresses what you want to say?

✓ Did you rely on the entertainment value of your commercial to sell the product?

✓ Did you ask if the opening shot will command attention?

✓ Did you check to see that the product is afforded enough visibility, in terms of time and closeness to the camera?

✓ Did you ask if you can get closer to the action to make the action more involving?

✓ Did you use supertitles to help viewers remember important points and, especially, the product name and the campaign theme?

✓ Did you end on the product, somehow?

✓ Did you choose words that add to the picture's meaning, not that mean the same thing as the picture?

✓ Did you make certain that important words are related to the pictures they've been chosen to represent?

● Suggested Activities

1. Watch at least five commercials on television this week, and take notes on the following:

   a. Was the product shown prominently the first time it was mentioned?

   b. Was the product featured visually in or near the final shot?

    c. Did the first shot get your attention? How?

    d. Was the first shot related to the product story? How?

    e. Which shot was most memorable? Why?

    f. How did you feel about the product as a result of the commercial? Did it change your feelings at all? How and why?

2. Write a television commercial. Begin with a scenario, progress to a script, and present it to the class in storyboard form. Use your classmates' suggestions to make revisions.

3. Go to *http://www.adcritic.com* and watch several commercials—either current or classic. Write a critique of at least two.

Search Online! Discovering More About Television Commercials

Using InfoTrac® College Edition, try these phrases and others for Key Words and Subject Guide searches: *visual storytelling, writing with pictures, scenario writing, slice of life, testimonial + advertising, camera framing, camera moves, video editing, camera point of view, classic TV commercials.*

BriefCase

Pepsi Finds a New Way to Poke Fun at "the Other Cola"

Michael Patti, executive creative director, and Don Snyder, senior vice president and senior creative director, were the team at BBDO/NY, along with co-CEO and chief creative officer Ted Sann, who crafted the memorable "Security Camera" television commercial for client Pepsi-Cola. Patti tells how they came up with the idea:

"We have a history of doing competitive ads that poke fun at Coca-Cola, but it seems every year it gets harder and harder to do a great one. Don and I work together as a team, one-on-one in my office day in and day out on Pepsi. Ted comes in as often as he can and sits down with us to throw ideas around. It's an ongoing process. Ted can stick his head in for five minutes and say, 'Jelly beans, I got an idea,' and walk away. And Don and I will sit there and think about it.

"One day he came in around lunchtime. He didn't have a lot of time. We were working on a bunch of other stuff, and he said, 'Security camera. I don't know what it means, but security camera.'

"He had just installed a security system in his house or something, and that was the real germ of the idea. We told him, 'Come on. That's boring. That's stupid.' Then he walked away. Then he came back, and we sat down. We talked about the spot as being a single-take thing, something that happened with no cuts. And we thought that was interesting for Pepsi, because we never do anything that simple and that focused.

"We thought it had competitive qualities. Don came up with the idea of putting the two coolers next to each other, and I think it took a day or two before we came up with maybe having the Coke guy going for a Pepsi. And we let it sit for a week.

"Don drew a key frame of these two coolers with this Coke guy there. The thing we settled on would be that the Coke delivery guy would go for a Pepsi, and at that moment he would be caught in the act by a woman coming around the corner with a shopping cart. He would get embarrassed and leave the frame and you would stay

REPRINTED FROM AGENCY MAGAZINE, SPRING 1996. USED WITH PERMISSION.

and stay on that empty frame. Then all of a sudden, from underneath the security camera, he would sneak back in, grab a Pepsi, and run like hell.

"The 'Cheatin' Heart' music—I don't know who came up with it. We might have been talking about music and bounced a bunch of titles around. Once we played it, we knew that if we ever shot the spot, it would be perfect. It just felt good.

"We thought the spot was okay, but it wasn't great. The CEO at Pepsi liked it a lot and said, 'Gee I think it could be a little funnier.' So we came up with an alternative ending. We said, 'Well, maybe it would be funny if he pulled one can and maybe 20 cans fell on him and he had to pick them up and he got embarrassed.'

"As a result, we created the spot with more than 20 cans. Which was Joe Pytka, the director, saying, 'Let's make it the mother of all spills! Let's keep it going until it's beyond belief.'

"Two takes was all we did. And we knew we had it in the can."

CHAPTER 10

Using Direct Marketing to Build Lasting Relationships

A Lands' End ad cuts to the chase: "Like, who has time to shop anymore? Maybe shopping at the mall was fun once. But not these days. You're too busy working, chauffeuring the kids around, doing a thousand other things. You simply can't afford the time to shop, can you?" The convenience of shopping at home may explain why 65 percent of respondents in a major survey for *USA Weekend* said they ordered a product by catalog in the past year and 44 percent ordered by phone or mail a product they saw in an ad. With the blossoming of the Internet as a virtual shopping mall for the world (see Chapter 11), the push by advertisers toward direct marketing is evident.

With the explosion of mass-media advertising and a continuing trend toward segmentation of target audiences, it's not difficult to understand why direct marketing is growing rapidly. Not only does direct marketing, of all advertising venues, inherently make it easiest to purchase products, it also delivers its messages to a highly targeted and therefore user-friendly group of prospects. More brands are competing for the same customers, and the market continues to fragment. So, as marketers peg more and more subgroups of consumers by demographics, lifestyles, and purchasing habits, companies need to be ever more specific in their marketing campaigns. Information-driven marketing helps companies do this by targeting prospects with far greater accuracy than other mass-media efforts.

● Direct Marketing: An Old Idea Improved Through Technology

A lthough the computer, the checkout scanner, the credit card, and the Internet have breathed new life into direct marketing, it has been a healthy and active industry for nearly 150 years. Direct marketing got its start at about the same time that the U.S. Postal Service established coast-to-coast delivery in 1847. Early, purveyors of direct-response advertising, called mail order in those days, were Sears, Roebuck & Company, founded in 1886, and the Montgomery Ward Company, established in 1872. Their early hand-illustrated, black-and-white catalogs brought the products of the industrialized world—in the form of appliances, farm tools, clothing, and even do-it-yourself home-building kits—to the most isolated farmhouses in America. And America never looked back. Direct marketing is one reason U.S. marketing techniques are eagerly emulated all over the world.

Early in the twentieth century, pioneers in industrial sales, such as National Cash Register, used letters to attract sales prospects. But little of the present revolution in direct marketing would have been possible without the computer, the credit card, and the 800-number. Computers and checkout scanners capture and assimilate detailed information about businesses and individuals, and then compile that information in narrowly targeted mailing lists. Names of individuals are now isolated not only by age, name, education, and other demographics but also by credit history, hobbies, and buying habits. Prospects are also targeted by size and type of business and exact job function.

● How Direct Marketing Differs from Mass-Media Advertising

While the goal of advertising is to build brand awareness or to create demand for a new product category, direct marketing is structured to sell *now*. Urgency is the key component. Also, the information flows two ways: from prospect to advertiser and back to the prospect. It's purposely interactive so that the lists that produce the greatest response can be identified early on. Once the list is analyzed by socio/demographic characteristics, marketers can obtain lists with the same characteristics but with new names. In a sense, direct response is a way to obtain marketing information through sales. Advertising sells products. Direct marketing sells offers, using deadlines to produce swift responses. Most importantly, subsequent efforts to sell to the same prospect work to strengthen the relationship between consumer and company. If, as we claimed in Chapter 1, all advertising works to build a relationship between the brand and the prospect, direct marketing works the hardest and is generally the most successful in building long-term brand loyalty.

Direct marketing is growing rapidly because it keeps bringing home the business. In a recent year, more than half the U.S. adult population ordered merchandise or services by phone, mail, or the Internet. More women ordered than men, while the greatest growth by age group was in the 18–24 category, followed by 45–54, and 55+. But buyers from all income classes participate, with annual growth skewing slightly toward incomes of $50,000 or more.

Even more interesting is what companies and marketers can find out about their customers:

- The dollar value of purchases
- The number of purchases annually
- The length of customer-company relationships
- Information on other purchase influencers at the same address
- Promotions aimed at customers
- Rentals of customers' names to other companies
- Nonresponders
- Socio/demographic information on customers

In 1994, more than 22 million adults said they watched home-shopping programs on TV, and close to 8 million bought merchandise through TV offers. And more than half the businesses that participate in direct-response mailings make their lists available for a price to other businesses, usually in the form of rentals or exchanges.

● Advantages of Direct Marketing over Other Forms of Advertising

Direct marketing has several distinct advantages over other forms of advertising, including the following:

- *Pinpointing of prospects.* A well-targeted database enables marketers to pinpoint a select group of prospects by lifestyles, demographics, purchasing patterns, and so forth.
- *Personalized messages.* The design and tone of the message can be easily personalized.
- *Faster sales.* Sales can be made sooner than through traditional advertising media.
- *A wide variety of packaging options.* Except for minor regulations imposed by the U.S. Postal Service, the creative team can develop a range of exciting packages, from multifold self-mailers to odd-shaped boxes and from tear-open packs to actual product samples.
- *Less "competition" from other media content.* Unfettered by the editorial environment of print and broadcast media, the direct-marketing piece must compete only with other messages in the mail. If the design and copy are successful in getting recipients to look inside, the message has their attention as long as they find something interesting in it.

● FIGURE 10-1

From the headline "Hear the Radio That Woke Up an Entire Industry," to the subheadline touting its status as "Best New Product," to its long, fascinating copy, this ad works hard for a response—and a direct one at that. Note the phone number and coupon integrated with the Bose logo. Why will interested prospects read this ad, aside from their interest in the radio? First, the copy is broken into short, easy-to-take paragraphs. The copy works hard to be reader-friendly—you'll find no scientific terms here, just reason after reason to enjoy the superb sound. Not only do the subheadings throughout break the long copy, but each one makes an important selling point. The little visuals inset throughout with their own captions reinforce what the copy is saying. Finally, the offer is practically irresistible.

HEAR WHY THE BOSE® WAVE® RADIO WAS NAMED A "BEST NEW PRODUCT OF 1994" BY *BUSINESSWEEK*.

Tabletop radios are popular for their convenience and small size. But their sound quality leaves much to be desired. No one really expects high-fidelity sound from a radio. Until now.

Bose presents the Wave radio. It's the one radio acclaimed by leading audio critics. Because it's the is our patented acoustic waveguide speaker technology. Just as a flute strengthens a breath of air to fill an entire concert hall, the waveguide produces room-filling sound from a small enclosure. This technology and performance is available in no other radio.

You'll touch a button and hear your favorite music come alive in rich stereo sound. You'll hear every note the way it's *meant* to be heard. The Wave radio measures just

Set six AM and six FM stations.

Easily connect your CD player, cassette player, TV, or VCR.

CALL NOW AND MAKE SIX INTEREST-FREE PAYMENTS.

The Wave radio is available for $349 directly from Bose, the most respected name in sound. Call 1-800-845-BOSE, ext. RIB233, or return the coupon for free information or to learn more about our in-home trial and satisfaction guarantee. When you call, ask about our six-month installment payment plan.

HEAR THE RADIO THAT WOKE UP AN ENTIRE INDUSTRY.

one radio that delivers big, rich, lifelike stereo sound *plus* a small, convenient size.

THE BEST-SOUNDING RADIO YOU CAN BUY.

We think the Wave radio is the best-sounding radio you can buy. And audio critics agree. *Radio World* called the sound "simply amazing… a genuine breakthrough in improved sound quality." *BusinessWeek* named the Wave radio a "Best New Product of 1994."

Popular Science called it a "sonic marvel," and gave it a prestigious "Best Of What's New" award. The key

The speakers in conventional radios cannot produce lifelike bass, which is essential for great sound.

Only the Wave radio with acoustic waveguide speaker technology produces high-quality sound with full, rich bass.

4.5"H × 14"W × 8"D and fits almost anywhere. So you can listen in your bedroom, living room, kitchen, or any room.

REMOTE-CONTROLLED CONVENIENCE.

Operate the radio from across the room with the credit card-sized remote control. Set six AM and six FM stations, and switch between them at the touch of a button. You can even bring great Bose sound to recorded music, TV programs, or movies by connecting the Wave radio to your CD or cassette player, TV, or VCR.

Wired magazine said, "The clean, sweet sound will have your friends wondering where you've hidden your fancy speakers." But you have to hear the Wave radio for yourself to believe it. Call today.

CALL 1-800-845-BOSE, EXT. RIB233.

When you call, ask about our six-month installment payment plan. (Available on telephone orders only.) Also ask about FedEx® delivery.

Mr./Mrs./Ms. _____
Name   (Please Print)

Address _____

City _____ State ____ Zip ____

(____) _____
Daytime Telephone

(____) _____
Evening Telephone

Mail to: Bose Corporation, Dept. CDD-RIB233, The Mountain, Framingham, MA 01701-9168, or fax to 508-485-4577.

BOSE®
Better sound through research®

© 1996 Bose Corporation. Covered by patent rights issued and/or pending. Installment payment plan option expires 6/30/96, and is not to be used in combination with any other offers. Price is subject to change without notice.

● Computer Databases:
The Key to Targeting the Best Prospects

Thanks to the computer, advertisers can locate their best prospects with an accuracy never before possible. Once they "merge and purge" names from a number of databases—trades with other companies, motor vehicle records, warranty card data from their own files, birth announcements, lists of college students, subscribers to selected magazines, and on and on—they can compile an ever-growing list of ideal prospects for their goods and services. Buy fat-free salad dressing and yogurt at the checkout, and a scanner labels you as a prospect for exercise equipment or fitness magazines. Join an airline's frequent-flyer plan, and your gasoline credit card statement arrives with an offer for luggage. Buy a new car, and you hear periodically from the manufacturer asking you to complete a satisfaction questionnaire and reminding you it's time for servicing. Purchase a new home, and a lawn-care service mails you a "welcome to the neighborhood" offer for a trial weeding and feeding.

Clearly, advertisers who depend on direct marketing know a great deal about their customers and are continually seeking data about potential additions to their customer list. For example, Vons, a major supermarket chain, knows the power of such information. Its VonsClub preferred shopping program is one of the oldest and largest such efforts in the United States. Membership is growing at 25 percent a year, and Vons has assembled an exceptional database on its customers. This enables Vons to work effectively with manufacturers and others to produce targeted marketing efforts.

The key to Vons' success is the way in which it builds this valuable database. As customers pass their VonsCards through scanners at checkout stands, they automatically receive discounts on items promoted that week. Little do they know that the computers are also collecting data about what they purchased. This data is combined with lifestyle information originally furnished during the VonsClub application process. This extensive database contains insights, for example, into which private-label products offer the most promise for Vons and which customers are the best prospects for each product.

But Vons does even more with its database. Its CheckOut for Children school donation program lets VonsClub members electronically assign their checkout purchases to the school of their choice without having to collect register tapes. In a joint effort with marketers of brand-name goods, Vons uses data on customer purchases to create direct-mail pieces that contain six to eight different promotional offerings, each aimed at specific households and based on their purchasing history of those brands.

Other companies are using databases to expand sales into new market segments. As we noted in Chapter 2, research shows that gays and lesbians are a loyal and sensitive audience. To win business from gay business owners, MCI naturally chose direct

marketing. Their direct-mail piece is delivered to a list obtained through the Gay &
Lesbian Business Alliance. It rewards gay business owners who sign up by a certain
date with free membership in the alliance, plus an offer for a new MCI calling card
with the alliance logo, a 5 percent discount on volume calling, and one free month of
MCI long-distance calling. The mailing includes both a letter from an openly gay
MCI employee (who describes MCI as a workplace free of discrimination) and material describing various discounts and special offers for gay business owners.

Direct-mail campaigns can also be vehicles for market research. To get Singapore
teens to divulge information about their pimple-control product usage—a sensitive
issue in this age group—Ogilvy & Mather Direct created a questionnaire mailer that
offered trendy prizes such as Doc Martens shoes. Using point-of-sale leaflets, direct-
response ads in teen magazines, and names of previous promotion respondents, the
agency amassed over 10,000 names for its mailing. The control group (5000 names)
then received a free gift (a small sample of the product), while the test group (the
remaining 5000 names) received the gift and a "Skinformation Kit" with skin care
advice and information on Oxy products. Adding the information in the test group
mailing upped the brand-purchase intention to three times that of the control group,
while the overall result of the mailing was a 34 percent increase in correct usage of
the product by teenagers.

And in New Zealand, Ogilvy & Mather Direct used a mailing list of 350 current
owners of BMW or rival luxury cars to introduce its new 7-series. This seven-part
mailing was designed to "treat, spoil, and reward prospective buyers just as the new
7-series would." Seven months before actual introduction of the car, the first of the
seven mailers was delivered. Each appealed to one of the senses, such as the chance to
win an all-expense-paid trip to the Auckland Flower Show, an appeal to the sense of
smell. The final mailing offered a test drive of the $150,000 car, an appeal to "pure
driving pleasure."

● Direct Marketing: A More Personalized Relationship

Jerry Pickholz, chair of Ogilvy & Mather Direct Worldwide and a leader in the
field of direct marketing, says that consumers have rejected many aspects of the
mass-marketing approach in favor of a more personalized and intimate one-on-one
relationship, a relationship made possible by visionary concepts and modern information technology. Among currently hot trends, he cites the following:[1]

- *Using traditional media to generate new leads*—as the California division of the
  American Automobile Association did with a television commercial aimed at
  increasing AAA membership among female drivers.

[1]Courtesy of Jerome Pickholz, Ogilvy & Mather Direct.

- *Using compelling offers to upgrade customers*—as the American Association of Retired Persons did when it used its vast membership database to promote related products such as insurance and credit cards.

- *Using high-impact mail to build traffic at the place of business*—as Jaguar did when it offered an upscale writing pen to members of a highly affluent prospect list for visiting the Jaguar dealership. Simply offering a prestigious item of small value compared to the cost of the car brought this elite audience to dealers in droves.

- *Gathering a list while increasing usage*—as Miracle Whip did when it invited TV viewers to contribute recipes using Miracle Whip to a newsletter that featured a photo of the recipe's creator. By including coupons for Miracle Whip and related products in each issue, the marketer not only increased consumption but also was able to track future sales.

- *Building loyalty*—as Ikea furniture stores did by mailing an informative home decorating newsletter to its "family" of customers. The newsletter included a questionnaire to track changes in the family unit and discount coupons to bring customers back.

- *Enhancing value*—as Microsoft did when it mailed a 30-minute videotape of its president, Bill Gates, talking "face to face" about the superiority of Microsoft programs, to convince "tekkies" who influence major software decisions for their companies. Because of specific targeting, Gates was able to use technical language that only this audience could appreciate.

For Emily Soell, vice chairman and chief creative officer of Rapp Collins Worldwide, the winners in direct marketing today are those who recognize that consumers have turned the tables on marketers. Suspicious of claims that promised they could "have it all," Soell maintains, consumers now have less faith not only in advertisers but also in doctors, police officers, teachers, financial advisors, and even religious leaders.

Soell contends that a perceptive direct marketer knows how to change old rules to conform to new consumer values. Instead of showing the product, she says, "show the promise." A woman's magazine found that showing glamour alone is not as powerful as promising that the magazine will help subscribers contain the costs of face creams, haircuts, and other, often overpriced, accoutrements of glamour. Instead of bribing the prospect, Soell adds, contemporary marketing endeavors to *involve* the prospect. To attract possible convention business, the city of Memphis sent a dog-eared package to a select list with a hand-scrawled address and the line "We found your wallet in Memphis" on the outside. Inside was a real wallet, stuffed with simulated "credit cards" that gave recipients numerous reasons to consider Tennessee's largest city as a convention site. While the claims were compelling, it was the magic of the highly involving package that made the difference.

Being personal is good but not enough. Soell stresses that marketers must also be relevant. Computer-generated statements that read "New York's best-dressed women:

Ivana and (consumer's name here)" will only draw derision and contempt from today's consumers. A much more savvy way to personalize is Gillette's mailing to young men on their eighteenth birthday, which includes a Sensor razor and a can of Foamy shaving cream, plus a coupon offering a reduced price on the next purchase of Sensor blades.

Finally, Soell says that, while "making the sale" may be old-fashioned, "building the relationship" certainly is not. It is this relationship that holds the promise of making many more sales.[2]

● The Three Musts for Successful Direct Marketing

The List

As the most important element of a direct campaign, the list should be narrowed to prime prospects for the product or service. The cost of outgoing and incoming messages and telephone calls constitutes the largest single expense of a direct-marketing campaign. There's no room for names that don't fit the target profile and won't offer the chance of a response.

The Message

Copywriters estimate they have only seconds to grab a consumer's attention with direct mail. As you will discover in Chapter 11, direct marketing on the Internet carries similar limitations. This is why great care should be devoted to the design of the envelope. Make it oversized. Print a message in boldface type on the front. Laser-print the recipient's name into the message on the envelope. Inside the envelope, a majority of offers contain a personalized "typewritten" letter, a brochure, and a response card. Stickers for "Yes" or "No" responses may be used to involve the consumer further.

The letter carries the letterhead of the company and a salutation in keeping with the list: "Dear Music Lover," "Dear Traveler," or simply, "Dear Friend." To grab attention, the letter digresses from a personal letter by adding a message in large boldface type before the salutation, a message linking the lure on the envelope to the letter that follows. This headline also takes advantage of its prominence to sell the third essential, the offer.

The Offer

The mailing always asks for a response, often in the form of a limited-time offer. This may be as simple as coupons offering reduced prices if you buy before the expiration date, merchandise at a reduced price for a limited time, or a chance to participate in a contest should you buy something now. To raise the odds for a response, use a prepaid business-reply card or envelope, or a toll-free number. The recipient must be told how to respond in the letter, in the brochure, and especially on the order blank or catalog page. Here, repetition makes sense, because the average direct-mail reader just skims the mailing. A significant number of prospects will only read the response coupon, ignoring the letter and brochure, because they know they will find a short

[2]Courtesy of Emily Soel, Rapp Collins Worldwide.

summary of the entire offer there. In addition to mentioning the offer in the letter's headline, you have other opportunities to urge the reader to respond as soon as possible. Look at the *Mother Jones* example in Figure 10-2, and note that the offer is mentioned practically throughout the message. The offer is made (1) in the letter's headline, (2) near the bottom of the first page (in the underlined subhead "It's yours free"), (3) near the end of the third page (beginning with "So—waste not a second" and even adding more incentive in the following paragraph), (4) toward the end of the letter on page 4, and (5, 6) twice in the P.S., or postscript, which is one of the most highly read portions of a direct-response letter. Six repetitions of the offer drive the point home even to skimmers.

Designing the Direct-Marketing Package

Want to try your hand at this? Perhaps the most common—and least expensive—design for direct marketing is the mailer designed on standard 8½ × 11-inch paper and folded into thirds. And this is where you begin. Fold a piece of paper this size, and rough in the design for each panel. In preparing your rough, you may wish to use the front panel for a teaser headline, with or without a visual. Consider continuing the message on the right-hand panel—or "flap"—which is where the eye generally looks next. The left-hand panel will become part of the inside once the flap is lifted, so whatever you place there must work with the flap opened or closed. While it's not always necessary to put something major on the back, because this gets the lowest readership, you should at least include a logo and perhaps an accompanying tag line.

Prepare your letter and envelope and—voilà—you have a direct mailer. Place the letter, brochure, and reply card inside the envelope, and mount the back of the envelope, with the flap open, on black matte board for presentation.

Direct Marketing as Part of a Total Advertising Campaign

Research indicates that a direct-marketing ad campaign launched in conjunction with a mass-media blitz produces a higher response than an isolated direct campaign. Also, when the direct campaign includes three mailings, varying in terms of the copy but not the offer, that continue over the duration of the media schedule, the response will be at least double that of a campaign with only a single mailing.

Fundraising Through Direct Marketing

Nonprofit organizations such as the March of Dimes and the American Lung Association use direct marketing as their major fundraising tool. In recent years, using creative and aggressive direct-mail campaigns, over $104 billion has

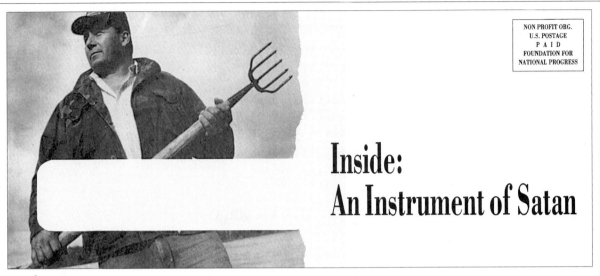

NON PROFIT ORG.
U.S. POSTAGE
P A I D
FOUNDATION FOR
NATIONAL PROGRESS

Inside:
An Instrument of Satan

Envelope

Brochure

● FIGURE 10-2

Mother Jones, the liberal investigative magazine published in San Francisco, has won the hearts (and subscriptions) of its readers by admitting exactly what it is: a publication unafraid of big business or big government. Note the provocative envelope, the attention-getting headline in the brochure, and especially the "tell it like it is" letter that contradicts the "satanic image" of the envelope by chronicling the success of the magazine in exposing questionable practices and products. Note how consistent the voice (a flippant kind of intellectual) is in these various parts: (1) the headline at the start of the letter; (2) the opening paragraph, which sets the tone and delivers the message instantly; (3) the offer on pages 1, 3, and 4; (4) the "handwritten" signature; and (5) the repeated offer in the postscript.

MOTHERJONES

"The Nation's Best Magazine for Investigative Journalism."
American Journalism Review

First they dismissed us as flaky and hysterical.
Then they branded us a threat to internal security.
Now they're calling us an instrument of satan.
Find out why. FREE

Dear Reader,

Ever get the queasy feeling you've just read the same six articles over and over again in a half-dozen different magazines?

Wackos in Waco. Yattering with Yeltsin. Soaping up with Schwarzkopf. Hobnobbing with Hillary. Disrobing (yawn) with Demi.

The same torpid insights from the same cast of "experts." The same shallow gossip. The same stale spin.

What's more, you have to wade through 40 glossy ad spreads for floral bed linen, designer perfume and Italian luggage... before you get to one slim nugget of real news.

When you're done, what more do you really know about the world? How will it help you put things in perspective?

No wonder things often look as bleak as a *thirty-something* rerun.

Now -- here's a prescription that will decidedly improve your outlook. Intrigue you. Enlighten you. Empower you. And give a lively new boost to your political IQ.

(In this dramatic year of Washington turnover, it might just make a difference.)

Just fire off the order card in this envelope, and I'll rush you, with my compliments, the latest issue of the all-new MOTHER JONES.

It's yours free. An uncompromising, uncensored, unapologetic journal teeming with the real people, politics and passions that have a daily impact on your world.

Plus some hardheaded tips on how <u>you</u> can make a daily impact for peace, social justice and a safer environment.

It's also a damn good read.

-2-

MOTHER JONES? Isn't she that feisty old gal who pulled the plug on the lethally defective Ford Pinto?...

Yanked the chain on the corporate criminals who were dumping hazardous junk in the Third World?...

Blew the whistle on federal bureaucrats who twiddled their thumbs while millions of Americans came down with AIDS?

Yep, yep and yep.

Like our namesake, orator and agitator Mary Harris "Mother" Jones, we have a bit of a history. (Including three National Magazine Awards in our first four years.)

Also like the original article, we get results. (In the case of Ford Pinto, a homicide indictment, $20 million in consumer lawsuits and the largest auto recall in history.)

How do we do it? By sponsoring the kind of gritty, time-consuming, often dangerous investigative journalism that the rest of the press just doesn't have the stomach for.

(Or doesn't respect your smarts enough to dig for.)

Result? In an era when corporate megamergers have gobbled up most news sources... tainting what you see, read and hear with fluff, euphemism or outright distortion...

MOTHER JONES remains the unchallenged leader in hard-hitting, between-the-lines, no-holds-barred, nose-to-the-street, no-nonsense news, analysis and consumer advocacy.

The kind you simply won't find in the New York Times, the Wall Street Journal, Esquire, Newsweek or Vanity Fair.

And today we're doing our job with more chutzpah, punch and audacity than ever before.

Just ask our quarter-million avid readers. Or, the media pros polled by the American Journalism Review, who voted us the nation's "Best Magazine for Investigative Journalism."

What do they find in every issue of MOTHER JONES?

In-Depth Exposés. Like the ones that awakened America to the health-threatening Dalkon Shield. Toxic breast implants. The pesticide peril at your breakfast table. The electronics industry's calculated decision to shred the ozone layer.

-3-

██

    <u>Thoughtful Essays</u>. Like our level-headed look at black urban poverty and America's growing trailer-home population. Gays in the military and the crisis in the Balkans. Women in the Men's Movement. Congressional reform.

    <u>Practical Advice</u>. Like what to do when job options and principles collide. How to conduct an ecological audit of your home. Protect yourself from skin cancer. Seize back the airwaves. Act up against AIDS. Lead a shareholder revolt.

    Also an unabashed point of view. A passion for uncovering government corruption and corporate shenanigans. An aversion to gridlock. A commitment to the little guy.

    Needless to say, all this attitude and insight doesn't sit very well with some of the self-appointed legislators of political correctitude and public morality.

    Demagogues on the right... who've branded us pro-terrorist, pro-feminist, pro-socialist, pro-hedonist, pro-humanist, pro-communist, pro-gay.

    Ideologues on the left... who've squealed when we skewered a few of their sacred cows.

    Or the fundamentalist kooks at the Coalition on Revival who denounced our coverage as "a powerful blow by Satan."

    Are we going to let this gutter-baiting gall us?... Naaah. You see, the old lady's still got her teeth, and she knows how to bite back.

    But she sure could use a few more independent thinkers like you along for the ride. After all, <u>you're</u> the reason we keep raking up the muck.

    So -- waste not a second. All you need do is return the enclosed card. Your trial issue comes FREE.

    If you like it, I'll round out your year with five more bimonthly issues of MOTHER JONES (6 total) for a full <u>33% off</u> our regular subscription rate.

    Send no payment now, if you like. We'll bill you later.

        But -- if you <u>do</u> send payment with your order, I'll sweeten the deal. Extending your subscription by <u>two more issues</u> (that's 8 in all) for the same low price.

-4-

██

And if at any time you're not thoroughly enthused, engaged and galvanized, simply cancel your subscription. I'll send you a full refund on all unserved issues.

MOTHER JONES. We're not just a mirror of events, but a catalyst. A Molotov cocktail of ideas. A prairie fire of inspiration.

Are we also an instrument of Satan? Well, perhaps not. (The fellow on the envelope is actually a Chippewa spear-fisher named Tom Maulson, one of our 1991 grassroots activist award-winners.)

But we <u>can</u> assure you a devilish good time. While we make things mighty hot for the powers that be.

Can you afford <u>just 23¢ a week</u> to put yourself in the know, and keep America's best investigative machinery humming? ... That depends.

Are you the kind of person who's a little disgruntled with the status quo? Ready for a fresh outlook?

The kind who's willing to read between the lines? See the writing on the wall? Punch a hole in some platitudes?

Are you really? ... Then come on. Take a chance. Fill out the card. Cross the median. Welcome to the other side.

Cheers,

Jeffrey Klein
Editor

P. S.   <u>Act now, risk nothing</u>. 33% off the regular subscription rate! And if you don't find MOTHER JONES completely indispensable, cancel at any time for a full refund on all unserved issues.

<u>Pay now, get more</u>. Two extra issues (that's 8 in all) for the same low price!

been raised annually for such causes. As state and federal funds for nonprofit organizations dwindle, more and more charities and cultural groups are turning to direct marketing for support. Competition for consumer donations is fierce and will only become more so. Those organizations that cultivate current givers and prove that donations directly benefit their causes will be the winners.

Another factor in the surge in direct-marketing pleas for donations is the attempt by advocacy and social-change organizations to rid themselves of corporate support and large donors, turning instead to hundreds of thousands of dedicated small donors. Such organizations have discovered that, with 85 percent of their contributions coming from small donors, direct marketing is a democratic way to fund social change.

Sophisticated fundraisers spend heavily to acquire donors. They know that, even if the initial donation fails to cover the marketing expense, people who donate that first time are highly likely to donate again. Accordingly, when a donor is first acquired, the contribution is swiftly and "personally" acknowledged to secure the donor's loyalty to the organization. Subsequently, the donor will be asked annually to renew the donation, even as the organization attempts to increase the amount of the donation each year.

Fundraising solicitations pose peculiar problems. Remember that a fundraiser asks for money without offering something in return (other than perhaps a tax deduction). Unless the case for support is made absolutely clear, the appeal may fall on deaf ears. Often, the benefit to the giver is a sense of helping the needy. In other cases, givers will respond to support a service, like public television, that they themselves enjoy.

● Catalogs: Bringing the Retail Store into the Home and Office

Catalog advertising has come a long way since the early days of Sears, Roebuck. Some tightening is evident in sales, and a number of marginal catalogs have fallen by the wayside, yet catalog sales have emerged as a major contender in the battle for the retail dollar.

Successful catalogs follow the trend of all successful direct advertising today: They target specific groups of buyers. So Americans' mailboxes are loaded with catalogs touting products to beautify their homes, control stress, organize their lives, groom their pets, update their computers, and so on. Each has a particular audience in mind for the types of goods it offers. There are catalogs for movie lovers, music lovers, cat lovers, and dog lovers. Catalogs for new parents, for older travelers, for gift givers, and for designer collections. And the list goes on and on. In 1998, 8000 catalog companies mailed about 14 billion catalogs nationwide. That's an average of 125 per household.[3]

[3]David Sharp, "L.L. Bean Feels Heat of Catalog Competition," *The State,* 15 Dec. 1998, p. G4.

To order merchandise, you don't even have to fill out an order form. You simply dial a toll-free number, place your order, and charge it to a major credit card. Return policies are generally liberal, so you need not be concerned about buying sight unseen.

In addition to being persuasive and interesting, catalog copy must anticipate questions and provide all the answers. Prospects who can't examine a knit shirt in person must know it's 100 percent washable cotton, and comes in sixteen colors and four sizes.

● Personalizing the Direct-Marketing Message

Specialists in writing direct-marketing copy claim that the key to success is the element of one-to-one human contact. "There's no mystery about the No. 1 social problem in the United States," claims Robert Haydon Jones. "It's loneliness and alienation. Every new research poll confirms this, year after year. In direct marketing, perhaps more than in any other medium, we can take advantage of that reality. . . . The simplest letter gives us the chance for a great platform for dialog. Someone has written to me. How interesting."

Keeping the "List of Lists" shown in the box on the facing page in mind, collect several direct-mail packages from friends and family. Choose one to analyze, paying particular attention to the following questions:

1. How well does the message on the envelope motivate the targeted audience to open it and read further? Inside the mailing, how strong is the relationship between the envelope message and the opening of the letter?

2. How is the letter put together? Specifically:

   a. If a headline begins the letter, does it succeed in getting the reader to read on?

   b. How does the salutation address the audience targeted?

   c. How are color, indented phrases or paragraphs, and subheadings used to break up the letter? What types of information are highlighted by such devices?

   d. What is the offer? How well does it relate to the product or service being offered? To the audience targeted?

   e. How much incentive is there to respond promptly?

3. What clues you into the socio/demographic characteristics of this mailing list? (Possibilities include age; gender; marital status; occupation; family income; level of education; own or rent home; special events such as just got married, had baby, bought home, remodeled home, moved, changed jobs, or retired; hobbies or special interests.)

List of Lists

To demonstrate the vast amount of data available from list sellers, here is a sample breakdown by life-styles and demographic data available from a typical organization. Lists are not free. Generally, the more names on the list, the higher the cost. List buyers may request that lists be narrowed by merging demographic characteristics with lifestyle and geographic data in virtually any combination to help the advertiser pinpoint the best potential market for the mailing.

LIFESTYLES

Affluent/Good Life
Community activities
Charities/Volunteer activities
Cultural/Arts events
Fine art/Antiques
Gourmet cooking
Own vacation home
Shop by catalog
Stock/Bond investments
Travel for business
Travel for pleasure
Foreign travel
Frequent flyers
Wine purchasers

Community/Civic
Current affairs/Politics
Donate to charitable causes
Military veteran
Wildlife/Environmental
   issues

Domestic
Automotive work
Bible reading
Book reading
Fashion clothing by size
Gourmet cooking
Grandchildren
Home decorating
Own cat/Own dog
Own microwave

Entertainment
Buy prerecorded videos
Cable TV subscriber
Casino gambling
Home video games
Home video recording
Own VCR
Stereo/Tapes/CDs
Own CD player
Watch sports on TV

High-Tech
Personal/Home computers
Use PC/Use Macintosh
New technology
Photography
Science fiction

Hobbies
Automotive work
Camping and hiking
Coin/Stamp collecting
Crossword puzzles
Do-it-yourself repairs
Fishing
Gardening
Gourmet cooking
Needlework

Self-Improvement
Dieting/Weight control
Exercise: walking for health
Health/Natural foods
Health improvement

Sports
Bicycling
Boating/Sailing
Fishing
Golf
Hunting/Shooting
Motorcycling
Snow skiing
Tennis

DEMOGRAPHICS

Gender: Male/Female (Mrs., Ms., or Miss)
Location: State, County, Zip Code
Age: 18–24, 25–34, 35–44, 45–54, 55–64, 65–74, 75+ (Year of birth available)
Home: Own or Rent
Marital Status: Married or Unmarried
Household Income: Increments from Under $15,000 to $100,000+
Occupation
   Professional/Technical
   Upper management
   Middle management

Sales and Marketing
Clerical
Craftsman/Blue-collar
Student
Homemaker
Retired
Self-employed business
Working women (Spouse's occupation available)
Credit Cards: Travel/Entertainment, Bank, Other
Children at Home: Exact ages of children from infant to 18 by selection; gender also available

Religion/Ethnicity: Asian, Catholic, Hispanic, Jewish, Protestant
Education: Some high school, finished high school, technical school, some college, completed college, some graduate school, completed graduate school
Other Available Information
   Motor vehicle registration
   Census data
   Your own company's consumer database
   Competitive-purchase information (from other list sources)

4. Based on the "List of Lists," what does the sender already know about the prospect? How does this knowledge strengthen the relationship value of the message?

Now select a product that lends itself to the sort of narrow targeting that direct marketing does so efficiently:

1. Who is your target? Can you narrow this description even further?

2. How can you narrow the field so as to mail to the prospects most likely to respond?

3. What incentive will you offer them so that they respond quickly?

4. Assuming you have a budget, what lists will you buy to find your best prospects?

5. What will your offer consist of? How will you connect it to the product and what you already know about the prospect?

6. What will your package say/show to gain their attention and make them want to read on?

● Ethical Aspects of Direct Marketing

While direct marketing represents the ultimate way to establish a relationship with a prospect, its detractors claim that computer technology has caused an unprecedented invasion of privacy. Not only can marketers amass data on your age, name, and address, they can also easily find out what your buying habits are and what your favorite charities are. Every time you pay with a credit card or check, every time you fill out the lifestyle section of a product warranty card or do any number of seemingly innocuous things, you are most likely contributing to a database. Your age, weight, and hair color come from driver's license records, your political leanings from your contributions, and the due date of your baby from the guest register at the maternity store where you shop. Marketers may know you have a weakness for Haagen-Dazs ice cream or prefer Naturalamb condoms, for every time you pay by check or credit card, the electronic scanner that totals your bill links each purchase to your name. Some fear that even your prescription drugs—birth control pills, tranquilizers, heart remedies—may be the next frontier for list harvesters. As you work on your direct-response package, keep such thoughts in mind.

● Suggested Activities

1. To demonstrate how much you can learn from databases, assume you are also the target consumer for your product, and fill out the form in Figure 3-1. Then

answer the following questions: What products or services might this "person" be a good prospect for? What clues, if any, suggest a basis for the relationship you might build with this person? What sort of offer/merchandise would appeal to this person? How would you work with this information to create an integrated marketing campaign?

2. Write a direct-response letter based on the "List of Lists" on page 209. Use all available tactics to get the prospect interested. And don't forget the offer—develop one that will make the prospect want to respond. Don't "give away the store," but suggest a premium, special price, limited deal, or other device that relates to your prospect and also to what your product represents to the prospect. Check how specifically you are targeting the direct-response package for your product. Remember, you can target much more narrowly using a good list than you can through typical mass media. That means you can restrict your appeal through direct response to the "ideal prospect." To narrow your search, assume you can buy any type of list you might dream of. Beside each applicable entry, specify precisely what characteristics you are seeking in that particular category. Now summarize who is going to be on your list. How will this affect the nature and tone of your copy?

3. You have been hired to attract subscribers to a monthly newsletter, *Wine Lines*. The mission of *Wine Lines* is to provide an up-to-the-minute guide that helps subscribers become connoisseurs of fine wines. Subscribers will learn how to select, store, serve, and savor the finest vintages; they'll be able to enjoy the history of wine making; and they'll discover what to look for in texture, taste, body, and shelf life. Add other features that you think a wine newsletter should include. The price for twelve monthly issues is $12.99. The offer is three months free when the reader subscribes by a specified date (you choose). The offer also includes a premium: a wine bottle coaster that looks expensive (but is actually cheap when purchased in volume). You are targeting upscale men and women age 35–50, urban and urbane. You have three testimonials (from Harrison Ford, Martha Stewart, and Julia Child)—use any or all of them. Design and produce (a) an envelope, (b) a letter, (c) a brochure, and (d) the response card.

4. Develop a direct-marketing piece for a nonprofit campus organization; target your mailing to college students who are most likely to become members or supporters of the organization. Before you begin, interview the staff of the organization, asking what might compel other students to use the services of this organization, join the organization, or donate money to it.

5. City Web, a local Internet provider that offers news and information about the local scene, needs direct marketing to find subscribers. Not all homes have computers. Not all computer owners have modems. Some computer homes already have Internet providers. How would you build a list of solid prospects for City Web? What would you say in your letter to convince your target audience to invest? What would you offer them for joining?

Search Online! Discovering More About Direct Marketing

Using InfoTrac® College Edition, try these phrases and others for Key Words and Subject Guide searches: *catalog shopping, Internet shopping, online shopping, direct marketing, universal product code, checkout scanner, relationship marketing, consumer database, gathering consumer data, direct-marketing offer, direct-mail letter, direct-mail envelope, fundraising, list of lists, direct-marketing lists.*

BriefCase

Father Seeks Revenge After Daughter Loses Virginity (or Just Another Night at the Baltimore Opera)[4]

You like this story line? Then you'll like *Rigoletto*. How about this story line: "Impotent blind man kills hundreds of pagans" (*Samson et Dalila*). Or "Young woman headed for convent gets steamy with two jealous lovers" (*Manon Lescaut*). Decadence? Immorality? Loose morals? Looks like Baltimore Opera's season is going to be fun. So you check the box alongside. Or you refuse (as if anyone could) by checking where it reads, "Call me a prude, but I'm not quite ready for your particular brand of entertainment."

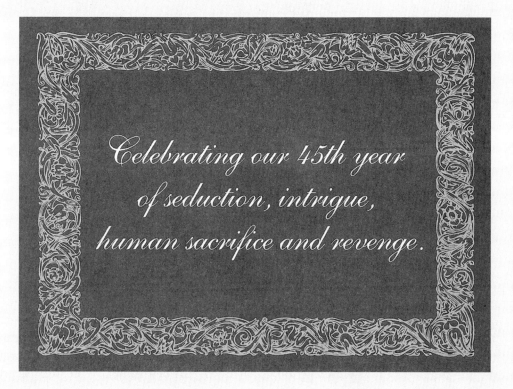

Celebrating our 45th year of seduction, intrigue, human sacrifice and revenge.

[4]With special thanks to Deborah Goetz, director of marketing and PR, Baltimore Opera Company.

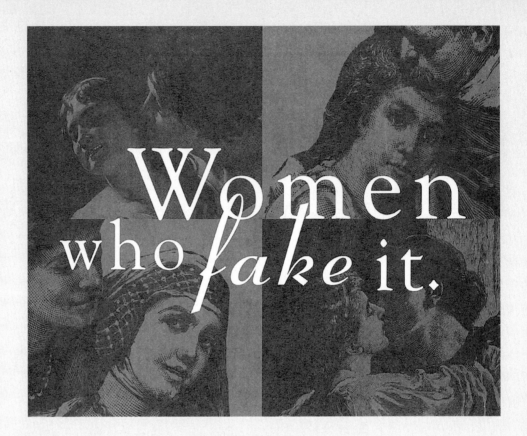

Women who *fake* it.

What's going on here? Opera is boring stuff, isn't it? That's what a random phone survey by the Baltimore Opera of arts preferences and habits turned up in the early 1990s. By fiscal year 1992, subscriptions were down 1 percent from the previous year, single-ticket sales were down 2 percent, and corresponding revenues were dropping dramatically. The subscriber base was stagnant, consisting mostly of long-time, aging devotees whose numbers were naturally decreasing.

But in 1994, the general director and the Board of Trustees took "dramatic" steps to rejuvenate the company by broadening the audience of both subscribers and single-ticket buyers. With a goal of a 20 percent revenue increase, the opera company used a repositioning campaign that embraced research, public education, new media choices, and a tongue-in-cheek approach.

On the positive side, the phone survey had confirmed that patrons of the arts really do love opera music and that current subscribers were continuing to pledge their support. But outweighing these positives was a long list of negatives—reasons many Baltimoreans couldn't imagine themselves enjoying opera: "foreign language," "hard to follow," "not for me," "boring," "not my kind of music." So instead of "preaching to the converted," the new campaign focused its energies on this uninitiated majority.

Next on OPERA

He loves her. She loves him not. She marries him. She cheats on him. He catches her. *La Gioconda* saves the day. October 1996. Featuring: Ghena Dimitrova, Nina Terentieva and Ermanno Mauro.

Is she a he or isn't she? Only *Fidelio* knows for sure. See what happens when a woman bends her gender to break her better half out of the big house. November 1996. Featuring: Frances Ginzer, Jan Grissom, Wolfgang Fassler and Gran Wilson.

She's not really his mom, she just plays it in *Il Trovatore*. Later, when junior gets reunited with his blood relatives, well let's just say things definitely get bloody. March 1997. Featuring: Chris Merritt, Stefka Evstatieva and Irina Mishura.

Everyone knows the story of *Roméo et Juliette*. Everyone except poor Roméo. When he realizes that his beloved Juliette is just pretending to be dead, it's too late. May 1997. Featuring: Leontina Vaduva and Fernando de la Mora.

1996-97 promises to be another exciting, dramatic and colorful season for The Baltimore Opera. So, in addition to a bit of feminine fakery, these four operas will share another common feature: fast selling tickets.

Don't you fool around. Become a season ticket holder. You'll save on the price of each opera, be guaranteed a better seat and have ticket exchange privileges. Just return the card below for complete season ticket information.

THE BALTIMORE OPERA
Opera. It's better than you think. It has to be.

All performances at the Lyric Opera House, 140 West Mount Royal Avenue, Baltimore.

Using humor, showcasing the beautiful music, and communicating that English surtitles are displayed at every performance, the Baltimore Opera worked a miracle through direct-response, telemarketing, public-service TV spots, and a radio campaign—which emphasized English surtitles—on stations with a younger demographic skew.

The results? Revenues are up, the subscriber base has grown 33 percent over four years, subscriber retention is up by 10 percent to an all-time high of 80 percent, and single-ticket sales have risen 28 percent in two years. And the company was able to add a fifth performance of each opera in 1995 *and* to expand the season from three to four productions in 1996.

Each year, the promotions become more irresistible. For a recent season, a square envelope teased the recipient with "Baltimore Opera on Disc." Inside, a paper disc with a rotating overlay allowed readers to review the four operas for the season in an interactive manner. (And without computers!) Turn the inner wheel to *La Traviata,* and you read, "A handsome guy gets together with a beautiful girl who has a questionable past. But she has a good heart—it's just the rest of her that's not in such great shape. In all, a consuming tale."

Opera was always like this. It's just that most of us never knew it. Now all of Baltimore knows that grand opera and great entertainment can coexist in pure harmony.

CHAPTER 11

The Internet: The Ultimate Direct

BY JIM SPEELMON

In the beginning, the Internet gave people information, and a lot of it. Anyone who created a Web site knew that people would visit. Today, people are more sophisticated about their use of information, and companies are more sophisticated about providing it. Rather than using the Internet exclusively, those companies who are reaping the full benefits of this medium are integrating their advertising efforts across most or all media forms to create a more engaging relationship between their brands and their customers.

Let's look at an example. A Web site selling computer equipment used two other media forms to promote an offer of 10 percent off all items purchased on the Web during the holiday season. The company (1) sent e-mail to everyone on its customer list (garnered from both Internet and print catalog sales) and (2) ran an ad in a leading national newspaper about the "Web only" discount. The site was so busy that many who tried were not able to complete their orders. Instead, they phoned the 800-number on the screen, placed their orders over the telephone, and were given the same discount as if they had ordered online.

This chapter is designed to give you your first peek into the world of Internet advertising design and development. At the end, you may not be creating the ultimate online brand experience, but you should be better at it.

● The Interactive Team

When you design ads for the Internet, your team is a bit larger than one for traditional advertising. You still need an art director and a copywriter, but you need a couple of other people as well. You'll need a programmer for technical expertise. You don't want the technology to overwhelm your creative thinking, but at some point you'll need to know whether your ideas are technically feasible. You'll also want to have a producer on hand. Internet sites and banner ads can be like jigsaw puzzles, and it's not unusual to have ten or fifteen people working on a project. The producer makes sure that everyone is on the same "page" and keeps track of the many details involved in completing the project.

● Designing for the Internet: A Four-Stage Process

Whether it's a 100-page Internet site or an advertising banner, there is a method to the madness of Internet design. As you read this chapter, you'll notice that much of the Internet design process is similar to that for print and TV. The Internet is not as different as you might think.

● Stage 1: Research and Planning

Anytime you see a great ad campaign, you'll find a great strategy behind it. Does this sound familiar? It should. In Chapter 4, you learned that good ads start with good strategies. Successful Internet sites and banner ads start the same way. Over the course of your career in advertising, you'll find that almost every project starts with research. And after working on a couple of projects without a clear strategy, you will really understand why it's so important.

Designing a Web Site: The Site Map

Suppose someone asked you to build a house. How would you start? Would you dash off to Home Depot for bricks, lumber, and plumbing supplies? Install the heating system and then build the walls? Shingle the roof before you poured the foundation? Probably not. You would likely start by asking some questions. How big will the house be? How many bedrooms will there be? Will the dining room be formal or just an extension of the kitchen? Will there be one bathroom or two? If you didn't ask questions, then you wouldn't know what to build or how to build it.

Designing for the Internet is a lot like building a house. One of the first things you need to do is get your idea down on paper. Look at the high-level site map shown in Figure 11-1. Just as a blueprint tells a construction manager how many rooms the house will have, where the doors and windows will go, and so on, the site map helps a creative team decide how many pages will be needed and how people will move through them. The map helps them make better decisions about how the site will look and work.

Understanding how people will move through a Web site is important. Your design approach will vary depending on how many options people have to select from. Look at the detailed site map shown in Figure 11-2. This version outlines all the specific details for the "demo" section. Not only does the site map identify the different pieces of content, but it also makes recommendations for using technology. The

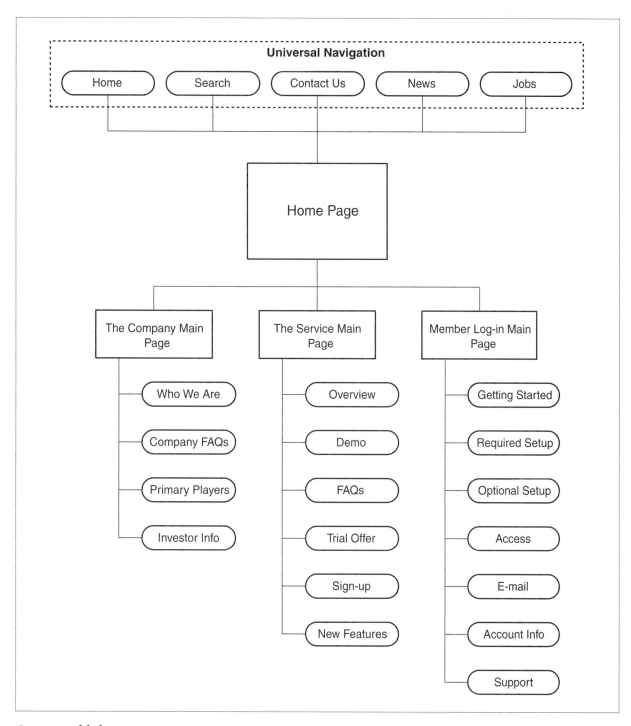

● FIGURE 11-1

This high-level site map provides an overview of the different sections planned for this Internet site. The universal navigation options identified at the top of the map would appear on every page. From the homepage, major content sections are identified, giving the creative team a better understanding of the amount of information they have to work with.

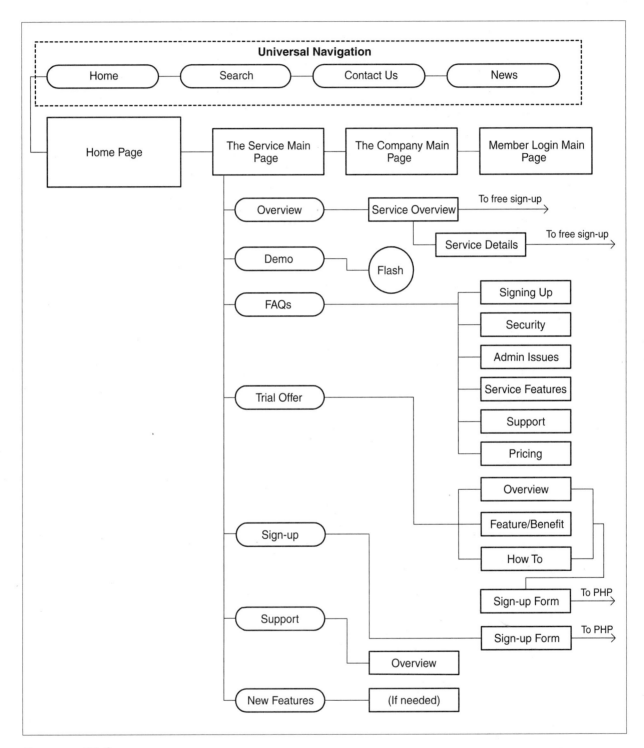

● FIGURE 11-2

The detailed site map provides the specific details about how the pages will work. In this example, boxes with rounded corners identify primary navigation options, and the rectangular boxes identify specific pages.

"demo" tab under "The Service Main Page" leads to an indicator for "Flash." When developing concepts for this section, the creative team will know that they need to design a demo using Macromedia Flash. They also know that the content window will need to be big enough to play the Flash movie. The demo will have a storyboard and script of its own.

● Stage 2: Concepts

Once you have an approved site map, you're ready to start developing design concepts. Because of the way Internet sites are built, you actually have to develop concepts for both the content and the page template. Think of it as developing the "look and feel" (page template) of a magazine first and then coming up with this month's editorial material (content).

Some art directors prefer to create their concepts, or roughs, as a simple sketch. Others prefer using a computer with illustration or design software. Whatever your preference, the idea is the same: You start by putting together a rough version of your design. This is not the time to be precise. It's more important to capture the basic concept than it is to come up with a completed design.

You might find it helpful to start with your page template, deciding where you want to place the constant elements like logos and navigation features. This helps you determine how much space you have for the actual content. And don't worry about whether your initial ideas are possible. At this stage, you want to give yourself plenty of options. Don't let the technology limit your thinking.

Remember that you're looking for interaction, not just a reaction. In traditional advertising, your ad is often considered successful if you stimulate a reaction in your audience. Janine Carlson, director of strategic marketing and principal at Icon Communications, points out the greater challenge facing online marketers: "You can't be satisfied with getting a reaction. You have to spark an interaction. One is simply a split-second exchange with your audience. The other opens the door for an ongoing relationship. And that should be the goal for anyone working in advertising or marketing."

Here are some guidelines to keep in mind as you start developing your rough concepts:

1. *Make sure your design works across a series of pages.* Internet sites almost always have more than one page, and not every page functions the same way. That means your design for the page template has to be flexible. Some of the pages might have graphic headlines, text, and supporting images. Other pages might include a Flash movie, a submit form, or some other kind of Internet technology. Your template has to accommodate all of these elements. It's usually easiest to start with your most complicated page. Figure 11-3 illustrates how a design works on both the homepage and a secondary page.

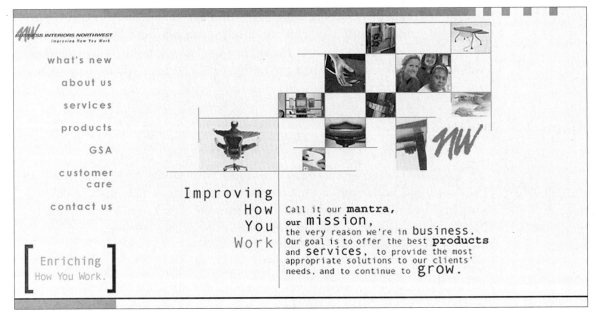

Homepage

Secondary Page

● FIGURE 11-3

This homepage design uses a navigation-focused approach, providing visitors with an overview of the information they can find on the site. The goal of this homepage is to quickly move users to the page that best meets their needs. The secondary page provides more specific information about the company's services. Notice that there are not huge design differences between the homepage and the secondary page. While they are not exactly the same, the art director for this site continued the initial theme to the lower-level pages, keeping brand and navigation elements in the same location on each page. The result is a consistent and attractive page that is easy to navigate.

2. *Keep some parts of the template constant.* When you design a page template, it's important to remember that some design elements won't change as you move from one page to the next. For example, you want to keep navigation elements in the same area on each page so people can find them. Logos are another design element that should stay in one place. Consistency makes your site easier to access and follow. Identifying the location of your constant elements first helps you determine how much space you have left over for everything else. Figure 11-4 gives an example of how a page might be broken into different sections to allocate space.

● FIGURE 11-4

This content guide identifies the art director's placement of the constant page elements. This helps determine how much room is required for the page template and how much space is left over for the content. Once the position has been identified, the art director can begin to refine the design of these elements.

3. *Keep the most important elements in first view.* There really is no limit to how long an Internet page can be, but there is a limit to how much of the page a person will see at one time. A person's first view of an Internet page depends on the screen resolution, or size, of the Web site. Your template design should put the most important elements at the top so they're easy for people to find.

4. *Pay attention to navigation.* Think of navigation as the highway system for your Web site, helping people to quickly get to the information they're looking for. And just like a real highway system, the navigational highway uses both primary and secondary systems. Primary navigation provides access to the major sections of content on a Web site. Secondary navigation helps users move around within a specific content section. Some sites also include universal navigation. These are navigation options that apply to all users on all pages. Examples of universal navigation include a "home" option for returning to the homepage, a "search" option for accessing a site's search capability and a "contact us" option for sending an e-mail or finding a phone number or address.

Having a lot of options can sometimes create problems. Remember that technology will never be a good substitute for solid strategic planning. Just because you can make a logo spin doesn't mean that doing so is a good idea. Julie Johnson, executive producer for Web design firm Elusive Little Fish, advises creative teams to strive for elegant simplicity, noting that too often the message gets lost in the technology. Movement for the sake of movement doesn't do anything to make your message more memorable or effective. It can, however, be incredibly distracting.

● Stage 3: Development

Refining the Design

Now it's time to start making decisions about your design and ironing out the details. An important part of development is comparing your concepts to the site map. You need to make sure that the final design works well on all the pages in your site. Sometimes, you find the right design quickly. Other times, you don't and find yourself back at the drawing board looking for a better idea.

You'll likely revise your design more than once before you finalize it. And the more complex your project, the more likely the need for revisions. When you're designing a complex Web site, it's a good idea to do a functional proof-of-concept before you get too far along in the project. You'll need your programmer for this. With your help, the programmer can mock up a section of the site and make sure that your design is technically feasible.

As you move through the development process and refine your design, you'll probably end up adding additional pages. Make sure you consider the impact this will have on the rest of the site. A Web page is useful only if people can get to it, and introducing new pages at the end of the development phase can cause problems with the rest of the site.

Writing Copy for the Internet

The development phase is also the stage at which the copywriter really starts working. If you start writing too early in the process, you won't know how the pages work, and your copy won't make sense. By waiting until you're a little further along in the design process, you save yourself from having to do a lot of rewriting.

Writing copy for the Internet is a lot different from writing for print. Why? Because people don't read on the Internet. They scan. According to usability expert Jacob Nielsen, principal partner of the Nielsen Norman Group, people rarely read Web pages word for word. Instead, they scan the page, picking out individual words and sentences. This means that, when you write copy for the Internet, you need to adjust your style to match how people read online.

While it's important to realize that writing for the Internet is different from conventional writing, it's equally important to note the similarities. Remember the guidelines for writing copy given in Chapter 6? They still apply. If you adhere to those guidelines and to the following guidelines for the Internet, your copy should be enjoyable and effective.

1. *Use highlighted keywords.* Adding visual emphasis to important words helps catch the scanning eye of the reader. Using boldface or italics is an effective way of highlighting keywords. If you have more detail related to a specific word, turning it into a hyperlink not only catches the readers eye but also provides easy access to additional information on a subsequent page. However, use highlights sparingly. If every other word is a link or is boldfaced, the reader will ignore them and move on.

2. *Make sure your subheads are meaningful and not just clever.* Subheads are a lot like highway signs. Just as motorists use highway signs to find their way through a unfamiliar city, readers on the Internet use subheads to find their way through your site. If your subheads aren't instructive, people will abandon your site and go somewhere else.

3. *Aim for one idea per paragraph.* Having a single idea makes it easier to get your point across. Readers will skip over any additional ideas if they're not captivated by the first few words in the paragraph. In traditional advertising, you shouldn't try to say everything in one ad. On the Internet, you should avoid trying to say it all in one paragraph.

4. *Present complex ideas with bulleted lists.* Sometimes, a single idea will have multiple parts, making it difficult to get the main idea across quickly and easily. A bulleted list is a great way of organizing complex ideas and presenting the major points. Another benefit is that the specific bulleted items can be turned into hyperlinks so

that additional details are just a mouse click away. Consider the "great deal" in this paragraph:

> The Acme Super Home Computer has everything you need. A 6 Gig hard-drive, 64 MBs of RAM, a 128 front-side bus, a DVD player, and tons of software. Only $1,999 at Acme Super Computer City.

Difficult to read, isn't it? Now see how a bulleted list makes this information much easier to read:

- $1,999 Acme Super Computer City Special
- 6 Gig hard-drive
- 64 MBs RAM
- 128 front-side bus
- DVD player
- Tons of software

5. *Write your copy using an inverted pyramid style.* Start with the conclusion, and then add the details. If people have to read the entire paragraph to get to your main point, they won't. Putting the conclusion or benefit right up front makes it easy for your readers to determine whether they're interested in this information.

6. Use half as many words (or less) as you would with conventional writing. Reading on a computer screen is a different experience from reading on paper. Studies show that people read about 25 percent slower on a computer than they do when they read from paper. Cutting the length of your copy helps compensate for the slower reading time. Another problem is that reading from a computer screen is hard on the eyes. Think about the last time you spent a lot of time reading from your computer screen. It probably didn't take very long before your eyes felt dry and tired. By writing concise copy and tightly focusing your ideas, you can get your point across before your reader wears out.

● Stage 4: Production

The final stage in designing an Internet site is putting all the pieces together. Your journey from initial idea to fully developed plan is almost complete. With the help of the producer and the programmer, you'll assemble the text, images, and various other parts of the site into the finished product.

Using Internet Technology

When you were coming up with your ideas and turning them into a great design, you didn't want the technology to limit your thinking. During production, the role of technology can't be avoided. And while Internet technology seems to change on a daily basis, some things do stay the same. Here are the most constant impacts of technology on your design:

- *Screen resolution.* Every Web site has a pixel dimension or screen size. This is known as the screen resolution. The most common screen resolutions are 640 × 480, 800 × 600, or 1040 × 780. It's important that you pick your target screen resolution before you start programming. Why? Imagine designing a full-page ad for a broadsheet newspaper and then learning that you actually only have a quarter of a page to work with. If you had known that size limitation before-hand, you probably would have developed your ad differently. For example, a horizontal navigation bar works very nicely on a Internet site designed for an 800 × 600 size, but not for a 640 × 480 size. It's quite similar to the landscape versus portrait setting on a printer. The screen resolution is usually determined by the size of the monitor used by the target audience. A screen resolution of 800 × 600 doesn't fit in the window of a 15-inch monitor, but it does on a 17-inch monitor.

- *Operating Systems.* When you watch a TV commercial, it doesn't really matter which kind of TV you see it on because the ad looks the same whether you see it on your own TV or on your friend's. Unfortunately, this does not hold true for the Internet. When you create a Web page, you have to accommodate differences between operating systems (OS). While most home computers use a Microsoft Windows OS, many people use an alternative such as Mac OS, Unix or Linux. Each OS results in a different user experience on the Web site. Some Internet technologies are optimized for performance on one OS and may not work on a different system. Make sure you're aware of the consequences before you decide on your final solution.

- *Browsers.* Browsers are the software applications used to view Internet content. They interpret the page code and make it possible to combine text, graphics, audio, video, and all the other technologies that make the Internet such an exciting place to be. The two main Internet browsers are Microsoft Internet Explorer and Netscape Navigator. While they both work about the same way, they do have their differences. It's important to check your finished Web page in both browsers. Just because your Web page looks great in Navigator doesn't mean it will in Internet Explorer. Different versions of the same browser might also affect your finished pages. Some technologies that work in a 4.0 version of Netscape Navigator won't work in the 3.0 version.

- *Internet-safe colors.* Different computer operating systems (Mac, Windows, and Windows 95) use different color palettes. An image containing 100 colors might look fine on a Mac. But a computer with a Windows OS may not contain all the same colors, and the image may look very different from the one on the Mac. Generally, you don't want such unpredictability in your Web page. How do you control the colors that will appear on your pages? Although the color palettes vary between the different operating systems, they all have 216 colors in common.

These 216 colors are considered browser-safe, and if you create images using only these colors, you'll avoid most of the inconsistencies between the different operating systems, computer platforms, and browsers.

- *Plug-ins.* Some Internet technologies require users to download and install plug-ins (small software programs) in order for the design to appear. Macromedia's Shockwave is an example of a plug-in-dependent technology. If your Web design includes a technology like Shockwave, users won't see your design unless they have installed the plug-in. You should never require a plug-in for content displayed on a Web site's homepage. Ideally, any content requiring a plug-in should be optional, meaning that not seeing it won't have a serious impact on the user experience. The final determination about whether a plug-in is appropriate depends on your target audience. A technically savvy audience is more likely to have a higher-end system, and requiring a plug-in may not be an issue.

Making It Live   After production is finished, the Web site is ready for the public. This last step doesn't require you to do anything except move the fully programmed Web site to the host server.

● Banner Ads

Many people on the Internet consider banners annoying and go out of their way to ignore them. But with the right approach, banners can be a very effective means of advertising. Consider the following story of a banner that doubled traffic to the destination Internet site:

You're browsing an online store looking for a Christmas gift for your best friend. You can't help but notice the banner at the top of the web page: "Need CA$H for the holiday?" The banner animates to the second frame: "Sell last year's gifts." Finally comes the call to action: "Online auctions everyday." You click on the banner and go to an online auction, where you buy the perfect gift for your friend.

Why was this banner so effective? First, it asked a question. It's more difficult to ignore a question than a statement because even a stupid question makes you pause and think about it. In this case, the use of a question was even more effective because many readers identified with the subject. Who hasn't needed extra cash for the holidays?

Second, it used humor. You certainly don't expect the second frame of this banner. Most of us have probably wished we could sell last year's presents. We just wouldn't say that out loud.

Third, it took a different approach. This banner's objective was to funnel traffic to an online auction. Most banner ads about online auctions focus on the "buy." This banner focused on the "sell," setting this auction apart from the competition and creating an intriguing invitation for both buyers and sellers.

Guidelines for Creating Banner Ads

Sometimes the simplest ideas turn out to be the most effective. Here are some guidelines that will help make your banner ads more effective:

1. *Keep it short and simple.* People usually don't visit a Web site to see banner ads, and they probably won't take the time to notice a complex message. You have only a few seconds to catch people's attention before they move on to the next page and away from your banner. That's not much time to grab their attention. Short and simple messages have a stronger focus and are more likely to result in a click-through. As a general rule, each frame of a banner ad should have at most seven words.

2. *Animate three times and then stop.* If you've spent much time on the Internet, you've probably noticed that constantly animating banners are annoying. In fact, most Web sites that accept banners advertising limit animations to a cycle of three. Even if the site doesn't have an animation limit, it's a good idea to use one. After all, you don't want people's reactions to your ad to be negative.

3. *End with the logo or the name.* If someone doesn't click on your banner, they might at least notice the name of your company. While it's not the best response you could hope for, it's better than nothing. Banner ads may not be the best tool for creating awareness about a brand, but every impression helps.

● A Look at the Future

A mere five years ago, most people considered the Internet a fad and quickly dismissed it. Back then, the closest thing to shopping online was picking up the phone and calling an 800-number. Today, it doesn't seem unusual that you can do everything from buying groceries to earning a master's degree online. Technology is finally catching up with our imaginations.

● Suggested Activities

1. You've been hired by a new company that sells socks. Create a site map for your new client, outlining how the site would come together.

2. Visit at least five different Web sites, and ask yourself the following questions:
   a. Was the navigation consistent from one page to the next, making it easy for you to move through the site?
   b. Was it easy to find what you were looking for? Why?
   c. Which site did you think had the best design? Why?
   d. If you could change anything about the sites, what would it be?

Search Online! Discovering More About Internet Advertising

Using InfoTrac® College Edition, try these phrases and others for Key Words and Subject Guide searches: *Internet advertising, Internet banners, Internet marketing, Web programmer, Web sites + design, Macromedia Flash, Macromedia Shockwave, interactive advertising + Internet, Web site homepage, Web site secondary page, HTML, writing for Internet, Internet links, Netscape Navigator, Microsoft Internet Explorer, Internet animation.*

BriefCase

Getting Banner Results on the Internet:
What's Creative Online?

BY STEVEN R. ROBINSON, VICE PRESIDENT, MARKETING,
ISG INTERNATIONAL, INC.

Internet advertising has come a long way since 1994, when www.zima.com became the first national consumer brand Web site. About the same time, McDonald's sponsored an online chat area on America Online, taking out space in *USA Today* to promote the sponsorship. And so the marriage between conventional media and what would soon be called "new media" began.

On the Internet, banner ads are generally placed toward the top of the Web page and come in many shapes and sizes. A visitor to a Web site who is attracted to the banner may click on the ad and be transported to another Web site featuring the advertised product or service.

The efficacy of the banner can be measured by using the "click rate," the percentage of clicks an ad receives per number of times the ad appears on a computer screen. While this figure is hardly conclusive, it does tell how much more effective one ad is at capturing attention and moving viewers to action than other ads.

At ISG International, an independent insurance agency, where I work as vice president of marketing, one of our most successful products is CCBsure (Computer Consultant Business Insurance), a group of commercial insurance policies bundled into a program that's tailored to reach small to mid-sized information technology companies and independent computer professionals. Our Web site is http://www.ccbsure.com.

Decision makers in our target are more likely to be men age 25-45 with a college degree and an average annual income of $100,000.

To determine the relative success of a number of different approaches, we developed a series of animated banner ads in four distinct groups:

- *Using basic information.* This banner had bold white text fading in and out of the black area:

ccbsure.com
The best way to insure IT.
Free Insurance Quotes

ccbsure.com
The best way to insure IT.
Real-time Advice Online

ccbsure.com
The best way to insure IT.
IT Developers

ccbsure.com
The best way to insure IT.
IT Developers
click here

The banner incorporated the look and feel of the CCBsure Web site and told how visiting the site would make the insurance research and buying process easy for the viewer (IT stands for "information technology").

- *Using fear to invoke action.* This ad featured purple text on white.

Is this your client calling you?

Nope.

It's your client's attorney.

> Insurance suddenly sounds like a good idea.

> Get the best. Get it fast. Get it here. NOW.

The text faded in and out and was accompanied by a photo of a man on the phone.

- *Using humor to invoke curiosity.* This banner ran on the www.monster.com site. Using a string of different-colored condoms hanging on a clothesline, the banner read:

> **WARNING:**
> Cutting corners in the insurance process can yield harmful results.

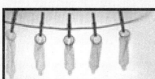

> If you're doing IT.

> Make sure you're protected with the right insurance.

> ccbsure.com

> ccbsure.com
> Business Insurance for IT Professionals.

BriefCase

Incidentally, risqué ads are more the norm than the exception in this market.

- *Using a functional approach to invite participatory action.* These ads took a different approach altogether. None were animated, and none mentioned the CCBsure name or Web site. They were not "adlike," but instead attempted to draw the interest of the viewer by blending in with the site on which they appeared. What they all shared was a device (buttons or fill-in windows) where the viewer could ask for specific information and be connected to the CCBsure Web site. Each ad was designed to resemble the Web site on which it was located.

Business Insurance for:

Programmers   Developers   Consultants   Designers   [   ]   Quote

What seemed to work best, after all was said and done, were the functional ads in the last group. While many traditional advertising rules don't apply to the Internet, at least one still stands: Information is king. In fact, the Internet may be the prime medium for the transmission of information through advertising. The study told us that people on the Internet aren't as interested in being entertained or scared or simply told about something. They want to be empowered. Perhaps this explains why the functionality of the ads in this study played a larger roll than the personality of the ads. Perhaps what Internet surfers really want is a magic button that will give them the answer they want when they want it.

David Ogilvy once said, "I do not regard advertising as an entertainment or art form, but as a medium of information. When I write an advertisement, I don't want you to tell me you find it 'creative.' I want you to find it so interesting that you buy the product."

Perhaps Ogilvy would have relished the power of this medium to do just that.

CHAPTER 12

Retail Advertising

I f you think retail advertising isn't for you, consider this: Both authors of this book began their careers in retail. Jewler began as a copywriter for Sears catalogs, while Drewniany landed a job right out of college as a junior copywriter at Bamberger's (now Macy's). What we didn't know at the time was that retail is a great place to learn all aspects of advertising and can itself become a very rewarding career. It's also a well-trod path to agency work on national accounts.

Our experiences are not unique. Many advertising majors work on retail accounts when they graduate from college. In fact, it is highly likely that you'll create retail ads sometime in your career. Even if you don't work directly for a retailer, chances are you will have retail accounts if you work for a local advertising agency or for the advertising department of a newspaper or radio or TV station.

But don't think that you have to be small-time to create retail ads. Many of the advertising greats, including David Ogilvy and Bill Bernbach, worked on retail accounts. Does that surprise you? It shouldn't. Retail advertising is big business. In 1998, retailers spent $11.5 billion on advertising media. That's more than was spent on media to advertise food, toiletries, cosmetics, beer, wine, and liquor combined.[1]

The size of the advertising budget isn't the only thing that sets retailers apart. And before you can create effective retail ads, you must understand the many differences between national and retail advertising.

[1] "100 Leading National Advertisers: Total Measured U.S. Ad Spending by Category and Media in 1998," *Advertising Age*, 27 Sept. 1999, p. S3.

● What Makes Retail Advertising Unique?

Retail advertising is unique for a number of reasons, including the following:

- *Retail ads tell two stories.* When you create an ad for a retailer, you want to get customers interested in the product, and you want them to buy it at your store. When you create ads for a national product, you usually aren't concerned with where the customer buys it.

- *Retail ads are sought out by customers.* Most people don't turn on their TV or flip through a magazine to see if brand X toothpaste comes in a new flavor, if brand Y detergent comes in a new package, or if brand Z medicine is stronger than before. However, they do open their local paper to find out what's on special at the grocery store, when the white sale starts at their favorite department store, and who has the best deal on air conditioners when the temperature starts to soar. In a sense, a retail ad is like a news story—it tells customers who, what, when, and where. Perhaps Thomas Jefferson said it best; "I read one newspaper and that . . . more for its advertisements than its news."

- *Retail advertisers have several clients to please.* Retailers receive co-op funding from national manufacturers to advertise their products. Although the money is great, sometimes the manufacturer's creative requirements can conflict with a store's image. For example, a manufacturer may require you to use a specific photograph, but your store's advertising format may only use illustrations. As you can imagine, it's not always easy to please both "clients." To add to the challenge, you may have several brands on the same page. Pleasing everyone takes diplomacy and imagination.

- *Retail ads promote competing brands.* There are times when several competing brands appear in the same retail ad. There are even times when the store's private label is promoted next to national brands. The challenge to the retail advertiser is to put each brand in a favorable light, give customers enough information to make intelligent decisions, and not offend any of the vendors. It's not always easy. It is much easier to sell only one brand, as national advertisers do.

- *Retail ads promote a broad range of products.* A retailer may carry everything from high tech to high fashion. Or a retailer may specialize in a product category and offer a vast variety of brands to suit a range of budgets. Therefore, you need to appeal to a variety of consumer needs while establishing a consistent image for your store.

- *Retail ads have a greater sense of urgency.* You want customers to know that, to get the best prices and the best selection, they should get to your store today. Not tomorrow. And certainly not a month from now. By contrast, most national ads imply, "The next time you go shopping for a particular product, buy our brand."

● FIGURE 12-1

In an era when off-price stores are becoming a mecca for virtually all socioeconomic levels, Stein Mart positions itself at the top of this category, claiming to offer better fashion at unbeatable prices. With copy lines such as "The exact same clothes from two different stores look exactly the same" and "You work five days a week, fifty weeks a year, for what? So you can give your money to some overpriced department store?" the advertisements reach out and build a meaningful relationship with their audience, reinforcing the idea that, at Stein Mart, "you could pay more, but you'll have to go somewhere else."

Studies prove that if you paid less for what you're wearing, you'd look exactly the same.

It's a scientific fact. The exact same clothes from two different stores look exactly the same.

That's something to keep in mind the next time you're out shopping.

Whether you need a new shirt, a new belt, or a whole new outfit, Stein Mart sells it for less than those overpriced department stores. Same merchandise.

Same designer labels.

Just one major difference. Up to 60% off every single thing every single day. Which leads us to one other undisputed fact: Discounts will always lead to saving money.

Stein Mart®
You Could Pay More, But
You'll Have To Go Somewhere Else.

- *Retail ads contain more details.* National brand advertisements don't usually contain details such as price, size, and color. In retail advertising, these details are extremely important and may be what separates a store from the competition.

- *Retail ads reflect local tastes.* When you create local retail advertising, you know your customers. They are your neighbors and friends and family. You know their tastes and their sense of humor; you know what's on their minds. When you create an ad for a national product, you deal with demographic and psychographic generalities. It's difficult to get very personal because the ad you create must appeal both to someone in New York, and to someone in New Orleans.

    Recently, many local stores have merged with national retailers, so their ads are now created at the national headquarters rather than locally. Although this may save money, it lessens the personal touch the retailer once had with its customers. Small retailers still can boast this advantage and should use it to differentiate themselves.

- *Retail ads are easier to track for success.* Just check a printout of the day's sales or stroll around the selling floor, and you will know your ad's results. The effects of a single ad are much more difficult to measure on a national level because the ad is part of a long-term multimedia campaign, and a variety of outside factors (including retailer support) can influence sales.

- *Retail advertising is more volatile.* Because merchants know the results of specific ads, they are often inclined to make changes in campaigns that aren't drawing in customers. These changes can be made right up to the last moment because retail's most widely used media, newspapers and radio, accept last-minute changes. While changes may be necessary, it's important not to overreact. Some of the most powerful national campaigns have been running for decades.

- *Retail advertisers produce a greater volume of work.* Tom McElligott, cofounder of Fallon McElligott, started his advertising career at Dayton Hudson's. "The wonderful thing about starting in retail is that you're forced to write quickly and produce a lot. Many copywriters don't know what it's like to have a tremendous work load. In an agency, an ad or a campaign can consume weeks of their time. There's nothing like coming into your office on Monday morning and knowing you're responsible for producing 18 different pieces of work by Friday."[2]

● How to Create Retail Ads

Creating retail advertising is quite challenging. You have to sell not only a variety of competing brands but also your store. You need to convince customers that your store is *the* place to shop, even though the competitor across the street may be selling the same merchandise at the same prices. You also need to convince customers

[2]Laurence Minsky and Emily Thornton Calvo, *How to Succeed in Advertising When All You Have Is Talent* (Lincolnwood, IL: NTC Business Books, 1995), p. 231.

● FIGURE 12-2

There are dust collectors. And then there are dust collectors. Target's Club Wedd uses parallel construction to tell couples how they can get gifts they will actually use.

A Typical Wedding Gift.

Atypical Wedding Gift.

When it comes right down to it, there are three kinds of wedding gifts. First, there's the kind that gets returned. (You already have something like it. Or you wouldn't be caught dead owning something like it.)

Second, there's the kind that gets put away. (You know, for those "special occasions" that come around two, maybe three times every other decade.)

And then there's the kind you really use. That's where Club Wedd™ comes in. Club Wedd is the gift registry service at Target. It helps guests choose gifts that

you need. Gifts you'll enjoy. Gifts that you'll really use.

Just stop by the Club Wedd kiosk at the Target locations listed below. Instead of pen and paper we'll give you a barcode scanner to instantly record each gift you'd like as you walk through the store.

It's fun to do and your wedding guests will be able to purchase gifts quickly and easily.

Just let them know you've registered at one of the participating Target Club Wedd locations. They'll thank you for it later. After, of course, you've thanked them.

CLUB
WEDD
GIFT REGISTRY

PLYMOUTH • WOODBURY • BROOKLYN PARK • SHOREVIEW   BLOOMINGTON • NORTHTOWN • MANKATO • APPLE VALLEY

◎ TARGET.

that the traditional way of shopping is better than buying things in the comfort of their own home through a catalog or online. This is not easy.

Before you write copy or draw a layout, ask yourself why you would shop at your store. Think about it. Carefully. The answers will tell you a lot about your store's personality, and that will give your ads direction. To get you started, here are some things to consider telling your customers.

Tell Them About Your Store's Personnel

Have you ever stood in line for several minutes, only to be told, "Sorry. This line is closed?" Have you ever waited patiently for a sales clerk to complete a personal phone call? Or have you ever asked a sales clerk a question about a product, only to get a vacant look? Did you leave the store in disgust? Well, you're not alone. In a survey sponsored by MasterCard International, 62 percent of shoppers said they'd abandoned a purchase in the last six months because the sales clerks were too busy to help. On top of that, 60 percent said store personnel weren't knowledgeable enough to be of help.

Smart retailers know that good service is key to their survival. After all, it's the face-to-face contact that sets traditional retailing apart from catalog and online shopping. Assuming you have the good fortune to work for a retailer that offers good service, you need to tell the story in your advertisements. But simply saying your store offers good service is not enough. You need to tell a more convincing story. So do some homework. Read letters from customers. Talk with the sales clerks. The dressing room attendant. The tailor. You'll be surprised at how interesting these stories can be.

Don't stop with the obvious personnel. Look behind the scenes. While your customers may never see the people who buy the merchandise for your store, they certainly see the results of your buyers' efforts. So talk about your buyers. Did an interesting thing happen to them on a buying trip? Were they able to negotiate an extraordinary deal? Did they go to the ends of the earth to find unique merchandise? Then tell these stories.

The buying trip doesn't have to be exotic to capture your readers' attention. Remember, you're trying to express your store's personality. So let the store be itself. A fashion-buying trip to New York can make an interesting story. So can a furniture-buying trip to North Carolina. Or a visit to a local craftsman's shop.

Tell Them About Your Location

Things certainly have changed from the days when people went shopping for entertainment and the motto was "Shop 'til you drop." Today, many customers have abandoned traditional shopping for the convenience and safety of shopping at home. Your job is to convince customers that they should leave the comfort of home and go to your store to shop. Don't just give customers your address—tell them why your location is an advantage. For example, is your store conveniently located? Is there plenty of free parking? Is it on a bus route? Is it near another popular store? Tell your customers about these things.

What happens if your store isn't in a convenient location? Then see if you can turn this disadvantage into an advantage. Perhaps your store provides a unique service and needs to be in a special location to attract quality employees. Or perhaps it's a matter of economics. Maybe your retailer can offer lower prices because it doesn't pay extra rent for a fancy address.

Tell Them About Your Store's Pricing Policy

Does your store offer everyday low prices? Value prices? Does it meet or beat the competitors' prices? Or does it offer such exclusive merchandise that price is no object? Whatever the case, the way you present the prices in your advertising says a lot about your store's personality.

Regardless of your store's pricing policy, you most likely will have to create sale ads for it, whether it's to announce that your everyday low prices are even lower or your exclusive store is having its annual clearance event. Don't moan. Sale ads don't have to be boring. In fact, they shouldn't be. They need to be innovative so they stand out from the clutter. And, most important of all, they should reflect the image of your store.

Tell Them About Your Products

Chances are, you will have hundreds of products to sell for your store. Your challenge will be to become an expert on them all. How do you do this? Examine the products on the selling floor. Ask questions of the buyers and the salespeople. Ask for a demonstration. Visit merchandise shows. Study vendor spec sheets. Analyze national ads. Read articles about products. Pay attention to what your friends and neighbors say. Soon you'll be an expert.

You owe it to your customers to be knowledgeable. Have you ever read vague copy along the lines of "You'll find great savings on a terrific collection of beautiful tops that will brighten your holiday wardrobe"? Remember how frustrated you were? The copy says nothing about the product. Who makes the tops? What styles are on sale? Do they have long sleeves? Short sleeves? Cap sleeves? What about the neckline? What about the fabric? And so on. Chances are, the writer never saw the tops and relied on generic copy to fill the space allotted by the art director. Don't do that. Go to the selling floor to check the merchandise. Phone the buyer. Do anything. But don't cop out.

The way you present the products should say something about your store. One thing you should tell customers about is your store's selection of products. Many customers want to shop at a store with a huge variety. As a result, many retailers want their ads to be jammed with merchandise. But don't let your ads get so busy that they're confusing. Try a few layouts. Try combining merchandise categories. Be creative. See how many products can be included on a page without losing the creative integrity.

What do you do if your store doesn't offer a huge selection? Your ad can take several directions. Perhaps your store only stocks the finest merchandise. Or perhaps your store's small size gives it a friendlier atmosphere. Your layout and copy should tell the story.

The quality of your store's merchandise is another important message to relate to customers. Even the smallest detail can help you tell a big story. For example, a close-up of a jacket's buttons can help you tell customers about fine tailoring. A single

Target knows that most wedding gifts get used only on "special occasions." Their strategy in this campaign is, "Why not ask for something you'll really use, like everyday flatware?"

About $100 Each. Three Uses Per Year.

About $2 Each. Three Uses Per Day.

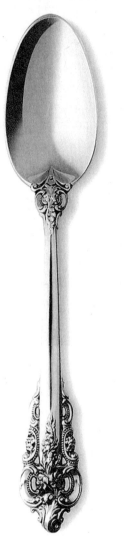

Not every wedding couple is into sterling silver gifts. Some prefer simple, unpretentious gifts they can use every day. For those couples, we suggest Club Wedd.℠

Club Wedd is the gift registry service at Target. It makes registering and shopping for a wedding gift simple, easy and affordable. Just stop by the Club Wedd kiosk at participating Target locations. We'll give you a barcode scanner to instantly record each gift you'd like as you walk through the store.

Then just tell your guests you've registered at Target Club Wedd. You won't end up with sterling silver. But you will end up saying "Now that, we can use."

CLUB
WEDD℠
GIFT REGISTRY

◎ TARGET

strawberry can tell the story about a grocery store's quest for freshness. The image of a strand of hand-knotted pearls can say reams about a store's beautifully crafted gifts.

Uniqueness is another important message. Does your store carry an exclusive line from a national manufacturer? Does your store carry private labels? What about special sizes? Get the idea? You want your store to seem special. You want to give customers a reason to shop in your store instead of going to the competitor across the street.

Tell Them About Your Store's History

Many people think of their favorite store as they would a friend. They enjoy hearing stories about it, particularly if it makes them look intelligent for choosing the store. Macy's history saved the advertising department one day. The department had released a catalog to the printer, and on each page, a special event (such as a celebrity appearance and contest) was highlighted in a color box. As it turned out, however, the special events feature had to be canceled. This created a major problem because the printer had already completed the color separations. Removing the color boxes would have been very costly. Leaving them blank would have looked foolish. Fortunately, tidbits from Macy's history worked perfectly in the special boxes. The fact that Macy's had invented the tea bag was placed on a page with kettles. The fact that Macy's had introduced the baked Idaho potato was highlighted on the microwave oven page. The fact that colored towels had been the brainchild of a Macy's buyer appeared on the domestics page. Macy's history saved the day. It looked as if the whole thing had been planned. The ad let customers know that creative merchandising had a long tradition at Macy's.

Even if your store doesn't have a history quite as glorious as Macy's, you still have important stories to tell. For example, has your store been managed by generations of the same family? Does your store's management still hold the same principles that were established years earlier? Maybe there's a story in the fact that your store no longer goes by the rules established by its founders.

Tell Them Where You Stand on Issues

Remember, your customers are your neighbors, and you need to show them that your store is involved in the community. Therefore, your ads should tell customers that your store participates in charity functions. They should tell where it stands on issues such as recycling. They should communicate that it cares about special groups. By telling customers where the store stands on issues, you're establishing an important rapport with them.

A retailer who understands the importance of being a good citizen is the Body Shop. Employees of the Body Shop are activists on such issues as protecting endangered species, fighting pollution, and stopping violence against women. The company's trade-not-aid policy gives opportunities to people who are less fortunate. Homeless people in New York make hand-rolled beeswax candles for the store, and in Baltimore, formerly at-risk youths make soap dishes from recycled wood pallets. Brochures, store signs, and even shopping bags tell customers how the Body Shop is making a difference.

● FIGURE 12-4

Why wait an eternity for furniture delivery? Rooms To Go has everything in stock, ready for you to take home.

Tell Them Just One Thing About Your Store

Don't send your customers mixed messages when you tell them about your store's personnel, location, pricing policy, products, history, and positions on issues. Instead, every ad you create should support one image in your customers' minds. The most successful retailers understand this concept, and it is reflected in everything they do. For example, Wal-Mart owns the word *value,* Nordstrom owns the word *service,* and Talbots owns the word *classics.* Unfortunately, many retailers send conflicting messages. For example, a men's clothier may take pride in its well-tailored clothing but contradict this image by constantly advertising mass-produced polyester slacks.

Tell Them the Truth

Remember, the ads you create are directed to your friends and neighbors. You can't fool them. If you do, you might lose their trust forever.

One time a copywriter was faced with the challenge of selling orange luggage. It was just plain ugly. What could she do? She *could* omit the fact that it was orange. After all, she wasn't taking mail and phone orders, so she didn't have to mention color at all. And, because the ad was going to run in black and white, no one would know the difference, right? Wrong. Customers would know the minute they came to the store. They would be furious. And the store could lose valued customers. So she wrote something along these lines: "Does your luggage get lost at the airline terminals? We've got the perfect luggage for you!" The luggage sold out because she turned a negative into a selling advantage. And she told the truth.

Telling the truth creatively isn't always easy. In fact, it's often hard work. Remember, retailers want to get customers into the store that day. They feel the message must be urgent, or it will go unnoticed. Your job as copywriter is to be the watchdog. If a merchant tells you that an item is going to be on sale for the "lowest" price, ask for substantiation. The same holds true if you're told that it's the "biggest" sale of the year.

The Better Business Bureau (BBB) has a code of advertising that all retailers should follow. If you're not familiar with these rules, call the bureau and ask for a copy. When Drewniany was a student, she did an internship with the BBB. Although she wasn't paid, it turned out to be a very valuable experience. One of the things that helped her get her first job was the fact that she understood the guidelines.

One area that seems to confuse many retailers is the difference between the terms *regularly* and *originally*. Actually, the difference is quite simple. If the item is going to return to its former price at the end of the sale, use the term *regularly* to describe the higher price. If the item is not returning to the higher price, use the term *originally*.

Another area that causes confusion is the term *manufacturer's list price*. Can you use it? Yes. But only if it is the actual selling price currently charged by "representative principal retailers" in your market area.

Still another area of confusion is the use of percentage savings. Perhaps you've seen "Save up to 50 percent" in an ad. Did you know what it meant? Were you saving

● FIGURE 12-5

There are guarantees. And
then there's the Company
Store's guarantee! Wonder
what happens after 76
years? Our bet is they'll
still honor their guaran-
tee. Now that should
make you sleep more
comfortably.

If you're not satisfied after 75 years, return for a full refund.

At the Company Store, we hand-stitch and hand-stuff our pillows to support you for a lifetime.

We're confident our pillows offer the best in comfort and quality.

But we know sleep styles change sometimes. Pillows get stained and ripped. New aches and pains creep in that you didn't have last year.

That's why we offer our "Rest Easy" guarantee.

We'll add or subtract fill to adjust the level of support. Dry-clean it if it's dirty.

Repair the tiniest rip, the biggest problem. For as long as you own your pillow.

We'll make it right...seven days or 75 years later. If you're still not happy, we'll replace your pillow or refund your money.

You see, it's our mission to help you sleep better.

We'll do whatever it takes to make sure that happens.

Call 1-800-777-DOWN for your free catalog.

5–50 percent? 20–50 percent? Or 40–50 percent? The customer has a right to know this. The BBB requires that you state both the minimum and maximum savings. Additionally, at least 10 percent of all items available should be at the maximum savings (unless local or state law requires otherwise).

Once you know the rules, you'll find that they are easy to follow. While it may take some effort to learn them, your customers deserve it. After all, you want to establish a lasting relationship with them, don't you?

● Suggested Activities

1. Create an image ad for your favorite store by describing your own personal experiences with it. Consider creating an image campaign by asking your friends to describe their experiences, too.

2. Find two stores in your town that sell similar merchandise at similar prices. Then determine what makes each store unique. Is it their personnel? Their location? Their history? Once you've determined what makes each store special, create an ad for each, using the same merchandise in each ad.

3. Spend 20 minutes brainstorming creative handles for sale ads. Some examples include "Friday the 13th sale," "leap year sale," and "spring cleanup sale days."

4. Remember the story about the orange luggage? Find an item in a local store that is just as unappealing, and write a newspaper ad and a radio spot that point out its advantages—without covering up the "ugly" truth.

5. Choose an item from one of your favorite catalogs, and create a retail ad for it. How will you convince customers to leave the comfort of their homes to shop at your store?

Search Online! Discovering More About Retail Advertising

Using InfoTrac® College Edition, try these phrases and others for Key Words and Subject Guide searches: *retail advertising, cooperative advertising, retail advertising + urgency, retail store image, retail advertising history, Better Business Bureau, JC Penney, Macy's, Sears, Nordstrom, retail sales, retail stores.* (Also search the Internet for retail Web sites, including those above.)

BriefCase

Pointy Shoes and Goodwill
Are Always in Style at Marshall Field's

Marshall Field's has been a Chicago institution since 1852. When Minneapolis-based Dayton Hudson Corporation acquired the store in 1990, they wanted to show they were still committed to the people of Chicago. They knew they couldn't reestablish the strong bond merely by telling customers of their commitment. They needed to prove it. So the idea for a new tradition was born.

In 1994, Marshall Field's presented Jingle Elves to the city of Chicago. Wearing pointy shoes with bells on their toes, these ambassadors of goodwill performed random acts of kindness throughout the greater Chicago area. They offered hot chocolate along Michigan Avenue. Paid bus and subway fares for commuters. Gave lip balm and hand lotion to pedestrians. Entertained travelers at O'Hare International Airport. Read stories at local libraries. Gave huggable bears to local hospitals. Delivered food to soup kitchens. Helped out with local food drives. And spread holiday cheer everywhere they went.

The following year, Marshall Field's formed a partnership with another great Chicago institution, the Lincoln Park Zoo. As sponsor of the month-long ZooLights Festival, Marshall Field's gave its customers coupons for discount admission. The zoo's "Caroling to the Animals" event set the stage for the introduction of the Jingle Elves. David Schwimmer, one of Chicago's favorite friends, read a giant copy of the storybook *The First Jingle Elf.* The story came to life as hundreds of elves jingle-jangled their way into the crowd. They danced. Performed. Sang carols. And delighted every child with a personal copy of *The First Jingle Elf.*

The creation of the storybook helped confirm Marshall Field's commitment to literacy. Jingle Elves gave 18,000 children their very own copies of the book. They read the story in libraries, schools, and hospitals. Local celebrities and leaders who were supporters of literacy were made honorary Jingle Elves. An official Jingle Elf hat, boots, and plaque were presented to Chicago Bulls coach Phil Jackson, Illinois First Lady Brenda Edgar, Illinois Secretary of State and State Librarian George Ryan, Chicago Bulls Community Relations Director Bob Love, and Chicago Bears players

POINTY SHOES
MAKE A COMEBACK
in Chicago.

The month of December finds the Marshall Field's Jingle Elves warming Chicago with hearts full of holiday cheer. Tradition has it that if you are lucky enough to be touched by their kindness, you must pass the spirit along. Because everyone can be an ambassador of goodwill. Even if you don't wear pointy shoes.

Marshall Field's
WHAT YOU'RE WISHING FOR

Book cover.

BriefCase

Opening pages of book.

It was the day before Christmas, and Santa's workshop was filled with the cheerful sound of jingling bells as the elves got ready for the big night. Everywhere you looked there was an elf hard at work, making sure the basketballs bounced high, the rocking horses rocked fast, and the sleds slid straight and true.

"This racing car is the grandest gift of all!" pronounced Holly Elf as she gave it the finishing touches with her elf-wrench.

"Oh, no!" cried Merry Elf, giving her elf bells an indignant shake. "This dollhouse has real lights! It's by far the best toy!"

"Pardon me!" called out Garland Elf from under a sea of wrapping paper. "This red bicycle with streamers is definitely the most wonderful toy this year!" And with that he tossed a bow at Merry.

$ELFISH

Today, Marshall Field's Jingle Elves will start traveling throughout Chicago performing random acts of kindness. Everything from paying someone's CTA fare to visiting hospital patients. Hopefully, the elves will serve as a reminder to all of us that the holiday spirit truly is about giving, not receiving. Happy holidays from Marshall Field's.

MAKING SPIRITS BRIGHT SINCE 1852

Todd Burger, Alonzo Spellman, Ryan Wetnight, and Chris Zorich. In addition, a $1000 donation was made on the behalf of each honorary Jingle Elf to Links to Literacy, a local organization that enhances literacy efforts in 150 Chicago public schools.

Stories about the Jingle Elves popped up everywhere in the media. They were shown shooting hoops with honorary Jingle Elf Phil Jackson. Playing trumpets at the "Caroling to the Animals" event. Signing the story of "The First Jingle Elf" to hearing-impaired children. And singing and dancing with children at O'Hare International Airport. Marshall Field's holiday program received more than 28 million media impressions. And hundreds of customers wrote and called to say how delighted they were with Marshall Field's acts of kindness. The ambassadors of goodwill won a place in people's hearts and helped Marshall Field's remain a symbol of Chicago's heart and soul.

CHAPTER 13

Convincing the Client

There's a wonderful scene in the British film *Honest, Decent, and True*—a send-up of advertising—in which the copywriter and art director do their best to convince the client that their TV commercial for his new brand of lager is just what the brand needs to become a success. If the scene didn't strike so close to home, we could enjoy the laughs less guiltily. But as in all good satire, this scene has been played, with variations, in nearly every advertising agency or client conference room. It goes something like this:

The writer ardently presents a TV storyboard, which is handsomely mounted and standing on an easel in full view of those present. These include, in addition to the client, members of the agency (the account executive, the planner or head of research, the media analyst, and, of course, the copywriter and art director, who have slaved feverishly for weeks to come up with this concept).

The commercial is a bit risky, however. It tells the story of a group of happy voyagers at the bar of a grand cruise ship. Some order embarrassingly toney drinks, while a few are "brave enough" to order what they really want—the client's new lager. Suddenly, there's a loud crash, and the ship begins to sink. In the final shot, we see survivors in a lifeboat, and they're all drinking the client's lager. Only then do we learn the name of the ship—it is the *Titanic*.

The client listens in silence and says nothing, even after the presentation is finished. The tense silence is at last broken by the researcher, who explains that this is a spoof, a big joke. The client answers, "Yes, I suppose some people would find this funny . . . Yes. Well it's just fine. Just fine." There is an audible sigh of relief. Then the client continues: "There are just a few very small things I'm having problems with. Nothing major, mind you. I wonder about the time frame here. After all, this is a contemporary product, and is it appropriate to do it in a period setting? Then there's the question of whether humor is appropriate to the selling of a lager. I also have a bit of a problem with the use of such a historic disaster to advertise our product. But nothing major." Silence again. A few clearings of throats. Then the various agency members attempt to brush these "small" problems aside, telling their conservative client that the young singles who are the market for this product don't care about the *Titanic,* that they will merely laugh at the disaster and get the message. But it's no use. He just isn't buying.

● The Presentation Is Half the Battle

Coming up with great ideas is a monumental task, but convincing your coworkers and your client to "buy" your ideas is no small task either. When you see great advertising, you can be fairly certain that those ideas saw the light of day because the client was willing to take a risk.

Regardless of your client's proclivity for taking risks, you must be prepared to sell the advertising just as thoroughly as you believe the advertising sells the goods. Generally, the presentation of the creative portion of an ad campaign should come after all other aspects of the campaign have been discussed. These other elements may include a summary of the marketing background for the product or service, a discussion of the research the agency has undertaken to conceive the strategy, and a proposed media plan that justifies the selection of certain media vehicles and the rejection of others.

Since your marketing summary will have touched on target markets and broad marketing goals, your presentation of the ad should be restricted to the communications aspects of your campaign. But where do you begin? Actually, you began weeks or months ago by establishing a comfortable, two-way relationship with your client. Clients don't like surprises. Nothing turns them off faster than walking into a presentation without the slightest inkling of what lies ahead. By staying in touch with your clients and making them feel that they are valued members of your team, you will put them in a more receptive frame of mind. This doesn't mean that you have to reveal your big ideas early, but you should certainly agree on the basic direction of the campaign before the actual presentation. Good clients are risk-takers who try not to throw barriers in the way of sound creative judgment. Part of your job is to nurture this attitude well before the day of the presentation. When that day arrives, here's what should happen:

1. *Begin with a brief recap of the assignment.* You were asked to solve a certain problem. Remind your client of the problem, and share your creative exploration of it. You might even share ideas that you rejected; this can indicate that you are concerned about the success of the campaign and not merely about selling your ideas.

2. *Discuss your creative strategy thoroughly.* You're not talking to the consumer, who doesn't need to understand the strategy to like the ads. You're talking to the people

who are going to be paying you handsomely for your efforts. Therefore, you must convince them in a highly logical manner that the ideas you are about to present— which may appear to be highly illogical—are the result of sound, perceptive thinking. So talk about what's going on in the minds of members of the target audience. Tell what they're saying now. Tell what you would like them to be saying. Tell why your campaign will stand out from the competition; you might even want to show competing ads to demonstrate how your campaign breaks through the clutter. Above all, when you get to your strategy, link it very clearly to the original goals of the project. Does it answer the problem? Exactly how does it do this?

3. *Make a big deal about the campaign's theme.* You may be so familiar with the theme by now that you forget that your client may never have seen or heard it before. Introduce the theme importantly by displaying it on a board or flashing it on a screen. If animation or music or sound is involved, use them as part of the presentation. If positioning, brand image, or other elements are critical, explain how the theme relates to them.

4. *Show how the big idea is expressed.* This involves the various advertisements and commercials, the sales promotion and collateral pieces, and everything else that is part of your campaign. For television and radio, try to have something as finished as possible (a demo tape for radio, a rough video or a set of computer-generated stills with an audio track for TV). When you present print, you obviously want to have crisp layouts in hand, appropriately mounted, with headlines and body copy set in type. With regard to the body copy, most seasoned presenters agree that it's best not to read it to your client. Instead, simply communicate what it expresses, and invite their review at a later time. What you're striving to communicate, obviously, is that the big idea—the central theme—runs through all of these ads and that this theme is a result of a well-devised strategy that delivers the intended message perfectly.

5. *Close with a summary statement, and ask for the order.* Remind the client how effective this campaign will be, how thoroughly it satisfies marketing and communications goals, and why it is the best choice for the problem at hand.

6. *Answer questions honestly.* If you don't know, say you don't know and promise to find out. Avoid direct confrontations, but don't come off as a "yes-man" or "yes-woman" to your client. Clients don't want that. If you disagree with your client's suggestions, explain why logically and politely. Compromise on minor issues, and speak with conviction about those issues you feel are essential to the spirit and intent of your work. If there is no agreement, your only choice may be to thank the client and go on to another job. Few good agencies will compromise their creative standards to produce what they feel is inferior work. It's a delicate situation. Knowing how to handle a client who disagrees demands a thorough understanding not only of that client's company culture but also of the personalities of the decision makers.

● Pitching with Pizzazz

Advertising is a creative business, so don't try to bore a client into buying your big idea. Have fun with your presentation, but make sure it's relevant. Consider this pitch from Merkley Newman Harty to members of the National Thoroughbred Racing Association. The Harty team started their pitch with a video that showed close-ups of a typical horse race—pounding hoofs, whips to the hindquarters, flaring nostrils, and a photo finish. Then came the line "The function of insanity is doing the same thing over and over again and expecting different results." This helped the agency make the point that the hackneyed approach that racetracks had used for years wasn't working. Racetracks needed a fresh, new approach. They needed Merkley Newman Harty. Members of the National Thoroughbred Racing Association agreed.

When Kevin Fisher presented his idea for a new ad campaign for the Riverbanks Zoo, he blared the song "Wild Thing" from a boom box and started dancing to the beat of the music. Mary Leverette, the zoo's marketing director, recalls her reaction: "When he was jumping around with the music just blasting, Satch (the director of the zoo) and I just cut our eyes at each other. It was a big departure from the sedate nature of the ads we had had in the past. But we loved it. We just loved it."[1] Fisher's performance sold the zoo directors on the idea of running commercials that featured animals keeping time to rock music while humans cut loose at the zoo.

Some agencies go to great extremes to win an account. Leo Burnett won the Heinz ketchup account by showing ads that made Heinz seem cool and teen-friendly. On the morning of the final pitch, the agency's team set up a hot dog stand in the lobby and lined the escalator walls with ketchup labels with catchy slogans. The conference room was turned into a diner with bar stools, a counter, and a short-order cook.

The Martin Agency's pitch for the advertising account of *Men's Health* magazine began even before the actual presentation. The magazine's representative encountered about 20 Martin Agency employees reading *Men's Health* on the sidewalk and throughout the agency's headquarters. When she got on the elevator, she found a framed sign that read, "If *Men's Health* was our client, your ad pages would go up faster than this elevator." The Martin Agency won the account.

Why do some agencies go to such elaborate lengths to win accounts? Consider this: According to the American Association of Advertising Agencies, the average account stays with an agency for 7.2 years. Harry Jacobs, the chairman emeritus of The Martin Agency, told the *Richmond Times-Dispatch,* "New business is the lifeblood of the advertising agency. Without perfecting it and being proficient at it, the agency is not going to grow."[2]

[1]Anna Velasco, "Swimming with the Big Fish: Fisher Communications Makes It Big, but Stays Small," *The State,* 29 Aug. 1999, p. G1.

[2]Otesa Middleton, "Here's the Pitch: Ad Agencies Reveal Their Strategies for Getting Accounts," *The Richmond Times-Dispatch,* 2 Sept. 1996, p. D16.

● Guidelines for Making Presentations

Whatever area of advertising you eventually wind up in, you're always going to have to present something to somebody. The more experience you have in presenting, the better you become. A great place to start presenting is in your classes. The following tips will help you discover how to do so comfortably, enthusiastically, and convincingly:

1. *Get the attention of your audience right away.* Open your talk with something that not only gains the attention of your audience but causes them to respect you as an authority and starts them thinking about your topic. Never apologize for yourself as an introduction—that only undermines your credibility.

2. *Remember how it feels to be a listener.* You have plenty of practice being a student. What do your most interesting professors do to keep your attention? Use them as role models.

3. *Be prepared for questions.* Don't let them throw you. No one is out to do that. If you don't know the answer, simply say you don't. Ask for others to answer.

4. *Rehearse out loud.* Practice before a mirror, unless that's uncomfortable. If it is, rehearse before a room, and pretend the room is filled. Or rehearse by asking one or more friends to listen and give you comments.

5. *Listen to your words and inflections.* If they sound wrong to you, they probably are. Underscore words you want to stress. Indicate pauses for a breath if that will help your pacing.

6. *Stand tall.* Your arms should be comfortably at your sides. Avoid sweeping gestures. Don't fiddle with rubber bands, paper clips, or caps of pens. It will be difficult at first, but you can learn to do it.

7. *Make eye contact.* If your audience is large, shift your focus now and then to a different person or a different side of the room. Include everyone. If one person is more important than the rest, spend a good deal of time making contact with him or her.

8. *Speak from your diaphragm.* Use one of the lower ranges of your voice. It will carry better and sound more authoritative.

9. *Use inflection for effect.* Avoid monotones. Emphasize important words as underscored in your notes. Pause for dramatic effect. A pause that seems eternal to you is probably short to your listeners.

10. *Use appropriate facial expressions and gestures.* These should be congruent with your spoken words. If something is funny, smile.

11. *Check out the room before you speak.* There's nothing more disconcerting than discovering when you're in the midst of your presentation that you can't use your visual aids. Before you speak, make sure all the audio/visual equipment you'll need is in the room and in working order. Are the seats arranged the way you want them? Is there a podium or table for your notes? If you plan on writing key points throughout your presentation, is there an easel with a pad, a chalkboard, or overhead projector? Are there appropriate pens or chalk?

● Perils and Pitfalls of Presenting

Ron Hoff, who in his long and distinguished career has been associated with Ogilvy & Mather and, more recently, with Foote Cone & Belding, has a lot of experience with the perils and pitfalls of presenting.[3] Here is what he says:

- The biggest problem we face is boring our audience. Sometimes, we even bore ourselves. Seldom do our true identities emerge in our professional selves. Perhaps this is why we're so boring when we make presentations.

- Visuals, when added to words, will more than double recall of your message. When you get the audience to *participate* in your presentation, recall will zoom to around 90 percent among the people who have actually taken part.

- The moment of judgment in presentations occurs within the first 90 seconds. That's when audiences decide to tune in or check out. If the presenter talks entirely about himself or herself, the audience disconnects. Or daydreams. Audiences are sitting there asking themselves, "When is that presenter going to start talking about me?"

Here are what Hoff identifies as key strategies for effective presentations:

1. *Know the people in the opposition, and know who is your best supporter.* Address your first words to the opponent. Then move to someone you know is favorable. You should feel refueled and reinforced at this point, so you can move on to the others. When you reach a seemingly negative person, go back to a friend. Keep warming up the group till it seems safe to invade the "enemy territory."

2. *Start with something you feel comfortable with.* It can be fun, but it must be relevant. Dr. Stephen Zipperblatt of the Pritikin Longevity Center in San Diego opens his workshop with these words: "Man doesn't die . . . he kills himself." He then goes on to tell participants how to live healthier lives. He's off and rolling.

3. *Appoint a DSW—a director of "So what?"* This person represents the grubby, selfish interests of the audience. Whenever you say something irrelevant, he or she says, "So what?" and you know you're off course.

---

[3] The authors thank Mr. Hoff for granting them permission to use these ideas.

4. *Start your agency presentations about halfway through.* That's where most of us stop talking about ourselves and start talking about our clients. Start with the audience's issue of primary concern instead of your issue of concern (get the business). Ask yourself, "How can we help the poor devils?"

Hoff also identifies "what bugs people about presentations," explaining that these come from people in the business who've suffered through numerous presentations that flopped:

- "You know so much more about this than I do." (The client wants someone who knows more than he or she does.)
- "I'm so nervous. I hope you can't see how much my knees are shaking." (A true confidence builder.)
- "I've got my notes so screwed up, I don't know what I'm going to do." (The client thinks, "What am I doing here?")
- "We know you're waiting for the creative, so I'll try to fly through the media plan." (And therefore miss lots of opportunities to sell the package. Or to set the stage for the big idea.)

Hoff also feels that every presentation should have a burning issue. Too often, we fall far short of this. We sputter. He adds that too many presenters act as if they don't know what slide is coming up next and that just as many don't know the first thing about eye contact. What is *so* interesting about that distant star they're looking at? Is it any wonder there's no connecting going on there?

How to Correct the Problems

Eye contact and connecting are extremely important. So keep the lights up, and get near members of the audience. Reduce the distance between you and them, both geographically and ideologically. People are nervous at the start of a presentation, when the distance is the greatest.

Don't be upset by interruptions. Answer, but never attack. Be professional. If there are rude people in the audience, continue to be polite. The group will take care of their own. Above all, never lose your temper. This is tantamount to losing the business.

People love to have lists. So give them lists: "Here are six things I think are really important."

How do you overcome nervousness? Tell yourself you're the best—and believe it. Relax. Present to yourself in the mirror, and watch and listen to yourself. Even better, videotape yourself presenting. Watch it once, a second time with the sound off, and a third time with sound only. Do you like your nonverbals? If not, take steps to improve them if you do not. Do you like your voice? What, if anything, could make you sound more convincing? Exercise your jaw just before presenting. Take several slow, deep breaths.

It all comes out in your voice—your joy, your nervousness, your anticipation, your boredom. Your voice gives your audience its first real clue about you. Yet we often neglect our voices. Deep voices communicate authority. And anyone can, with practice, present in a voice deeper than their normal speaking voice. Spend a day working on your voice by narrating your day into a cassette recorder: "It's 9 A.M. and I'm waiting for the bus. I see it coming now. A few people are here, but it's not a busy day. . . ." Then listen to it. Then do it again, and listen again.

Most important of all, says Hoff, is to remember that the client may not always be right, but the client is always the client.

● Suggested Activities

1. Contact an account executive or creative director in an advertising agency, or the advertising manager of a company, and ask that individual to explain how a particular creative strategy was devised. Make a presentation to your class on your findings.

2. Choose one of the case studies in this book, and imagine you've been chosen to sell the client on the idea. Make a presentation to the class as if you were selling the campaign to the client.

3. Read a book on salesmanship, or interview a speech professor at your school, and prepare a report that identifies the key elements in making a sale. How can you apply these principles to the selling of an idea?

 ## Search Online! Discovering More About Convincing the Client

Using InfoTrac® College Edition, try these phrases and others for Key Words and Subject Guide searches: *advertising agency + client, presentation style, advertising campaign, unusual advertising presentations, presentation techniques, speaking tips, eye contact + presentation, posture + presentation, overcoming nervousness, rehearsing presentation.*

BriefCase

Hail Happens. How Pro-Dent Got the Word Out on Getting the Dings Out

BY DAVID SLAYDEN, A.K.A. ADVERTISING
(CAMPAIGN BY DAVID SLAYDEN, WADE ALGER, AND JAY RUSSELL)

It hails in Dallas. Shopping carts roll freely in parking lots. And Bubba throws open his door on his pickup without looking at what's next to it. Hail and all these other hazards make little dings in cars. And among the jetsetters who drive Lexus, Mercedes, Porsche, BMW, Jaguar, and Infiniti, car disfigurement often is a threat to identity. In four words, "I am my car."

Body shops do repairs. They smooth, they sand, they prime, they paint, they polish. And they charge. In Dallas, there's a less expensive alternative: paintless dent removal. Trouble is, some of these "firms" are little more than a guy with a van who chases hail.

Pro-Dent Paintless Dent Removal is different. First, it has an actual facility and is a stable and reputable business. Second, Pro-Dent takes a craft approach to its work, employing only skilled people who care about the quality of their service. For the advertising campaign, we chose not to emphasize cost or savings, as this might suggest parity with other paintless operations. Instead, we recommended a position that would pit them against body shops, who do much of the work Pro-Dent can do but at a much higher price. And we had to explain precisely what sort of damage Pro-Dent could repair.

Pro-Dent makes its living through minor misfortunes to cars. In interviews with the client and with satisfied customers, we realized that Pro-Dent has a distinct personality. While they are sympathetic to their customers' plights, they also hold a crafter's respect for fine cars and pride in their ability to restore them.

Furthermore, we knew the campaign would be most effective if we could get drivers to think about imminent damage while they were in their cars and decide that, when and if that happened, Pro-Dent would be a more practical answer than any body shop. Initially, we wanted radio, but the cost to reach our target—an upscale market

IT'S A LAW OF NATURE THAT
SHOPPING CARTS ARE ATTRACTED
ONLY TO REALLY NICE CARS.

Pro Dent
paintless dent removal
867.9324

OUR IDEA OF BAD WEATHER
IS CLEAR BLUE SKIES AND
PLENTY OF SUNSHINE.

Pro Dent
paintless dent removal
867.9324

HAIL HAPPENS.

Pro Dent
paintless dent removal
867.9324

FOR ALL OF YOU TOO CHEAP
TO PAY FOR COVERED PARKING,
BLESS YOU.

Pro Dent
paintless dent removal
867.9324

IN A PERFECT WORLD,
PARKING LOTS WOULD ALWAYS
BE NEXT TO DRIVING RANGES.

Pro Dent
paintless dent removal
867.9324

FOR ALL YOU GUYS IN FANCY
SPORTS CARS, REMEMBER:
NO MATTER HOW LITTLE
YOUR DING IS, WE CAN FIX IT.

Pro Dent
paintless dent removal
867.9324

with one or more luxury cars—was prohibitive. Busboards proved to be the answer. They would be seen in the right location, and since we bought a three-month rotation, a variety of messages would be seen repeatedly by drivers in our market.

The idea for the somewhat irreverent approach came from two insights, one associated with the consumer, the other with the company. Most of us like to think that accidents happen to others, and this evokes a feeling that the accident may have been deserved. Our insight into the company came when the owner's wife revealed that he regularly watches The Weather Channel to see if hail is on its way. Although TV was out of our reach, we instantly visualized a TV commercial in which his heartbeat increased as he watched a report of a severe storm warning crawling across the screen.

We translated this quality into a campaign using ten busboards running on 20 buses in targeted portions of the Dallas metroplex. The response was immediate, with increased business and a number of callers commenting on the boards and asking for rates, range of services, and location.

We think it worked so well because we followed some simple rules of good advertising: Know your target, know your client, know who you're up against, be ready to take some prudent risks with your ideas, and realize that relevant humor can soften the blow when your car is having a ding of a day.

CHAPTER 14

Now It's Time to Land That Job

If you know how to market products and services, you know how to market yourself. The principles you've learned in this book that help you sell frozen peas and laundry detergent also work when you're selling yourself. What do you do? The same thing, only now *you* are the product. So you develop objectives, pinpoint your strongest selling points, assess the competition, do some research and get a thorough understanding of the target market. Only then do you go about creating the message that will land you a job.

● Step 1: State Your Objectives

Your career objectives should be as specific as possible. Do you want to work at a creative hot shop in Minneapolis? At a major agency in New York? For a small firm in your hometown? What about a Chicago agency that specializes in package-goods accounts? Or a direct-marketing company? Or the advertising department of a national retailer?

If you tell yourself you'll settle for any job, that's just what you'll do. Settle. Why not go after the job you really want? After all, you can always regroup if your first choice doesn't work out, *and* you will have learned a lot in the process.

When Ed Chambliss graduated, he wanted to move to Atlanta and work for a major agency. After studying the *Standard Directory of Advertising Agencies* (the "Red Book"), talking with professors, and reading the trade journals, Ed knew he wanted to work for BBDO-South. Rather than send a mass mailing of his résumé to every agency in Atlanta, Ed targeted BBDO with a self-promotion piece, *EDWEEK*, shown in Figure 14-1. Ed got the job and never had to fall back on his second or third choice.

EDWEEK

Vol. I No. 1   SOUTHEAST EDITION   INVALUABLE

BBDO/Atlanta Hires Chambliss
Other Atlanta Agencies Mourn Their Loss

By Ed Chambliss

ATLANTA—BBDO/Atlanta made creative history this week when it hired talented Atlanta copywriter Ed Chambliss. Gregg Dearth, executive creative director, announced the decision after meeting with Chambliss and viewing his portfolio.

"What initially got my attention," Dearth said, "was his parody of ADWEEK. It was unique. It caught my eye in a very memorable way."

The parody, received by Dearth early in the summer, featured several cover stories about Chambliss. Inside the four-page publication was an impressive resume detailing (among other things) four years of advertising experience. And, as final reminder, an ad for Chambliss appeared on the back.

Later, Chambliss called and set up an appointment to show Dearth his portfolio. "That was what clinched his sale," Dearth said. "It was an excellent mix of effective print, television, and radio." It was then that Dearth offered Chambliss a job.

Industry analysts are predicting that Chambliss's creative talents will have a "strong positive effect" on BBDO/Atlanta's creative product and its billings.

USC Ad Team Competes in D.C.

By Ed Chambliss

WASHINGTON—Garnett & Black, the University of South Carolina's student-run advertising agency, has placed 7th in the 1989 National Student Advertising Competition.

The team competed against 14 other regional winners by creating a campaign for a new Kellogg cereal. The campaign included the naming of the product, package design, and broadcast and print advertisements, all of which were supervised by Creative Director Ed Chambliss from Atlanta, Georgia.

WHAT'S INSIDE

What a Case Study

While most college students spend their summers eating in greasy fast food joints and trying to bronze their bods, the University of South Carolina's Outstanding Advertising Senior spent his summers preparing himself for more than clogged arteries or skin cancer.

(See page 2)

Experience The Key for Graduates
Atlanta's Hottest New Creative Tells How He Did It

By Ed Chambliss

ATLANTA—After Ed Chambliss, a recent college graduate, was offered a job by BBDO/Atlanta *(see story above)*, EDWEEK asked him a few questions concerning the way he got the job.

"Your book makes or breaks you. But first you have to get the creative director's attention so you can show your book," Chambliss said.

"One attention-getter that I'm proud of is the amount of actual experience I have in advertising. A good

Chambliss

college program won't give you a job, just the basic tools you need. It takes experience to know how to use those tools," he said.

In the past four years Chambliss has worked constantly, both at school and during the summer. On the list of recent summer employers are Fahlgren & Swink, Inc., and Turner Broadcasting Systems, both in Atlanta.

"Most people I know hated their summer jobs," added Chambliss. "For them, their jobs were work; mine were fun."

● FIGURE 14-1

Ed Chambliss created *EDWEEK,* a parody of the advertising trade magazine *Adweek,* to land a job at BBDO-South. He believes it worked for three reasons. First, everyone in advertising reads *Adweek,* so the creative directors understood the parody. Second, everyone loves to see their name in print. Notice that Ed incorporated the name of BBDO's creative director in the lead story. Third, it reinforced Ed's name.

● Step 2: Pinpoint Your Strongest Selling Points

This is not the time to be modest. Jot down every compliment you've ever gotten from professors, employers, and peers. Jog your memory for ways you've demonstrated creativity and leadership and entrepreneurship. What's your greatest accomplishment? Your proudest moment? The biggest hurdle you've overcome? What would your best friend say about you? Your favorite professor? Your current employer or internship supervisor?

Jot down reasons your educational or work background is superior. For example, if you've completed a journalism program that's accredited by the Accrediting Council on Education in Journalism and Mass Communications, you should have a well-rounded liberal arts education. This will be viewed as a plus by most employers, who want copywriters well versed in literature, the arts, philosophy, sociology, and psychology.

● Step 3: Assess the Competition

Start by looking around your classes. How does your work compare? Do you consistently earn praise from your professors and peers? Does your work get displayed as an example of excellence?

Check out the competition outside your school. Many advertising schools display the work of their best students on their walls and in their catalogs. How does your work compare to the work done by advertising students at such trade schools as the Portfolio Center or the Creative Circus in Atlanta? The Miami Ad School? Parsons School of Design or the School of Visual Arts in New York? The Art Center in Pasadena, California?

Also, compare your work to the industry's standard of excellence. Study the award books and publications devoted to creativity. *Communication Arts, Print, HOW, Advertising Age's Creativity*, and *Archive* are filled with creative work from the pros. Pay attention to the agencies that are doing great work, and see if your style and theirs are a good match.

● Step 4: Research Your Target Audience

Major agencies receive thousands of job inquiries every year. How do you set yourself apart from the hordes? By knowing your target audience. If you send a form letter, you're bound to receive a form rejection letter—or no response at all. However, if you demonstrate that you really want to work at a specific agency, you're more likely to capture its interest. Write to specific individuals. In your letters, say something about them. Mention an account they just landed. Compliment them on an award they just won. Refer to a write-up about them you read in *Advertising Age* or *Adweek*. And if you learned about the opening through a personal contact, be sure to mention that right up front. A letter that starts outs, "So-and-so suggested that I write to you" is bound to be noticed.

Also be sure that you're the right match for the company you're targeting. If your creative style is outrageous and a bit irreverent, don't bother with an agency that is known for its conservative advertising. If you hope to land a job at a creative hot shop, make sure everything you show pushes the boundaries. If you want to work in New York, develop strong package-goods and print campaigns. Smaller markets want to see spots for things like hospitals and banks, plus some strong radio and newspaper ads. Direct marketers want to see copy that intrigues while containing a lot of detail. Retailers want to see a range of things, from high fashion to high tech.

How will you learn about the agency or company you're targeting? The same way you learn about a product. Through research.

Secondary Research

As with any research project, you should start out by reviewing the information that already exits. There are excellent reference guides that will point your job search in the right direction, including the following:

- The *Standard Directory of Advertising Agencies* (also known as the "Red Book") lists 8,700 agency profile and includes the names of key personnel.

- The *Adweek Agency Directory* lists more than 4,300 agencies and media buying services.

- *Advertising Age* publishes special editions that are useful in a job search. *Leading National Advertisers*, a special annual issue that comes out at the end of September, profiles the 100 top U.S. marketers by media spending and includes the names of their advertising agency and the names of key advertising and corporate personnel. The *Agency Report* comes out in mid-April and lists gross income, volume, number of employees, and offices of the 25 largest global advertising organizations.

Annual publications are a great starting point, but they can't reflect all the changes that are constantly taking place. After all, agencies are winning and losing clients all the time. People are being promoted, retiring, and changing jobs. Therefore, you should set aside some time each week to peruse *Advertising Age, Adweek,* the marketing section of the *Wall Street Journal,* and the advertising column in the *New York Times.* These publications will keep you apprised of client moves, changes in agency personnel, and job openings. By being current, you'll show your passion for the business. You'll also save yourself the embarrassment of sending a letter to a person who no longer works at the agency or of complimenting the agency on work it did for a client it just lost.

Be sure to check out the agency's homepage on the Web. Call the public relations department, and ask for an annual report or clippings they have on file. Ask your professors and professional contacts what they know about the agency.

Primary Research

Now that you have a good foundation, it's time to customize your search. It's time to find out if you'll fit in with a particular agency or company. So where do you start?

1. *Go for an informational interview.* You may hear, "We don't have any positions open, but I'd be happy to talk to you." Do it. The feedback you receive on your portfolio will be worth it. Always end by asking for other names. Advertising is a small business, a name can get you over a variety of moats and walls, not to mention past the receptionist. And when you get home, be sure to write them a thank-you note.

2. *Network.* Networking is a key component of your job search. At first, some people are uncomfortable doing this because they think they'll be perceived as being pushy or obnoxious. Don't feel this way. Politely ask your professors, internship supervisors, parents' friends, and neighbors if they have contacts or know of any openings, and you may be pleasantly surprised. Also be sure to take advantage of every networking opportunity offered while you're in school. Join the student chapter of the American Advertising Federation, the American Marketing Association, the Public Relations Student Society of America, or all three. If your school doesn't have one of these chapters, consider starting one—it'll be a great way to demonstrate your leadership abilities to prospective employers.

3. *Attend professional meetings.* Local advertising clubs will often invite students to attend their meetings for free or at a reduced rate. When you go to these meetings, don't stand in the corner. Mingle. Make contacts. Get business cards. You'll be surprised at how receptive most people will be. Even if you're not job hunting locally, there's a good chance you'll bump into someone who knows someone in the town you want to move to. And contacts can open doors.

4. *Search online.* There are a variety of Web sites for jobs in advertising. Here are a few:

- *Advertising Job Bank.* Courtesy of *Advertising Age* and the Monster Board, this site lets you search on any number of advertising, marketing, or creative jobs, including account management, media, media sales, and production. Go to adage.monster.com.

- *Adweek Online.* Simply choose from a list of locations, companies, or categories. Go to www.adweek.com/careernetwork/index.asp.

- *Career Mosaic.* Career Mosaic has a vast job-search engine, but the jobs aren't necessarily aimed at recent college graduates. The site includes a résumé posting service and a somewhat helpful college connection section. Go to www.careermosaic.com.

- *JobSource Careers for College Grads: Monster Board.* Monster Board, the mother of all job-search sites, provides a specific section for entry-level jobs. You can search by location, category, or keyword. Go to jobsource.monster.com.
- *NationJob.* NationJob lists hundreds of jobs, ranging from entry-level to senior positions. For advertising and media jobs, go to www.nationjob.com/media. For marketing and sales jobs, go to www.nationjob.com/marketing.

● Step 5: Develop a Creative Communication Message

You've got a clearly defined objective. You understand your target audience and the competition. You know your key selling points. Now it's time to launch your campaign. You will need a cover letter, a résumé, and a portfolio. You may also want to create a self-promotion piece. And you'll certainly want to develop your interviewing skills.

Your Cover Letter

Your letter must not merely say, "Here's my résumé, and do you have a job?" It must demonstrate how well you write, how passionate you are about advertising, and how much potential you have.

Thousands of applicants never make it to the interview because their letters are poor. So how do you enhance your chances for an interview? Start by addressing your letter to an actual person. Do *not* use "To whom it may concern." Find out the name of the creative director by looking up the agency in the *Standard Directory of Advertising Agencies* or by calling the agency. Be sure to get the spelling and the gender correct. Robin can be a man or woman. So can Leslie, Pat, Lee, Kim, Beverly, and many others. When in doubt, call the receptionist and ask.

Now you've got your salutation. Start your letter by telling why you are writing. Then mention something nice, but not phony, about the company you're writing to, or simply plunge into your sales pitch. The main body of the letter should tell this person why you should get the job. Be sincere and forthright. Use plain English and avoid jargon. Personalize your letter by mentioning something about your background or personality that gives some insight into you, but don't be too flip or casual. In closing, state that you will provide additional information if required. Don't ask the recipient to call you. Tell the recipient you'll be calling him or her. And be sure to follow through. Look at the two letters shown in Figures 14-2 and 14-3. Which one do you think is more persuasive, and why?

Self-Promotion Ads

The same rules that apply for great advertising work for self-promotion pieces. Combine an unexpected headline and visual to make a relevant selling point. One such ad featured the headline "President Seeks Entry-Level Job." Your attention is captured right away, and you want to read further. In the body copy, you learn that the person was president of his fraternity and that this helped him learn how to motivate people. That's relevant. And unexpected.

● FIGURE 14-2

Here's what not to do: Don't send a letter to the personnel department— send it to the creative director. Don't send it to "sir or madam"—send it to a specific person. Don't bore this person with details about your past— intrigue him or her by showing how your past fits into the agency's future. Don't mention negative publicity about the agency. And don't expect this person to call you.

```
Personnel Department
McCann-Erickson Worldwide
485 Madison Avenue
New York, NY 10098

Dear Sir or Madam:

This spring I will earn my B.A. in Journalism from the University
of South Carolina with a major in advertising and public
relations and a cognate in marketing.

I will be seeking a position with an advertising agency in the
New York area, preferably as a copywriter, and would like to
talk with you about the possibility of employment with McCann-
Erickson.

I really enjoy writing copy and have taken two courses in
creative strategy with Professor A. Jerome Jewler at Carolina. I
have also completed courses in media, campaigns, ad research, ad
management, and graphic production. I believe I have much to
offer your agency and could make important contributions with my
unique ideas and marketing expertise.

By the way, I note in the trade press that you are in trouble
with the Nescafe campaign. I have been working up some roughs for
Nescafe and would be happy to share them with you, if you're
interested.

I look forward to hearing from you.

Sincerely,

Victoria Smith
```

Another ad had a Florida lottery ticket attached to it with the headline "Call Me on Monday to See If You Won." The ticket was for a multimillion-dollar lottery and was sent to a Dallas agency by a student from Florida who wanted to relocate. A mere investment of one dollar got the student something money can't buy—a phone call from the creative director.

Toby Jenkins landed a summer internship driving the Oscar Mayer Wienermobile by writing new lyrics to the famous jingle "Oh I wish I were an Oscar Mayer Wiener." Her lyrics demonstrated that she had the kind of spunk that's needed to travel around the country in a 4-ton orange hot dog.

Some people play on their own names to make an impression. A writer named Randy Rensch sent agencies wrenches with the inscription "When it's a copywriter, it's spelled Rensch." Patrick Fox invited employers to "Catch the Fox." Jim Brickman sent brick paperweights with his name inscribed on them.

Some people try to stand out by doing something outrageous. One student sent a roll of toilet tissue with the message "They said advertising is full of shit. But I don't

● FIGURE 14-3

This letter's got it right. It's written to the creative director, demonstrates a passion for advertising, offers examples of creativity, and shows initiative.

Roger C. Franklin
Executive Creative Director
McCann-Erickson Worldwide
485 Madison Avenue
New York, NY 10098

Dear Mr. Franklin:

I am writing at the suggestion of Brad Cummings, who is a longtime friend and mentor, and who knows of my desire to enter the world of advertising.

To be perfectly honest, I want to be a copywriter, and I've prepared myself for this difficult task from the time I was about thirteen--devouring advertising on radio, TV, in magazines and newspapers every chance I could get. The walls of my bedroom were literally plastered with my favorite ads. It didn't make Mom happy, but I couldn't resist clipping 'em and hanging 'em.

It's no wonder I pursued a degree in advertising at the University of South Carolina. And while my peers were earning C's and B's, I was getting A's in creative strategy, graphic design, campaigns, and marketing. My professors told me I was one of the best students they had seen in years. I began to believe it.

Now I want you to judge me. I have a portfolio of what I consider to be my best work, and I would be honored if you would grant me a few brief moments to share this with you.

I'm planning to be in New York the week of April 27, and will call you that Monday to see if you can see me sometime during that week.

In the meantime, I'm enclosing my résumé and a few samples. Once again, thanks for hearing me out. I'm excited about the prospect of meeting you and having you critique my work.

Cordially,

Victoria Smith

mind starting at the bottom." This concept won an award in *How* magazine's self-promotion contest. But be forewarned before you consider something over the top like this—not everyone will agree with this type of humor. And many will find it offensive.

How should you go about creating an ad for yourself? Start by jotting down such attributes as these:

- Something unusual, unique, or interesting about yourself from any period in your life

- Your interests, hobbies, collections, and spare-time activities

- A compliment paid you by a friend, family member, professor, advisor, or employer

- Your passion for advertising
- Details about the agency or company you want to be hired by, and how you will fit in

Your Résumé   Employers want to know what you did, where, and for how long. Be thorough, but don't overembellish. One page should be enough to convince an employer to invite you for an interview. More than two pages will indicate you don't know how to be concise.

Writing your résumé   Your résumé should be attractive, with no misspellings or errors in either punctuation or grammar. Organize it with titles and block sections. At the top of your résumé, put your name, address, and phone number. Should you include your career goals? Some say absolutely; others say never. If you can work your goals into your cover letter, you won't have to include them here. It's a good idea to list the position you are seeking, such as "copywriter." Most businesses will want to know at least that much. It confuses companies when you say you'll take any kind of job with them.

The main body of your résumé should have three basic sections: (1) educational background, (2) work experience, and (3) personal information. Whichever is more important should come first. Reasons for leaving former jobs (left for a better opportunity, wanted more pay and more challenging work, etc.) need not be mentioned. You can explain (if asked) during the interview, but never blame a former employer.

Avoid "I" and "me" sentences. Start with such phrases as "improved the service procedures," "supervised ten people," "managed three departments," "created . . . ," "designed . . . ," "introduced . . . ," and so on. Emphasize your accomplishments, not your duties. Emphasize assets, not liabilities. Omit anything unfavorable, but always tell the truth. You will most likely be checked.

In terms of personal information, include only what you think is relevant. Do not include a photo or such things as number of children or health. Include memberships in associations related to your profession, travel, experience, and language fluency. Hobbies and other interests can show employers how you spend your leisure time and reveal a side of you that the rest of your résumé cannot show. References may or may not be included. But if your references are prominent people, and you have their permission, definitely include them.

You may wish to follow the format of a chronological résumé, a functional résumé, or a combination of the two. A chronological résumé, shown in Figure 14-4, works best for people who want to show accomplishments over time and should start with the most current position. A functional résumé, shown in Figure 14-5 can be useful if your job history is not long or neatly categorized. Here, you pinpoint what job skills you used in each situation, with less emphasis on the particular job you held. This is especially helpful if you want to include community service, other volunteer jobs, student organization work, and so on.

Lisa Wilhelm
10401 Cave Creek Road, #113
Phoenix, AZ 85020
(602) 997-2635

Career Objective: To write and edit creative copy, preferably in an ad-related position.

Education: B.A., Journalism & Mass Communications, University of South Carolina - Columbia. May 1993. Major: Advertising/Public Relations

GPA: 3.96, Magna Cum Laude

Phi Beta Kappa

Honors: 1996 Two Addy Awards, Columbia Ad & Mktg. Federation
1995 Two InShow Awards, Columbia Communicating Arts Society
1995 Addy Award, Columbia Ad & Mktg. Federation
1993 Addy Award, Columbia Ad & Mktg. Federation
1993 Outstanding Advertising Senior--USC College of Journalism
1993 District 3 Champions--AAF Student Competition Team

Additional Training:

Computer graphics	Creative writing
Consumer behavior	Graphic design
Copy editing	Core advertising curriculum

Experience:

8/93 - 1/96   Writer at Chernoff/Silver and Associates, the second largest ad agency in South Carolina. Responsible for creative concepting of and writing copy for print ads, brochures, video and audio scripts, cards, speeches, presentations, proposals, posters, flyers, positioning lines and billboards.

1/90 - 5/93   Full-time student at the University of South Carolina. I also worked part time at Prudential Securities Inc. and as a desktop publishing assistant at the Carolina Coliseum/Koger Center for the Arts.

2/80 - 12/89   Various positions within the stock brokerage industry. Began as an operations clerk and earned three licenses within three years, including two administrative principal's licenses. Positions held included Operations Manager at The Robinson Humphrey Company, Inc. and Registered Sales Associate at Prudential-Bache Securities, Inc. (now Prudential Securities, Inc.).

● FIGURE 14-4

Lisa's chronological résumé outlines some impressive accomplishments but it lacks personality. Figure 14-5 shows how Lisa was able to give prospective employers a sense of her creative flair.

LISA WILHELM
10401 CAVE CREEK ROAD, #113, PHOENIX, AZ 85020
602.997.2635

My objective:

To continue my career as a copywriter—in California—with an agency that's known and respected for its creative product.

Skills you may find of interest:

• I'm especially good at writing clear, persuasive copy, using everyday language. I'm versatile and intelligent, so I can handle the complicated, technical jobs, too.

• My knowledge of grammar is thorough. I know how to bend the rules PROPERLY, and I know how to be concise.

• Proofreading is something I truly enjoy, and I'm good at it. But please don't think I'm entirely strange.

• I've had training in graphics and am a visual thinker, so I work well with art directors.

Most recently:

From 8/93 through 1/96, I was an award-winning writer of print ads, presentations and radio/TV/video scripts at Chernoff/Silver and Associates, the second largest ad agency in South Carolina. Among the accounts I worked on:

• Fleet Mortgage Services
• BMW
• South Carolina Electric& Gas
• United Way
• Hydril Tools (Houston, TX)
• American Cancer Society
• a MULTITUDE of healthcare-related accounts, including hospitals and physicians in four states

Before that:

I spent 10 years in the brokerage business. I've discovered I'm much better at—and happier—convincing people to spend their money than I was at telling them how to invest it.

Between careers:

I earned a B.A. in journalism from USC (the one on the east coast) from 1/90 through 5/93.

Ironic but true: I graduated magna cum laude with a 3.96 GPA, attained Phi Beta Kappa membership, presented for USC's 1993 ad team (which placed sixth nationally out of 133 teams) and was named Outstanding Advertising Senior by the J-school faculty. Still, it seems I'm best remembered for earning an A in copyediting from Dr. Henry Price. And I wasn't even required to take the course. Go figure.

● FIGURE 14-5

Lisa's lighthearted approach to a functional résumé allows her to boast about her accomplishments without seeming overbearing.

Posting your résumé online   A variety of sites allow you to post your résumé online. For example, Monster Board offers résumé posting and a personal job-search agent that allows you to specify the types of jobs in which you're interested and then sends you information about matching job openings.

Before you post your résumé online, be aware of the pitfalls. There are horror stories of employees being caught by their bosses who have access to online résumés. In some cases, it's a perfectly innocent mistake, such as when a résumé is posted before the person found the current job. In other cases, it can be the work of an unscrupulous headhunter who has duplicated and reposted the person's résumé.

To protect yourself, *Fortune* magazine suggests doing the following:[1]

1. Date your résumé.

2. Include a legend that forbids unauthorized transmission by headhunters.

3. Ask the job site's administrator if résumés are ever traded.

4. Keep your résumé off Usenet news groups.

5. Cloak your résumé by not including your name or employer.

Your Portfolio or "Book"

Students need more than "good" books—they need *great* books to even be considered by a major agency, according to top creative directors who spoke to a group of advertising educators in a weekend creative symposium. Agencies admire books that break rules instead of complying with them—books that stand apart in smart ways, just as great advertisements stand apart.

The person behind the portfolio   What are agencies looking for in beginning writers and art directors? Here are some key qualities:

- *Originality in thinking.* Granted, that's highly subjective. But you don't even get an interview unless your work is special. Furthermore, the work and the person being interviewed have to connect in the mind of the interviewer.

- *Passion for the work.* This involves the ability to enthuse about how you came up with the ideas and bounce back from mistakes.

- *Enthusiasm for the world.* More than a fleeting knowledge of music, film, theater, art, and current trends in humor is highly regarded. So is travel, especially to places that are off the beaten track. Such is the stuff that good ideas come from.

- *A love affair with words and design.* This affair should be ongoing and all-consuming.

- *Raw imagination.* For the book, the ideas don't have to be feasible. The agency can pull you back. It's much harder to push you further.

---

[1]Jerry Useem. "Read This Before You Put a Résumé Online," *Fortune,* 24 May 1999, p. 290.

- *Knowledge of research and marketing.* This means you can converse intelligently about those subjects, but not to the extent that it restrains your creative product.

- *The guts to try the dumbest ideas.* Strike the emotions. Touch people. But don't do too much of a good thing. Too many puns can hurt you. Bad puns can hurt you. Then again, it's subjective.

The look of your portfolio   What type of portfolio should you use? A spiral book with acetate pages is a popular choice because it allows you to arrange and rearrange your work until everything has the best flow. You may wish to place your mounted works in a compact portfolio or briefcase, arranging them in a way that shows off each piece to its best advantage. However, this approach can get cumbersome. Some students spend extra money to laminate their work so that it has a professional look. Others display their techno-savvy by putting their work on disk or CD-ROM.

Keep in mind that the quality of your work will be what lands you the job, not how much money you spend. A typo will hurt your chances whether the piece is laminated, on disk, or photocopied. However, given a choice between two would-be creatives who both have great books, the individual who puts in the extra effort will probably rate higher.

Also keep in mind that you will often be asked to leave your book for later review. Therefore, you may need to develop several books or create a small "leave-behind" piece consisting of photocopies of your work.

The contents of your portfolio   John Sweeney offers this advice about what to include in your book:[2]

1. *Demonstrate the campaign concept.* Make sure your first campaign is absolutely your best. And close with a flourish. First and last impressions carry weight.

2. *Adjust your portfolio to meet the needs of the interview.* But if you want a simple formula, try this: one package-goods campaign (toothpaste, deodorant, trash bags, etc.), one hard-goods campaign (stereos, cameras, computers, refrigerators, etc.), one food or fashion campaign, one public service or tourism campaign, and one new product idea and an introductory campaign for it. At least one campaign should include TV, print, radio, and outdoor—a complete demonstration of the campaign concept. Use music once, demonstration once, and testimonials once. Give a range of solutions to a range of products.

3. *Choose products you like when possible.* Be forewarned, however. It's easy to write for products you like. You won't always have such freedom in the business. Also, if you try to beat American Express, Coke, and Macintosh, you will probably fail. Choose products that are not currently celebrated for their creative work. Also, don't

---

[2]John Sweeney, "Step Up Persistence to Get in Agency Door," *Advertising Age,* 2 May 1985. Used by permission.

do work on one of the agency's accounts. You may choose a strategy that was rejected by research.

4. *Include at least two long-copy campaigns.* Many creative directors are suspicious of beginners. They are leery of smooth-talking, glitzy TV types who have no fundamental writing skills. Demonstrate your ability to write body copy conclusively by including at least two long-copy print ads that are substantially different in content. Show your ability to handle at least 300 words per ad.

5. *Make sure your scripts time properly.* The first sign of an amateur is a 30-second commercial that runs 58 seconds. Learn the proper scripting format. It's an easy way to look professional.

6. *Keep audience and strategy statements brief.* Agencies are looking for original thinking and strong writing skills, not marketing or research potential.

7. *Monitor your feedback.* If you get the same comment in many interviews, listen to it. If you get a range of responses to the same ad, welcome to the business.

Mistakes to avoid Based on a survey of top U.S. creative directors, Alice Kendrick and her colleagues report that the biggest mistakes students make in their portfolios include the following:[3]

- Creating fancy storyboards that couldn't be produced for under $500,000 (some even questioned the appropriateness of TV storyboards in portfolios)
- Offering weak ideas or clever pieces that don't demonstrate what advertising can do
- Failing to develop campaigns
- Doing what has already been done instead of taking risks with new ideas
- Doing ads for products that already have great campaigns
- Revealing a noticeable lack of writing, thinking, and conceptual skills
- Showing too much work—and having too much finished work
- Overemphasizing execution and underemphasizing content
- Overusing puns
- Forgetting that the real challenge of advertising often involves making small differences important to consumers
- Putting more weight on polished work than on creative work
- Showing work that does not apply to advertising

---

[3]Alice Kendrick, David Slayden, and Sheri J. Broyles, "'Real Worlds and Ivory Towers': A Survey of Top U.S. Agency Creative Directors." Used by permission.

The Interview   Relax! You shouldn't be nervous in an interview. The reason you've been invited for an interview is because they're interested in you. Feel confident. But don't be so relaxed that you look as if you don't care. You need to show professionalism through appropriate attire, proper attitude, and preparation for the interview. Laura McGowan, supervisor of training and development, and Laurie Brady, recruiter at J. Walter Thompson, Detroit, recall an unfortunate occasion when a candidate started the interview by opening a can of soda and then consumed it during the interview. Don't be mannequin-stiff, but don't put your feet up on the desk and gulp down a Coke either. Or a Pepsi.

Many interviewers state you shouldn't rehearse answers to questions because they will sound rehearsed. Instead, they recommend that you carefully consider your answer at the time the question is asked. However, many employment consultants say the opposite and insist that you must prepare yourself for an interview by anticipating the questions. So what's the answer? It's probably somewhere in between. Prepare for the interview, but don't memorize your answers.

Although no two interviewers are alike, here are some typical questions:

1. *"Why do you want to work here?"* In other words, what do you know about the company? Do you really want to work there, or will you jump at any job offer?

2. *"Tell me about yourself."* It's a simple request, but if you're not prepared, you will probably either ramble on or shrug your shoulders and say something dumb like "Shucks! There's not much to tell" or "Gee, I don't know where to start."

3. *"What are your strong points?"* Talk about things such as your ability to work on a team, your willingness to work long hours on creative projects, and your inquisitive nature—whatever you feel are qualities that will help you succeed in the job. But be honest.

4. *"What are your weak points?"* Try to come up with a weak point that will somehow show off a strong point. For example, you may have little patience with incompetent people. Or you may be terrible in math. Although this may hurt your chances of getting a job in the media or research department, most creative people aren't expected to have this talent.

5. *"What ad campaign do you love the most?"* You could choose one of the agency's campaigns, but don't do this unless you really think it's good. The next logical question is, "Why?"

6. *"What's the last book you read?"* They're not looking for the title of a textbook; they want to get a sense of who you are. Other similar questions include, "What's your favorite movie? Your favorite artist?"

● FIGURE 14-6

Kristin Gissendanner further demonstrated her creativity by wrapping her portfolio in gift paper and tying it with a ribbon. Inside were samples of her work and her résumé.

7. *"Why did you leave your last job?"* Never say anything negative about your former employers. Instead, say something about how you're looking for new opportunities. How you want to move to a larger/smaller city. Or how you were caught in corporate downsizing, which happens to the best of people.

8. *"What questions do you have?"* This is usually the last question, and in your quest to end the interview, you may be tempted to say you don't have any questions. *Don't* do this. By asking no questions, it will seem as if you're not that interested in the job. Or that you're uninquisitive, a definite no-no in this business. Remember, this is the last impression in the interview, your last chance to shine. When in doubt, ask the interviewer about his or her career at the agency. Ask about future growth opportunities. Ask when the hiring decision will be made. Don't be shy here—show you want the job!

After the Interview

Send a follow-up letter within two days of the interview. Reaffirm your interest in the position. Highlight one or two interesting points from the interview. Call about a week later and ask about the status of the opening.

What do you do if you feel the job interview didn't go well? Is it possible to get a second chance? Yes. Consider what happened to Stacey Staaterman. She wanted to switch from *Life* magazine to *Sports Illustrated for Kids.* Both magazines are owned by

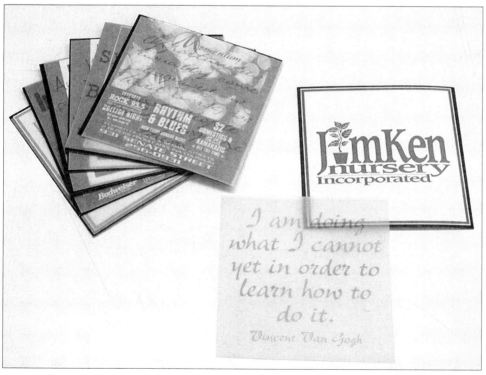

● FIGURE 14-7

Stacey Staaterman used a feature found in *Sports Illustrated for Kids* to win a position with the magazine's promotions department. After she won the job, she let her professional contacts know she had been traded.

Let's trade.

You're trying to fill that final spot to make your team complete.

Someone who can hit a homerun to take the game. Someone to pinch hit when you're down a man. Someone who won't throw too many curve balls when you're not looking. A real team player.

I've got what you're looking for. Let's trade. My creativity, experience and dedication to the game for a spot in your lineup.

the same parent company, Time Warner, so it seemed a sure thing—until the interview. Stacey could tell the person who interviewed her just wasn't interested. After some investigating, Stacey learned the interviewer already had someone else in mind. How could she convince him she was the best person? Why not pitch him like a client? Inspired by the trading cards that are found in *Sports Illustrated for Kids*,

I got traded.

Sports Illustrated KiDS *Stacey Staaterman*

ALL ★ AROUND TEAM PLAYER

Starting November 2nd, I'll be going to bat for a new team.

After nearly three years at *LIFE magazine*, I've accepted a position at *Sports Illustrated for Kids*. As Marketing Production Supervisor, I will be responsible for desktop design, art direction and production of all sales and marketing materials.

***SI for Kids* is the children's sports magazine started by Time Inc. in 1989. It represents the cutting edge of publishing for children.**

I am excited to be added to their team roster and to have a chance to hit a few homeruns.

So, batter up.

Stacey created an ad with the headline "Let's trade." The ad had a removable base-ball card with—you guessed it—Stacey's picture. The back of the card featured her career highlights and positions played. After she won the job, Stacey informed her professional contacts through a self-promotion piece. This time, she was able to say, "I got traded" (see Figure 14-7).

● Other Job-Hunting Suggestions

Enter the Awards Competitions

What's the first thing you see in the lobby and offices of just about every agency? Awards, awards, and more awards. According to an American Advertising Federation/*Advertising Age* poll, 60 percent of client/advertiser respondents felt that their ability to attract business was influenced by the awards they had won.[4] You don't need to have published work to win an award. There are a number of competitions that allow speculative work. Some of the student competition sponsors include the American Advertising Federation, the Clios, the Direct Marketing Association, and the Promotional Products Association. Some competition sponsors reward the winners with cash prizes, trips, and internships. All of them give the winners an accomplishment to highlight on résumés.

Practice Persistence

One creative director told all applicants that there were no jobs available and then interviewed only those who called back in spite of the lack of jobs. Agencies can be closed to job applicants for months and suddenly be in desperate need of people. You have to get used to it.

Explore All Your Options

The advertising agency is by no means the only place for a rewarding career in copy or design. Many manufacturing and service companies maintain in-house advertising departments. Likewise, many retailers have sizable advertising departments that offer impressive growth opportunities. Also, check the printing firms, which might need creative assistance for some of their clients. See what creative positions exist within the media—at newspapers and magazines, radio and TV stations, and cable TV companies. Consider the burgeoning fields of direct marketing and business-to-business advertising. Don't forget graphic design studios and production houses, which may need writers and art directors. Above all, be patient and persistent. If you know you are talented, the right job will come along. Best of luck!

● Suggested Activities

1. Write a résumé for a job in advertising. Try both a functional and a chronological résumé. Which works best for you, and why?

2. Write a cover letter to accompany your résumé. In preparation, jot down anything unusual about yourself that might be of interest, and carefully evaluate what you've written before you decide what to include. Remember that your cover letter should communicate something about the kind of person you are, as well as express your interest in and enthusiasm and qualifications for the position.

[4] "Awards Bring Laurels but No Guarantees," *Advertising Age,* 17 April 1995, p. 14.

3. Create a self-promotion piece using the guidelines in activity 2.

4. Interview a local advertising professional about the proper way to apply for a job. Assuming you would be applying for a position in copy or design, ask what sort of portfolio you would need to develop and how you should present your work.

 Search Online! Discovering More About Landing That Job

Using InfoTrac® College Edition, try these phrases and others for Key Words and Subject Guide searches: *career objectives, job resume, job cover letter, advertising agency hiring trends, hiring trends in advertising, advertising jobs, networking + jobs, advertising portfolio, interviewing.*

Assignments

● General

Use the following information as the basis for creating ads and commercials for print, radio, television, or other media. In completing these assignments, you may want to do additional research. In any event, you should know by now that it's important to identify your target audience, consider the competition, and devise a workable strategy before developing your ideas.

The Itty Bitty Book Light by Zelco

Popular for ten years. Clip this tiny light on your favorite hard- or soft-cover book, and cool light floods the pages. Optical-quality lead crystal bulb. Distortion-free. Will not cast shadows that can cause eye fatigue. Will not damage or weigh down your books, like some imitations. Only the book light attaches to your book, not the battery. Folds to store in book or its own travel case. At better stores and bookshops.

Tabasco 7-Spice Chili Recipe

For more than 100 years, the world's premier marketer of red pepper sauce has been churning out its mainstay product with no sense of urgency about diversifying its line. The family-owned McIlhenny Co., makers of the Tabasco sauce that all but owns the hot sauce market, started marketing other products only in 1973, when they introduced a Bloody Mary mix, followed by a picante sauce in 1982. Now they offer Tabasco Brand 7-Spice Chili Recipe mix, which plays off the strong heritage and widespread awareness of the Tabasco brand.

Tabasco is to red pepper sauce what Xerox is to copiers. Despite repeated buyout offers, the McIlhenny family has remained dedicated to preserving the old family recipe. The sauce is aged in oaken vats on remote Avery Island, deep in Louisiana Cajun country and headquarters for the company. The fiery sauce is difficult to duplicate because of the Central American Capiscum peppers used in the aging process, which involves mixing them with the local salt and vinegar.

Tabasco got its start in 1865 when Henry McIlhenny used peppers brought from Mexico's Yucatan Peninsula to create the sauce. For four generations, each patriarch has taken a daily walk, dressed in suit and tie, through the fields of peppers during the fall harvest to personally inspect the crop's quality, examine the mash in the vats, and watch the shipment of bottles. For more than a century, neither the bottle nor the name nor the logo has changed.

The chili is made from the finest vine-ripened tomatoes, green chiles, diced onions, genuine Tabasco pepper sauce, and a blend of seven herbs and spices known only to the company. All you add is fresh beef. The sauce comes in a "spaghetti sauce" jar. The label reads, "Tabasco Brand 7-Spice Chili Recipe. McIlhenny Co."

Tabasco dominates the hot sauce category with 30 percent of the market. And it is a growing market, riding the crest of a wave of popularity for spicy foods.

Device That Gets Rid of That Chatty Caller

Got a nuisance phone caller, but you're too embarrassed to end the one-way conversation? An electronic device called Gotta Go can simulate the clicking sound made by the phone company's call-waiting service. The gadget is a small white box activated by pushing a button. It can be hooked up to any single-line phone. Its inventor came up with the idea after trying to find a polite way to end rambling phone conversations with his rather chatty girlfriend. She was calling every day at his busiest times and just gabbing. One day she actually offered to end the conversation after she heard the click-click sound of call waiting and realized he had another call coming through. It struck him that he was very relieved when someone else would call and he'd hear the click, because *he* didn't have to end the call himself. Gotta Go sells for $14.95, less than some call-waiting services provided by the telephone companies, which usually charge a recurring monthly fee for the service.

Pet Drinks

Think of them as a cross between Gatorade, Evian, and Ensure . . . for dogs and cats. Dr. George Hill Pet Drinks are beef-flavored concoctions for dogs and cats (two formulations). They can be added to dry food or lapped up as a treat. Both are fortified with twelve vitamins and minerals and with brewer's yeast, commonly used to control fleas.

The products are packaged in 32- and 64-ounce "milk jug" bottles. The smaller ones sell for $1.39. Dr. Hill is a veterinarian from Salisbury, North Carolina, who feels that dogs and cats don't get a balanced diet.

Meanwhile a competitor, Original Pet Drink Co., has signed four beverage bottlers to make and distribute its Thirsty Dog! and Thirsty Cat! products.

These vitamin- and mineral-enriched waters are intended to replace tap water in a pet's bowl. A one-liter bottle of either the Crispy Beef flavor Thirsty Dog! or the Tangy Fish flavor Thirsty Cat! sells for $1.79. Two new flavors are in the making, as are formulations for puppies, kittens, and older pets. Research shows that many pet owners give Evian and Perrier to their pets. "Once you give people more than water to drink, they do. Why shouldn't pets have that option, too?" asks president Marc Duke.

Great Guiltless Flavor

Fat is not a nice word among health-conscious Americans, and it's no longer just a comment about weight. Why? Because Americans are convinced that reducing fat in their diet is one of the most important things they can do for their health. Enter new kinds of snack foods that promise to satisfy America's need for munching while delivering only tiny amounts of fat.

A popular brand in this growing market is Guiltless Gourmet, a company based in Austin, Texas. In 1989, a small group of slightly overweight snack food devotees (as company literature would have it) with expectations as high as their cholesterol counts scoured grocery shelves for snacks that wouldn't clog their arteries with bad things. They went away hungry. So they created their own tortilla chips—and thus was born the family of Guiltless Gourmet no-oil chips, dips, and salsas. Guiltless Gourmet chips are baked, not fried. You taste the full flavor of natural corn. A bag of fried chips can be up to 35 percent oil by weight. But in a 7-ounce bag of Guiltless Gourmet Tortilla Chips, you get as many chips as you find in a 10-ounce bag of fried chips. These chips are lighter because they have no oil. In a serving of about 22 chips, you'll get 1.5 grams of fat. That's low! Other products include no-fat bean dips, quesos, and salsas.

Lipton Kettle Creations Home-Style Soup Mix

Cooks in 30 minutes. Just add water. A fresh way to make soup. Makes 32 fluid ounces or four servings. No soup tastes better than homemade, but these days nobody's got the time. So just choose Lipton—their home-style soup mix is a wholesome mix of beans, grains, and pastas with herbs and spices. In other words, the ingredients are mixed for you. You add the water and let it simmer for 30 minutes. Four varieties: chicken with pasta and beans, bean medley with pasta, minestrone, and chicken and onion with long grain and wild rice. Packaged in attractive sealed bags with windows to show ingredients. Sell against canned soups, which heat in about 5 minutes.

A Handy Guide in Paperback

The Toilets of New York by Ken Eichenbaum. Here are the best and the worst public and semi-public relief stations for those who need to know. Includes walking and trotting maps. Over 100 detailed descriptions of men's and women's toilets all over Manhattan.

Comments: "If you're in the Big Apple with a Small Bladder, you need this book!" "Data on cleanliness, wheelchair access, number of stalls! This book gets four stars!" Funny, but practical. At your bookstore, or fax order 414-354-7714.

Pizza Chef Gourmet Pizza

Locally owned and operated. Recipes prepared fresh on premises. Fresh herbs and spices used in sauce and on pizzas. Gourmet salads of fresh romaine lettuce are tossed with homemade salad dressings. Bake their own sub buns and offer pizzas on freshly made whole wheat dough or traditional hand-tossed dough. All pizzas available baked or unbaked. All made to order.

Eat in, delivery, or pickup. Beer and wine on premises. Traditional pizza toppings plus "designer pizzas." Garden, Caesar, antipasto, southwestern chicken salads. Set this operation apart from the giants: Pizza Hut, Domino's, and so on.

Lawn "Makeup"

Possibly inspired by those infomercials for spray-on hair, this aerosol can of colored spray is for folks who don't want their lawns to look "browned out" come fall and winter. You can even choose the color to match your lawn or your mood, from Palm Green to Cedar Green to Spring Green to Kentucky Blue. The label promises that Lawn Makeup is virtually nontoxic and suggests that you spray a test area for color match. Definitely not for nature purists, so don't target them. Find your market, and convince them it's better to have a healthy-looking lawn than a healthy lawn (just kidding).

Fizzies Drink Tablets

Okay, this is definitely not for the young, upwardly mobile type. It's not for parents or the over-50 group. It's for kids. Adolescents. Those seventh- and eighth-graders who love to do "yucky" things. And it's called Fizzies. Fizzies are instant sparkling-water drink tablets in cherry, grape, root beer, and orange.

Fizzies have a strong nostalgic appeal for folks who were around in the late 1950s— the "golden age of bomb shelters"—for this is when they were originally introduced. In the intervening years, they faded from the shelves. Now revived, they're an unusual novelty item for children (or perhaps for their parents who remember "the good ole days").

One particularly disgusting aspect—you don't even need a glass of water to get in on the fun. Just stick a Fizzies tablet on your tongue, and soon you'll "spew blue goo" and have "colored foam oozing out of your mouth." Now how would you advertise this?

Heater Meals

Looks like a typical TV dinner until you open the package. The meal, which requires no refrigeration, is packed inside a sealed plastic container sitting face down on a foam tray. Affixed to the base of the tray is a flat tablet made of iron and magnesium, which—believe it or not—functions as a stove. Lift the meal, pour a few ounces of water on the tablet, replace the meal in the tray, and slide it all back into the box. The water causes a thermonuclear reaction (really); you actually see steam emerging from the box. Fourteen minutes later, you can enjoy hot grilled turkey breast, cheese ravioli, pepper steak, chili, and a few more varieties. A 2-ounce packet of water is included, just in case. Targets? Truckers, construction workers, campers, hikers, busy office workers eating at their desks, college students, hunters, fishermen. Who else can you target?

Body Glue

When clothes won't stay put, why not glue them in place? Droopy socks, baggy shirttails, shoulder pads, collars, cuffs, slips, bustiers, wigs and toupees, bathing suit bottoms, earrings—you name it—all stay put when you add Body Glue, a roll-on, water-soluble adhesive packaged like a deodorant stick (*don't* use it under your arms). Just roll a little on your skin, press the garment in place, and sit still for 3 minutes. There's a market out there somewhere. Find it. And sell it.

The Koolatron Portable Refrigerator

It looks like a cooler. It's just as portable. But it's really a refrigerator and food warmer all in one. NASA developed the technology for the Koolatron. They needed something less bulky and more dependable than traditional refrigeration coils and compressors. They found it in a solid-state component called the thermoelectric module, no bigger than a matchbook, that delivers the cooling power of a 10-pound block of ice. Aside from a small fan, this electronic fridge has no moving parts to wear out or break down. Costs the same as a good cooler plus one or two season's supply of ice (about the same as five family dinners out).

With the switch of a plug, the Koolatron becomes a food warmer for a casserole, burger, or baby bottle. It heats up to 125 degrees. Empty, it weighs only 12 pounds. Full, it holds up to forty 12-ounce cans. On motor trips, plug the Koolatron into your cigarette lighter. For picnics or fishing, it holds its cooling capacity for 24 hours. If you leave it plugged into your battery with the engine off, it consumes only 3 amps of power. $99 plus $12 shipping and handling. Optional ac adapter lets you use it in your rec room, patio, or motel room. 1-800-number for orders.

Electronic Kid Alarm

Out with the old-fashioned way to locate your lost youngster—that is, by shouting his or her name at a volume that blows out store windows. Enter the new millenium. You can now track your kid electronically. The Child Safety Corporation of Miami markets a child-tracking monitor system. The system consists of a battery-operated transmitter, attached with a safety pin to the kid, and a receiver carried by the parent. Each system sells for $99.

The device allows parents to log in an alarm range of 30 to 60 feet on the child's transmitter, which he or she wears like a pendant about the size of a silver dollar. If he wanders farther than the preset range, an alarm is triggered on the parent's receiver. The alarm also sounds if the transmitter is switched off or immersed in water.

Resorts Sportswear

A new line of exclusive designs on T-shirts and sweatshirts, representing the most popular resorts in the world.

Fifteen beach resorts captured on T-shirts of top-of-the-line Hanes beefy 100 percent cotton in colors plus white and ash: Acapulco, the Bahamas, Bimini, Cancun, Hawaii, Jamaica, Key West, Malibu, Nassau, Rio de Janiero, St. Croix, St. Tropez, San Diego, West Palm Beach, and Venice Beach. Large and Extra Large, $19.95.

Ten luxurious 9-ounce heavyweight 50-50 cotton-polyester blend, long-sleeve sweatshirts in ten original ski resort designs: Aspen, Breckenridge, Gstaad, Innsbruck, Purgatory, St. Moritz, Snowbird, Snowmass, Steamboat Springs, and Vail. White or ash only. Large and Extra Large, $31.95.

Available by mail only. Phone 1-800-number for color catalog or to place order.

Soundmate Personal Safety Device

This small plastic cylinder fits into the palm of your hand. Simply squeeze it and it screams. Literally. Loud and long. Rugged enough to withstand shock. Non-violent design cannot be used against the owner (as can Mace). Can be legally carried on an airplane. Has unique battery tester. Individually coded deactivation—it stops only when you want it to. $129.95. Full 30-day money-back guarantee and full 3-year warranty. Call 1-800-882-5778, ext. NY 122 to order.

Every 17 seconds another violent assault occurs. The SoundMate has the power of a unique, piercing 120-decibel "supersiren" that oscillates and strobes from 12 outlets.

Phonejak

Turns an electrical wall outlet into a phone extension. No installation required. Uses ordinary electrical wiring as telephone circuit. Better sound quality than the best cordless phones. Pay no fees to the phone company; save hundreds of dollars each year. Up to 20 telephone extensions from one number. Works with any phone device, cord or cordless, speaker phones, answering machines, fax machines, computer modems, and so on. $79 per system (includes transmitter and movable receiver/extension device. Additional receiver/extension devices for more phone outlets, $49 each.

The Value of Independent Higher Education

America's private (or independent) colleges are doing well but see that they must strive to increase enrollment. So they have decided to pool funds to advertise their advantages and thereby increase inquiries and enrollments. One region, the Midwest, is combining its efforts through the Midwest Partnership of Independent Colleges (Illinois, Indiana, Michigan, Ohio, and Wisconsin) and needs to develop a print campaign.

The facts Print advertising will run in regional editions of national news weeklies, which have agreed to run some of the ads as a public service. This information on private colleges is not well known:

- Independent colleges perform an important service to our society, although many of their contributions go unrecognized, perhaps because of the stronger "clout" of major state-funded colleges and universities.

- They have an average faculty-student ratio of 14:1. Their enrollments represent all races and income brackets.

- The Midwest group enrolls 390,000 students, of which 48,000 are minorities. Eighty percent of students receive some form of financial aid, 20 percent of which comes from the schools' budgets—double that of ten years ago.

- They award 30 percent of all bachelor's degrees in the region, and 66 percent of their students go on to postgraduate studies.

- They contribute an estimated $10 billion and 350,000 jobs each year to their local economies.

- Six out of ten Fortune 500 CEOs attended an independent college.

It is clear, therefore, that these colleges are strong contributors to the educational, cultural, and economic well-being of our society.

The audience Several choices are appropriate, but for this campaign, think in terms of parents of junior and senior high school students in the Midwest region served by this group of colleges. Since financial aid is available, it is important to reach middle- and low-middle-income families, especially those who find it difficult to believe they can afford to send their children to anything but a large state university, where tuition tends to be more affordable and where grants are often available for lower income levels. And since roughly 5 out of 40 college students are minorities, this is an audience that should not be overlooked. Essentially, the message should appeal to whites and minorities who believe in the value of diversity and who see or can be made to see the value in low faculty-student ratios and other appealing features of these schools that set them apart from the competition.

The competition This is a broad category. People in the target market might consider the competition to be large state universities and community and technical colleges (lower cost). But you might also think of the competition as not going to college at all. Remember, this is an era of inflated costs for everything, and education is no exception. Students from this pool will almost certainly have to finance part of their education, either by working or through grants and scholarships. The general perception is that the smaller and more private the school, the less opportunity for any sort of financial support.

● New Products

Think up a new product that satisfies certain needs of a particular group of consumers. Use the following guidelines to help you determine what your new product should offer. Then develop an advertising campaign for it.

1. What is the nature of the product? Give uses, description of packaging, approximate selling price, type of store carrying it, sizes available, and general shape and appearance.

2. What is its name? What does the name signify?

3. Who is the target audience, in demographic, lifestyle, and relationship terms? Is there a secondary audience?

4. What products will this one replace for this audience? In what ways will it be better than the products they were using before?

5. What is the key selling idea for this product?

● Campaign

Using one of the products or services in this section, or another product or service you have been assigned, prepare a multimedia creative campaign, and present it to the class. It should include, minimally, the following items.

- A comprehensive creative strategy

- Three print ads

- A 60-second *and* a 30-second (or another 60-second) radio script

- A 30-second TV storyboard

- A direct-response folder with letter and envelope

- An outdoor board

Your project may be judged on the following criteria:

- *Strategy.* Is your strategy appropriate for the product, competition, and target market?

- *Attention.* Does each message come through loud and clear, whether through the headline, visual, opening shot, or first words of the piece?

- *Continuity.* Do your pieces work as one? Is there an obvious theme running through your campaign? Does each part contribute to the overall strategic goals?

- *Liveliness.* Does your passion blaze through each message? Do you believe as much in the product as you want the audience to? Is your writing clear, concise, and lively?

Suggested Readings

● Creativity

Baldwin, Huntley. *How to Create Effective TV Commercials.* Lincolnwood, IL.: NTC Business Books, 1989.

Bendinger, Bruce. *The Copy Workshop Workbook.* Chicago: The Copy Workshop, 1993.

Bernbach, Evelyn, and Bob Levenson. *Bill Bernbach's Book.* New York: Villard Books, 1987.

Bond, Jonathan, and Richard Kirshenbaum. *Under the Radar (Talking to Today's Cynical Consumer).* New York: Wiley, 1998.

The Book of Gossage. Chicago: The Copy Workshop, 1995.

Brady, Philip. *Using Type Right.* Lincolnwood, IL: NTC Business Books, 1988.

Garchik, Morton. *Creative Visual Thinking: How to Think Up Ideas Fast.* New York: Art Direction Book Company, 1982.

Haag, Dan. *Practioners: One-on-One.* Boston: Houghton Mifflin, 1999.

Higgins, Denis. *The Art of Writing Advertising: Conversations with Masters of the Craft.* Lincolnwood, IL: NTC Business Books, 1989.

Kanner, Bernice. *The 100 Best TV Commercials . . . and Why They Worked.* New York: Random House, 1999.

Keding, Ann, and Thomas Bivins. *How to Produce Creative Advertising: Proven Techniques and Computer Applications.* Lincolnwood, IL: NTC Business Books, 1991.

Keil, John M. *How to Zig in a Zagging World.* New York: Wiley, 1988.

Lewis, Herschell Gordon, and Carol Nelson. *World's Greatest Direct Mail Sales Letters.* Lincolnwood, IL: NTC Business Books, 1996.

MacKenzie, Gordon. *Orbiting the Giant Hairball: A Corporate Fool's Guide to Surviving with Grace.* New York: Viking Penguin, 1998.

Marra, James L. *Advertising Creativity: Techniques for Generating Ideas.* Englewood Cliffs, NJ: Prentice-Hall, 1990.

Norins, Hanley. *The Young & Rubicam Traveling Creative Workshop.* Englewood Cliffs, NJ: Prentice-Hall, 1990.

Ogilvy, David. *Confessions of an Advertising Man.* New York: Atheneum, 1963.

———. *Ogilvy on Advertising.* New York: Random House, 1985.

O'Toole, John. *The Trouble with Advertising.* New York: Random House, 1985.

Roman, Kenneth, and Jane Maas. *The New How to Advertise.* New York: St. Martin's Press, 1992.

Sroge, Maxwell. *How to Create Successful Catalogs.* Lincolnwood, IL: NTC Business Books, 1995.

Sullivan, Luke. *Hey Whipple, Squeeze This: A Guide to Creating Great Ads.* New York: Wiley, 1998.

Von Oech, Roger. *A Kick in the Seat of the Pants.* New York: Harper Perennial, 1986.

———. *A Whack on the Side of the Head.* New York: Warner Books, 1990.

Wasserman, Dick. *That's Our New Ad Campaign . . . ?* New York: Lexington Books, 1991.

Weinberger, Marc G., Leland Campbell, and Beth Brody. *Effective Radio Advertising.* New York: Lexington Books, 1994.

● Diversity

Demographics of Minority Markets. Ithaca, NY: American Demographics Press, 1993.

Dunn, William. *The Baby Bust: A Generation Comes of Age.* Ithaca, NY: American Demographics Books, 1993.

Guber, Selina S., and Jon Berry. *Marketing to and Through Kids.* New York: McGraw-Hill, 1993.

Hollander, Stanley C., and Richard Germain. *Was There a Pepsi Generation Before Pepsi Discovered It?* Chicago: American Marketing Association, 1992.

Lazer, William. *Handbook of Demographics for Marketing and Advertising.* New York: Lexington Books, 1994.

Leeming, E. Janice, and Cynthia F. Tripp. *Segmenting the Women's Market.* Chicago: Probus, 1994.

Lukenbill, Grant. *Untold Millions: Positioning Your Business for the Gay and Lesbian Consumer Revolution. New York:* Harper, 1995.

McNeal, James U. *Kids as Customers.* New York: Lexington Books. 1992.

Morgan, Carol M., and Doran J. Levy. *Segmenting the Mature Market: Identifying and Reaching America's Diverse, Booming Senior Markets.* Chicago: Probus, 1993.

Moschis, George P. *Gerontographics: Life-Stage Segmentation for Marketing Strategy Development.* Westport, CT: Quorum Books, 1996.

———. *Marketing Strategies for the Mature Market.* Westport, CT: Quorum Books, 1994.

Reedy, Joel. *Marketing to Consumers with Disabilities.* Chicago: Probus, 1993.

Ritchie, Karen. *Marketing to Generation X.* New York: Lexington Books, 1995.

Rossman, Marlene L. *Multicultural Marketing: Selling to a Diverse America.* New York: American Management Association, 1994.

Seelye, Ned, and James Alan Seelye. *Culture Clash: Managing in a Multicultural World.* Lincolnwood, IL: NTC Business Books, 1995.

Valdés, Isabel, and Marta Seoane. *Hispanic Market Handbook: The Definitive Source for Reaching This Lucrative Segment of American Consumers.* New York: Gale Research, 1995.

Wolfe, David B. *Marketing to Boomers and Beyond.* New York: McGraw-Hill, 1993.

Wong, Angi Ma. *Target the U.S. Asian Market. A Practical Guide to Doing Business.* Los Angeles: Pacific Heritage Books, 1993.

Woods, Gail Baker. *Advertising and Marketing to the New Majority: A Case Study Approach.* Belmont, CA: Wadsworth, 1995.

● Research

Alreck, Pamela L., and Robert B. Settle. *The Survey Research Handbook: Guidelines and Strategies for Conducting a Survey.* Burr Ridge, IL: Irwin Professional, 1995.

Berkman, Robert I. *Find It Fast: How to Uncover Expert Information on Any Subject.* New York: Harper & Row, 1990.

Greenbaum, Thomas L. *The Handbook for Focus Group Research.* New York: Lexington Books, 1993.

Haskins, Jack B., and Alice Kendrick. *Successful Advertising Research Methods.* Lincolnwood, IL: NTC Business Books, 1992.

Krueger, Richard A. *Focus Groups: A Practical Guide for Applied Research.* Newbury Park, CA: Sage, 1994.

Larson, Erik. *The Naked Consumer: How Our Private Lives Become Private Commodities.* New York: Penguin Books, 1994.

Piirto, Rebecca. *Beyond Mind Games: The Marketing Power of Psychographics.* Ithaca, NY: American Demographics Books, 1991.

● Strategy

Aaker, David A. *Managing Brand Equity.* New York: Free Press, 1991.

Bogart, Leo. *Strategy in Advertising.* Lincolnwood, IL: NTC Business Books, 1996.

Jones, Susan K. *Creative Strategy in Direct Marketing.* Lincolnwood, IL: NTC Business Books, 1991.

Loden, D. John. *Megabrands: How to Build Them, How to Beat Them.* Homewood, IL: Business One Irwin, 1992.

Marconi, Joe. *Beyond Branding: How Savvy Marketers Build Brand Equity to Create Products and Open New Markets.* Chicago: Probus, 1994.

Murphy, John M. *Brand Strategy.* Englewood Cliffs, NJ: Prentice-Hall, 1990.

Randazzo, Sal. *Mythmaking on Madison Avenue: How Advertisers Apply the Power of Myth and Symbolism to Create Leadership Brands.* Chicago: Probus, 1993.

Rothenberg, Randall. *Where the Suckers Moon: The Life and Death of an Advertising Campaign.* New York: Vintage Books, 1995.

Schultz, Don E., Stanley Tannenbaum, and Anne Allison. *Essentials of Advertising Strategy.* Lincolnwood, IL: NTC Business Books, 1992.

Schultz, Don E., Stanley Tannenbaum, and Robert R. Lauterborn. *Integrated Marketing Communications.* Lincolnwood, IL: NTC Business Books, 1992.

Steel, Jon. *Truth, Lies and Advertising.* New York: Wiley, 1998.

● Presentations

Fletcher, Leon. *How to Speak like a Pro.* New York: Ballantine Books, 1983.

Hoff, Ron. *I Can See You Naked.* Kansas City: Andrews and McMeel, 1992.

Moriarty, Sandra, and Tom Duncan. *Creating and Delivering Winning Advertising and Marketing Presentations.* Lincolnwood, IL: NTC Business Books, 1995.

Schloff, Laurie, and Marcia Yudkin. *Smart Speaking.* New York: Plume, 1992.

Stuart, Cristina. *How to Be an Effective Speaker.* Lincolnwood, IL: NTC Business Books, 1989.

● Advertising Careers

Barry, Ann Marie. *The Advertising Portfolio.* Lincolnwood, IL: NTC Business Books, 1990.

Field, Shelby. *Career Opportunities in Advertising and Public Relations.* New York: Facts on File, 1990.

Minski, Laurence, and Emily Thorton Calvo. *How to Succeed in Advertising When All You Have Is Talent.* Lincolnwood, IL: NTC Business Books, 1994.

Morgan, Bradley J. *Marketing and Sales Career Directory.* Detroit: Invisible Ink Press, 1993.

Paetro, Maxine. *How to Put Your Book Together and Get a Job in Advertising.* Chicago: The Copy Workshop, 1990.

Pattis, S. William. *Careers in Advertising.* Lincolnwood, IL: NTC Business Books, 1996.

● Reference

Ammer, Christine. *Have a Nice Day—No Problem: A Dictionary of Clichés.* New York: Dutton, 1992.

Encyclopedia of Consumer Brands. Detroit: St. James Press, 1994.

Hulbert, James. *Dictionary of Symbolism.* New York: Meridian, 1993.

Moran, Hal. *Symbols of America.* New York: Penguin Books, 1986.

Wiechmann, Jack G. *NTC's Dictionary of Advertising.* Lincolnwood, IL: NTC Business Books, 1993.

Index